ATS-21a   ADMISSION TEST SERIES

This is your
PASSBOOK for...

Scholastic Aptitude Test (SAT) - Writing and Language

Test Preparation Study Guide
Questions & Answers

COPYRIGHT NOTICE

This book is SOLELY intended for, is sold ONLY to, and its use is RESTRICTED to individual, bona fide applicants or candidates who qualify by virtue of having seriously filed applications for appropriate license, certificate, professional and/or promotional advancement, higher school matriculation, scholarship, or other legitimate requirements of education and/or governmental authorities.

This book is NOT intended for use, class instruction, tutoring, training, duplication, copying, reprinting, excerption, or adaptation, etc., by:

1) Other publishers
2) Proprietors and/or Instructors of "Coaching" and/or Preparatory Courses
3) Personnel and/or Training Divisions of commercial, industrial, and governmental organizations
4) Schools, colleges, or universities and/or their departments and staffs, including teachers and other personnel
5) Testing Agencies or Bureaus
6) Study groups which seek by the purchase of a single volume to copy and/or duplicate and/or adapt this material for use by the group as a whole without having purchased individual volumes for each of the members of the group
7) Et al.

Such persons would be in violation of appropriate Federal and State statutes.

PROVISION OF LICENSING AGREEMENTS – Recognized educational, commercial, industrial, and governmental institutions and organizations, and others legitimately engaged in educational pursuits, including training, testing, and measurement activities, may address request for a licensing agreement to the copyright owners, who will determine whether, and under what conditions, including fees and charges, the materials in this book may be used them. In other words, a licensing facility exists for the legitimate use of the material in this book on other than an individual basis. However, it is asseverated and affirmed here that the material in this book CANNOT be used without the receipt of the express permission of such a licensing agreement from the Publishers. Inquiries re licensing should be addressed to the company, attention rights and permissions department.

All rights reserved, including the right of reproduction in whole or in part, in any form or by any means, electronic or mechanical, including photocopying, recording, or by any information storage and retrieval system, without permission in writing from the Publisher.

Copyright © 2025 by
National Learning Corporation

212 Michael Drive, Syosset, NY 11791
(516) 921-8888 • www.passbooks.com
E-mail: info@passbooks.com

PASSBOOK® SERIES

THE *PASSBOOK® SERIES* has been created to prepare applicants and candidates for the ultimate academic battlefield – the examination room.

At some time in our lives, each and every one of us may be required to take an examination – for validation, matriculation, admission, qualification, registration, certification, or licensure.

Based on the assumption that every applicant or candidate has met the basic formal educational standards, has taken the required number of courses, and read the necessary texts, the *PASSBOOK® SERIES* furnishes the one special preparation which may assure passing with confidence, instead of failing with insecurity. Examination questions – together with answers – are furnished as the basic vehicle for study so that the mysteries of the examination and its compounding difficulties may be eliminated or diminished by a sure method.

This book is meant to help you pass your examination provided that you qualify and are serious in your objective.

The entire field is reviewed through the huge store of content information which is succinctly presented through a provocative and challenging approach – the question-and-answer method.

A climate of success is established by furnishing the correct answers at the end of each test.

You soon learn to recognize types of questions, forms of questions, and patterns of questioning. You may even begin to anticipate expected outcomes.

You perceive that many questions are repeated or adapted so that you can gain acute insights, which may enable you to score many sure points.

You learn how to confront new questions, or types of questions, and to attack them confidently and work out the correct answers.

You note objectives and emphases, and recognize pitfalls and dangers, so that you may make positive educational adjustments.

Moreover, you are kept fully informed in relation to new concepts, methods, practices, and directions in the field.

You discover that you are actually taking the examination all the time: you are preparing for the examination by "taking" an examination, not by reading extraneous and/or supererogatory textbooks.

In short, this PASSBOOK®, used directedly, should be an important factor in helping you to pass your test.

SCHOLASTIC APTITUDE TEST

Reading Test

In the Reading Test, students will encounter questions like those asked in a lively, thoughtful, evidence-based discussion.

The Reading Test focuses on the skills and knowledge at the heart of education: what you've been learning in high school and what you'll need to succeed in college. It's about how you take in, think about, and use information.

- All Reading Test questions are multiple choices and based on passages.
- Some passages are paired with other passages.
- Informational graphics, such as tables, graphs, and charts, accompany some passages—but no math is required.
- Prior topic-specific knowledge is not tested.
- The Reading Test is part of the Evidence-Based Reading and Writing section.

When you take the Reading Test, you'll read passages and interpret informational graphics. Then you'll use what you've read to answer questions.

Some questions ask you to locate a piece of information or an idea stated directly. But you'll also need to understand what the author's words imply. In other words, you have to read between the lines.

To succeed in college and a career, you'll need to apply reading skills in all sorts of subjects. Not coincidentally, you'll also need those skills to do well on the Reading Test.
The Reading Test always includes

- One passage from a classic or contemporary work of U.S. or world literature.
- One passage or a pair of passages from either a U.S. founding document or a text in the Great Global Conversation they inspired. The U.S. Constitution or a speech.
- A selection about economics, psychology, sociology, or some other social science.
- Two science passages (or one passage and one passage pair) that examine foundational concepts and developments in Earth science, biology, chemistry, or physics.

A lot more goes into reading than you might realize—and the Reading Test measures a range of reading skills.

Some questions ask you to:
- Find evidence in a passage (or pair of passages) that best supports the answer to a previous question or serves as the basis for a reasonable conclusion.
- Identify how authors use evidence to support their claims.
- Find a relationship between an informational graphic and the passage it's paired with.

From the official announcement for educational purposes

Many questions focus on important, widely used words and phrases that you'll find in texts in many different subjects. The words are ones that you'll use in college and the workplace long after test day.

The SAT focuses on your ability to:

- Use contextual clues in a passage to figure out which meaning of a word or phrase is being used.
- Decide how an author's word choice shapes meaning, style, and tone.

The Reading Test includes passages in the fields of history, social studies, and science. You'll be asked questions that require you to draw on the reading skills needed most to succeed in those subjects. For instance, you might read about an experiment then see questions that ask you to:
- Examine hypotheses.
- Interpret data.
- Consider implications.

Answers are based only on the content stated in or implied by the passage.

Writing and Language Test

The SAT Writing and Language Test asks you to be an editor and improve passages that were written especially for the test—and that include deliberate errors.

When you take the Writing and Language Test, you'll do three things that people do all the time when they write and edit:

1. Read.
2. Find mistakes and weaknesses.
3. Fix them.

- All questions are multiple choices and based on passages.
- Some passages are accompanied by informational graphics, such as tables, graphs, and charts—but no math is required.
- Prior topic knowledge is never tested.
- The Writing and Language Test is part of the Evidence-Based Reading and Writing section.

To answer some questions, you'll need to look closely at a single sentence. Others require reading the entire piece and interpreting a graphic. For instance, you might be asked to choose a sentence that corrects a misinterpretation of a scientific chart or that better explains the importance of the data.

The passages you improve will range from arguments to nonfiction narratives and will be about careers, history, social studies, the humanities, and science.

Questions on the Writing and Language Test measure a range of skills.

Questions that test command of evidence ask you to improve the way passages develop information and ideas. For instance, you might choose an answer that sharpens an argumentative claim or adds a relevant supporting detail.

Some questions ask you to improve word choice. You'll need to choose the best words to use based on the text surrounding them. Your goal will be to make a passage more precise or concise, or to improve syntax, style, or tone.

Analysis in History/Social Studies and in Science

You'll be asked to read passages about topics in history, social studies, and science with a critical eye and make editorial decisions that improve them.

Some questions ask about a passage's organization and its impact. For instance, you will be asked which words or structural changes improve how well it makes its point and how well its sentences and paragraphs work together.

This is about the building blocks of writing: sentence structure, usage, and punctuation. You'll be asked to change words, clauses, sentences, and punctuation. Some topics covered include verb tense, parallel construction, subject-verb agreement, and comma use.

Math Test

The SAT Math Test covers a range of math practices, with an emphasis on problem solving, modeling, using tools strategically, and using algebraic structure.

Instead of testing you on every math topic there is, the SAT asks you to use the math that you'll rely on most in all sorts of situations. Questions on the Math Test are designed to mirror the problem solving and modeling you'll do in:

- College math, science, and social science courses
- The jobs that you hold
- Your personal life

For instance, to answer some questions you'll need to use several steps—because in the real world a single calculation is rarely enough to get the job done.

- Most math questions will be multiple choices, but some—called grid-ins—ask you to come up with the answer rather than select the answer.
- The Math Test is divided into two portions: Math Test–Calculator and Math Test–No Calculator.
- Some parts of the test include several questions about a single scenario.

The Math Test will focus in depth on the three areas of math that play the biggest role in a wide range of college majors and careers:

- Heart of Algebra, which focuses on the mastery of linear equations and systems.
- Problem Solving and Data Analysis, which is about being quantitatively literate.
- Passport to Advanced Math, which features questions that require the manipulation of complex equations.

The Math Test also draws on Additional Topics in Math, including the geometry and trigonometry most relevant to college and career readiness.
The Math Test is a chance to show that you:

- Carry out procedures flexibly, accurately, efficiently, and strategically.
- Solve problems quickly by identifying and using the most efficient solution approaches. This might involve solving a problem by inspection, finding a shortcut, or reorganizing the information you've been given.

You'll demonstrate your grasp of math concepts, operations, and relations. For instance, you might be asked to make connections between properties of linear equations, their graphs, and the contexts they represent.

These real-world problems ask you to analyze a situation, determine the essential elements required to solve the problem, represent the problem mathematically, and carry out a solution.

Calculators are important tools, and to succeed after high school, you'll need to know how—and when—to use them. In the Math Test–Calculator portion of the test, you'll be able to focus on complex modeling and reasoning because your calculator can save you time.

However, the calculator is, like any tool, only as smart as the person using it. The Math Test includes some questions where it's better not to use a calculator, even though you're allowed to. In these cases, students who make use of structure or their ability to reason will probably finish before students who use a calculator.

The Math Test–No Calculator portion of the test makes it easier to assess your fluency in math and your understanding of some math concepts. It also tests well-learned technique and number sense.

Although most of the questions on the Math Test are multiple choices, 22 percent are student-produced response questions, also known as grid-ins. Instead of choosing a correct answer from a list of options, you'll need to solve problems and enter your answers in the grids provided on the answer sheet.

SAT Essay

The redesigned SAT Essay asks you to use your reading, analysis, and writing skills.

The SAT Essay is a lot like a typical college writing assignment in which you're asked to analyze a text. Take the SAT with Essay and show colleges that you're ready to come to campus and write.

- Read a passage.
- Explain how the author builds an argument to persuade an audience.
- Support your explanation with evidence from the passage.

The prompt (question) shown below, or a nearly identical one, is used every time the SAT is given.

As you read the passage below, consider how [the author] uses evidence, such as facts or examples, to support claims.

- evidence, such as facts or examples, to support claims.
- reasoning to develop ideas and to connect claims and evidence.
- stylistic or persuasive elements, such as word choice or appeals to emotion, to add power to the ideas expressed.

Write an essay in which you explain how [the author] builds an argument to persuade [his/her] audience that [author's claim]. In your essay, analyze how [the author] uses one or more of the features listed above (or features of your own choice) to strengthen the logic and persuasiveness of [his/her] argument. Be sure that your analysis focuses on the most relevant features of the passage. Your essay should not explain whether you agree with [the author's] claims, but rather explain how the author builds an argument to persuade [his/her] audience.

You can count on seeing the same prompt no matter when you take the SAT with Essay, but the passage will be different every time.

All passages have these things in common:

- Written for a broad audience
- Argue a point
- Express subtle views on complex subjects
- Use logical reasoning and evidence to support claims
- Examine ideas, debates, or trends in the arts and sciences, or civic, cultural, or political life
- Always taken from published works

All the information you need to write your essay will be included in the passage or in notes about it.

The SAT Essay shows how well you understand the passage and use it as the basis for a well-written, thought-out discussion. The two people who score your essay will each award between 1 and 4 points in each of these three categories:

Reading: A successful essay shows that you understood the passage, including the interplay of central ideas and important details. It also shows an effective use of textual evidence.

Analysis: A successful essay shows your understanding of how the author builds an argument by:

- Examining the author's use of evidence, reasoning, and other stylistic and persuasive techniques
- Supporting and developing claims with well-chosen evidence from the passage

Writing: A successful essay is focused, organized, and precise, with an appropriate style and tone that varies sentence structure and follows the conventions of standard written English.

You don't have to take the SAT with Essay, but if you do, you'll be able to apply to schools that require it. Find out which schools require or recommend the SAT Essay.

Key Content Features

Many questions on the SAT focus on important, widely used words and phrases found in texts in many different subjects. Some questions ask you to figure out a word's meaning based on context. The words are ones that you will probably encounter in college or in the workplace long after test day.

The Evidence-Based Reading and Writing section and the SAT Essay ask you to interpret, synthesize, and use evidence found in a wide range of sources. These sources include informational graphics, such as tables, charts, and graphs, as well as multiparagraph passages in the areas of literature and literary nonfiction, the humanities, science, history and social studies, and on topics about work and career.

For every passage or pair of passages you'll see during the Reading Test, at least one question will ask you to identify which part of the text best supports the answer to the previous question. In other instances, you'll be asked to find the best answer to a question by pulling together information conveyed in words and graphics.

The Writing and Language Test also focuses on command of evidence. It asks you to do things like analyze a series of sentences or paragraphs and decide if it makes sense. Other questions ask you to interpret graphics and to edit a part of the accompanying passage so that it clearly and accurately communicates the information in the graphics.

The SAT Essay also tests command of evidence. After reading a passage, you'll be asked to determine how the author builds an argument to persuade an audience through the use of evidence, reasoning, and/or stylistic and persuasive devices. Scorers look for cogent, clear analyses supported by critical reasoning and evidence drawn from the text provided.

The redesigned SAT Essay asks you to read a passage and explain how an author builds an argument to persuade an audience. This task closely mirrors college writing assignments because it is asking you to analyze how the author used evidence, reasoning, and stylistic and persuasive elements.

The new Essay is designed to support high school students and teachers as they cultivate close reading, careful analysis, and clear writing. It will promote the practice of reading a wide variety of arguments and analyzing how authors do their work as writers.

The essay prompt will be the same every time the SAT is offered, but the source material students are asked to write about will be different each time.

Not all students will take the SAT with Essay, but some school districts and colleges require it. The SAT is the only assessment in the SAT Suite that includes the Essay.

The Math Test focuses in-depth on three essential areas of math: Problem Solving and Data Analysis, Heart of Algebra, and Passport to Advanced Math.

Problem Solving and Data Analysis is about being quantitatively literate. It includes using ratios, percentages, and proportional reasoning to solve problems in science, social science, and career contexts.

The Heart of Algebra focuses on the mastery of linear equations and systems, which help students develop key powers of abstraction.

Passport to Advanced Math focuses on more complex equations and the manipulation they require.

Current research shows that these areas are used disproportionately in a wide range of majors and careers. The redesigned SAT also includes questions on other topics in math, including the kinds of geometric and trigonometric skills summary that are most relevant to college and careers.

SUMMARY

Throughout the SAT, you'll be asked questions grounded in the real world, directly related to work performed in college and career.

The Evidence-Based Reading and Writing section includes questions on literature and literary nonfiction, but also features charts, graphs, and passages like the ones students are likely to encounter in science, social science, and other majors and careers.

Questions on the Writing and Language Test ask you to do more than correct errors; they ask you to edit, revise, and improve texts from the humanities, history, social science, science, and career contexts.

The Math section features multistep applications to solve problems in science, social science, career scenarios, and other real-life situations. The test sets up a scenario and asks several questions that give you the opportunity to dig in and model it mathematically.

The redesigned SAT asks you to apply your reading, writing, language, and math knowledge and skills to answer questions in science, history, and social studies contexts. In this way, the assessments call on the same sorts of knowledge and skills that you'll use in college, at work, and throughout your life to make sense of recent discoveries, political developments, global events, and health and environmental issues.

The redesigned SAT includes a range of challenging texts and informational graphics that address these sorts of issues and topics in the Evidence-Based Reading and Writing section and the Math section. Questions will require you to read and understand texts, revise texts to be consistent with data presented in graphics, synthesize information presented through texts and graphics, and solve problems that are grounded in science and social science.

When you take the SAT, you'll be asked to read a passage from U.S. founding documents or the global conversation they inspired.

The U.S. founding documents, including the Declaration of Independence, the Bill of Rights, and the Federalist Papers, have been inspired by and have helped to inspire a conversation that continues to this day about the nature of civic life.

The SAT includes texts from this global conversation. The goal is to inspire a close reading of these rich, meaningful, often profound texts, not only as a way to develop valuable college and career readiness skills but also as an opportunity to reflect on and deeply engage with issues and concerns central to informed citizenship.

———

HOW TO TAKE A TEST

You have studied long, hard and conscientiously.

With your official admission card in hand, and your heart pounding, you have been admitted to the examination room.

You note that there are several hundred other applicants in the examination room waiting to take the same test.

They all appear to be equally well prepared.

You know that nothing but your best effort will suffice. The "moment of truth" is at hand: you now have to demonstrate objectively, in writing, your knowledge of content and your understanding of subject matter.

You are fighting the most important battle of your life—to pass and/or score high on an examination which will determine your career and provide the economic basis for your livelihood.

What extra, special things should you know and should you do in taking the examination?

I. YOU MUST PASS AN EXAMINATION

A. WHAT EVERY CANDIDATE SHOULD KNOW
Examination applicants often ask us for help in preparing for the written test. What can I study in advance? What kinds of questions will be asked? How will the test be given? How will the papers be graded?

B. HOW ARE EXAMS DEVELOPED?
Examinations are carefully written by trained technicians who are specialists in the field known as "psychological measurement," in consultation with recognized authorities in the field of work that the test will cover. These experts recommend the subject matter areas or skills to be tested; only those knowledges or skills important to your success on the job are included. The most reliable books and source materials available are used as references. Together, the experts and technicians judge the difficulty level of the questions.
Test technicians know how to phrase questions so that the problem is clearly stated. Their ethics do not permit "trick" or "catch" questions. Questions may have been tried out on sample groups, or subjected to statistical analysis, to determine their usefulness.
Written tests are often used in combination with performance tests, ratings of training and experience, and oral interviews. All of these measures combine to form the best-known means of finding the right person for the right job.

II. HOW TO PASS THE WRITTEN TEST

A. BASIC STEPS

1) Study the announcement

How, then, can you know what subjects to study? Our best answer is: "Learn as much as possible about the class of positions for which you've applied." The exam will test the knowledge, skills and abilities needed to do the work.

Your most valuable source of information about the position you want is the official exam announcement. This announcement lists the training and experience qualifications. Check these standards and apply only if you come reasonably close to meeting them. Many jurisdictions preview the written test in the exam announcement by including a section called "Knowledge and Abilities Required," "Scope of the Examination," or some similar heading. Here you will find out specifically what fields will be tested.

2) Choose appropriate study materials

If the position for which you are applying is technical or advanced, you will read more advanced, specialized material. If you are already familiar with the basic principles of your field, elementary textbooks would waste your time. Concentrate on advanced textbooks and technical periodicals. Think through the concepts and review difficult problems in your field.

These are all general sources. You can get more ideas on your own initiative, following these leads. For example, training manuals and publications of the government agency which employs workers in your field can be useful, particularly for technical and professional positions. A letter or visit to the government department involved may result in more specific study suggestions, and certainly will provide you with a more definite idea of the exact nature of the position you are seeking.

3) Study this book!

III. KINDS OF TESTS

Tests are used for purposes other than measuring knowledge and ability to perform specified duties. For some positions, it is equally important to test ability to make adjustments to new situations or to profit from training. In others, basic mental abilities not dependent on information are essential. Questions which test these things may not appear as pertinent to the duties of the position as those which test for knowledge and information. Yet they are often highly important parts of a fair examination. For very general questions, it is almost impossible to help you direct your study efforts. What we can do is to point out some of the more common of these general abilities needed in public service positions and describe some typical questions.

1) General information

Broad, general information has been found useful for predicting job success in some kinds of work. This is tested in a variety of ways, from vocabulary lists to questions about current events. Basic background in some field of work, such as sociology or economics, may be sampled in a group of questions. Often these are principles which have become familiar to most persons through exposure rather than through formal training. It is difficult to advise you how to study for these questions; being alert to the world around you is our best suggestion.

2) Verbal ability

An example of an ability needed in many positions is verbal or language ability. Verbal ability is, in brief, the ability to use and understand words. Vocabulary and grammar tests are typical measures of this ability. Reading comprehension or paragraph interpretation questions are common in many kinds of civil service tests. You are given a paragraph of written material and asked to find its central meaning.

IV. KINDS OF QUESTIONS

1. Multiple-choice Questions

Most popular of the short-answer questions is the "multiple choice" or "best answer" question. It can be used, for example, to test for factual knowledge, ability to solve problems or judgment in meeting situations found at work.

A multiple-choice question is normally one of three types:
- It can begin with an incomplete statement followed by several possible endings. You are to find the one ending which best completes the statement, although some of the others may not be entirely wrong.
- It can also be a complete statement in the form of a question which is answered by choosing one of the statements listed.
- It can be in the form of a problem – again you select the best answer.

Here is an example of a multiple-choice question with a discussion which should give you some clues as to the method for choosing the right answer:

When an employee has a complaint about his assignment, the action which will best help him overcome his difficulty is to
    A. discuss his difficulty with his coworkers
    B. take the problem to the head of the organization
    C. take the problem to the person who gave him the assignment
    D. say nothing to anyone about his complaint

In answering this question, you should study each of the choices to find which is best. Consider choice "A" – Certainly an employee may discuss his complaint with fellow employees, but no change or improvement can result, and the complaint remains unresolved. Choice "B" is a poor choice since the head of the organization probably does not know what assignment you have been given, and taking your problem to him is known as "going over the head" of the supervisor. The supervisor, or person who made the assignment, is the person who can clarify it or correct any injustice. Choice "C" is, therefore, correct. To say nothing, as in choice "D," is unwise. Supervisors have and interest in knowing the problems employees are facing, and the employee is seeking a solution to his problem.

2. True/False

3. Matching Questions

Matching an answer from a column of choices within another column.

V. RECORDING YOUR ANSWERS

Computer terminals are used more and more today for many different kinds of exams.

For an examination with very few applicants, you may be told to record your answers in the test booklet itself. Separate answer sheets are much more common. If this separate answer sheet is to be scored by machine – and this is often the case – it is highly important that you mark your answers correctly in order to get credit.

VI. BEFORE THE TEST

YOUR PHYSICAL CONDITION IS IMPORTANT

If you are not well, you can't do your best work on tests. If you are half asleep, you can't do your best either. Here are some tips:

1) Get about the same amount of sleep you usually get. Don't stay up all night before the test, either partying or worrying—DON'T DO IT!
2) If you wear glasses, be sure to wear them when you go to take the test. This goes for hearing aids, too.
3) If you have any physical problems that may keep you from doing your best, be sure to tell the person giving the test. If you are sick or in poor health, you relay cannot do your best on any test. You can always come back and take the test some other time.

Common sense will help you find procedures to follow to get ready for an examination. Too many of us, however, overlook these sensible measures. Indeed, nervousness and fatigue have been found to be the most serious reasons why applicants fail to do their best on civil service tests. Here is a list of reminders:

- Begin your preparation early – Don't wait until the last minute to go scurrying around for books and materials or to find out what the position is all about.
- Prepare continuously – An hour a night for a week is better than an all-night cram session. This has been definitely established. What is more, a night a week for a month will return better dividends than crowding your study into a shorter period of time.
- Locate the place of the exam – You have been sent a notice telling you when and where to report for the examination. If the location is in a different town or otherwise unfamiliar to you, it would be well to inquire the best route and learn something about the building.
- Relax the night before the test – Allow your mind to rest. Do not study at all that night. Plan some mild recreation or diversion; then go to bed early and get a good night's sleep.
- Get up early enough to make a leisurely trip to the place for the test – This way unforeseen events, traffic snarls, unfamiliar buildings, etc. will not upset you.
- Dress comfortably – A written test is not a fashion show. You will be known by number and not by name, so wear something comfortable.
- Leave excess paraphernalia at home – Shopping bags and odd bundles will get in your way. You need bring only the items mentioned in the official notice you received; usually everything you need is provided. Do not bring reference books to the exam. They will only confuse those last minutes and be taken away from you when in the test room.

- Arrive somewhat ahead of time – If because of transportation schedules you must get there very early, bring a newspaper or magazine to take your mind off yourself while waiting.
- Locate the examination room – When you have found the proper room, you will be directed to the seat or part of the room where you will sit. Sometimes you are given a sheet of instructions to read while you are waiting. Do not fill out any forms until you are told to do so; just read them and be prepared.
- Relax and prepare to listen to the instructions
- If you have any physical problem that may keep you from doing your best, be sure to tell the test administrator. If you are sick or in poor health, you really cannot do your best on the exam. You can come back and take the test some other time.

VII. AT THE TEST

The day of the test is here and you have the test booklet in your hand. The temptation to get going is very strong. Caution! There is more to success than knowing the right answers. You must know how to identify your papers and understand variations in the type of short-answer question used in this particular examination. Follow these suggestions for maximum results from your efforts:

1) Cooperate with the monitor

The test administrator has a duty to create a situation in which you can be as much at ease as possible. He will give instructions, tell you when to begin, check to see that you are marking your answer sheet correctly, and so on. He is not there to guard you, although he will see that your competitors do not take unfair advantage. He wants to help you do your best.

2) Listen to all instructions

Don't jump the gun! Wait until you understand all directions. In most civil service tests you get more time than you need to answer the questions. So don't be in a hurry. Read each word of instructions until you clearly understand the meaning. Study the examples, listen to all announcements and follow directions. Ask questions if you do not understand what to do.

3) Identify your papers

Civil service exams are usually identified by number only. You will be assigned a number; you must not put your name on your test papers. Be sure to copy your number correctly. Since more than one exam may be given, copy your exact examination title.

4) Plan your time

Unless you are told that a test is a "speed" or "rate of work" test, speed itself is usually not important. Time enough to answer all the questions will be provided, but this does not mean that you have all day. An overall time limit has been set. Divide the total time (in minutes) by the number of questions to determine the approximate time you have for each question.

5) Do not linger over difficult questions

If you come across a difficult question, mark it with a paper clip (useful to have along) and come back to it when you have been through the booklet. One caution if you do this – be sure to skip a number on your answer sheet as well. Check often to be sure that you have not lost your place and that you are marking in the row numbered the same as the question you are answering.

6) Read the questions

Be sure you know what the question asks! Many capable people are unsuccessful because they failed to read the questions correctly.

7) Answer all questions

Unless you have been instructed that a penalty will be deducted for incorrect answers, it is better to guess than to omit a question.

8) Speed tests

It is often better NOT to guess on speed tests. It has been found that on timed tests people are tempted to spend the last few seconds before time is called in marking answers at random – without even reading them – in the hope of picking up a few extra points. To discourage this practice, the instructions may warn you that your score will be "corrected" for guessing. That is, a penalty will be applied. The incorrect answers will be deducted from the correct ones, or some other penalty formula will be used.

9) Review your answers

If you finish before time is called, go back to the questions you guessed or omitted to give them further thought. Review other answers if you have time.

10) Return your test materials

If you are ready to leave before others have finished or time is called, take ALL your materials to the monitor and leave quietly. Never take any test material with you. The monitor can discover whose papers are not complete, and taking a test booklet may be grounds for disqualification.

VIII. EXAMINATION TECHNIQUES

1) Read the general instructions carefully. These are usually printed on the first page of the exam booklet. As a rule, these instructions refer to the timing of the examination; the fact that you should not start work until the signal and must stop work at a signal, etc. If there are any special instructions, such as a choice of questions to be answered, make sure that you note this instruction carefully.

2) When you are ready to start work on the examination, that is as soon as the signal has been given, read the instructions to each question booklet, underline any key words or phrases, such as least, best, outline, describe and the like. In this way you will tend to answer as requested rather than discover on reviewing your paper that you listed without describing, that you selected the worst choice rather than the best choice, etc.

3) If the examination is of the objective or multiple-choice type – that is, each question will also give a series of possible answers: A, B, C or D, and you are called upon to select the best answer and write the letter next to that answer on your answer paper – it is advisable to start answering each question in turn. There may be anywhere from 50 to 100 such questions in the three or four hours allotted and you can see how much time would be taken if you read through all the questions before beginning to answer any. Furthermore, if you

come across a question or group of questions which you know would be difficult to answer, it would undoubtedly affect your handling of all the other questions.

4) If the examination is of the essay type and contains but a few questions, it is a moot point as to whether you should read all the questions before starting to answer any one. Of course, if you are given a choice – say five out of seven and the like – then it is essential to read all the questions so you can eliminate the two that are most difficult. If, however, you are asked to answer all the questions, there may be danger in trying to answer the easiest one first because you may find that you will spend too much time on it. The best technique is to answer the first question, then proceed to the second, etc.

5) Time your answers. Before the exam begins, write down the time it started, then add the time allowed for the examination and write down the time it must be completed, then divide the time available somewhat as follows:
   - If 3-1/2 hours are allowed, that would be 210 minutes. If you have 80 objective-type questions, that would be an average of 2-1/2 minutes per question. Allow yourself no more than 2 minutes per question, or a total of 160 minutes, which will permit about 50 minutes to review.
   - If for the time allotment of 210 minutes there are 7 essay questions to answer, that would average about 30 minutes a question. Give yourself only 25 minutes per question so that you have about 35 minutes to review.

6) The most important instruction is to read each question and make sure you know what is wanted. The second most important instruction is to time yourself properly so that you answer every question. The third most important instruction is to answer every question. Guess if you have to but include something for each question. Remember that you will receive no credit for a blank and will probably receive some credit if you write something in answer to an essay question. If you guess a letter – say "B" for a multiple-choice question – you may have guessed right. If you leave a blank as an answer to a multiple-choice question, the examiners may respect your feelings but it will not add a point to your score. Some exams may penalize you for wrong answers, so in such cases only, you may not want to guess unless you have some basis for your answer.

7) Suggestions
   a. Objective-type questions
      1. Examine the question booklet for proper sequence of pages and questions
      2. Read all instructions carefully
      3. Skip any question which seems too difficult; return to it after all other questions have been answered
      4. Apportion your time properly; do not spend too much time on any single question or group of questions
      5. Note and underline key words – all, most, fewest, least, best, worst, same, opposite, etc.
      6. Pay particular attention to negatives
      7. Note unusual option, e.g., unduly long, short, complex, different or similar in content to the body of the question
      8. Observe the use of "hedging" words – probably, may, most likely, etc.

9. Make sure that your answer is put next to the same number as the question
10. Do not second-guess unless you have good reason to believe the second answer is definitely more correct
11. Cross out original answer if you decide another answer is more accurate; do not erase until you are ready to hand your paper in
12. Answer all questions; guess unless instructed otherwise
13. Leave time for review

b. Essay questions
1. Read each question carefully
2. Determine exactly what is wanted. Underline key words or phrases.
3. Decide on outline or paragraph answer
4. Include many different points and elements unless asked to develop any one or two points or elements
5. Show impartiality by giving pros and cons unless directed to select one side only
6. Make and write down any assumptions you find necessary to answer the questions
7. Watch your English, grammar, punctuation and choice of words
8. Time your answers; don't crowd material

8) Answering the essay question

Most essay questions can be answered by framing the specific response around several key words or ideas. Here are a few such key words or ideas:

M's: manpower, materials, methods, money, management
P's: purpose, program, policy, plan, procedure, practice, problems, pitfalls, personnel, public relations

a. Six basic steps in handling problems:
1. Preliminary plan and background development
2. Collect information, data and facts
3. Analyze and interpret information, data and facts
4. Analyze and develop solutions as well as make recommendations
5. Prepare report and sell recommendations
6. Install recommendations and follow up effectiveness

b. Pitfalls to avoid
1. Taking things for granted – A statement of the situation does not necessarily imply that each of the elements is necessarily true; for example, a complaint may be invalid and biased so that all that can be taken for granted is that a complaint has been registered
2. Considering only one side of a situation – Wherever possible, indicate several alternatives and then point out the reasons you selected the best one
3. Failing to indicate follow up – Whenever your answer indicates action on your part, make certain that you will take proper follow-up action to see how successful your recommendations, procedures or actions turn out to be
4. Taking too long in answering any single question – Remember to time your answers properly

EXAMINATION SECTION

EXAMINATION SECTION

TEST 1

DIRECTIONS: Each question or incomplete statement is followed by several suggested answers or completions. Select the one that BEST answers the question or completes the statement. *PRINT THE LETTER OF THE CORRECT ANSWER IN THE SPACE AT THE RIGHT.*

Questions 1-11.

DIRECTIONS: Questions 1 through 11 are to be answered on the basis of the following passage and supplementary material.

    Climate science measures changes that occur to a large geographical area over a long period of time, making it difficult to provide definitive answers to climate change questions. [1]However, multiple studies have been conducted since the 1990s to determine how the scientific community collectively views anthropogenic climate change. These studies [2]are including surveys as well as analysis of peer-reviewed articles and have come to the conclusion that at least 97 percent of actively publishing climate scientists around the world agree that human activities have contributed to rising global temperatures.
    Surveys suggest, however, that most Americans either disagree with these findings or are unaware of them. [3]A study found that only 48 percent of American adults surveyed shared the belief that increased global temperatures resulted from human activities. Skeptics of global warming and climate change have noted, for instance, that Earth has experienced cyclical changes to its climate patterns for millennia and that recent climatic shifts are not as severe as indicated or necessarily a consequence of human activity alone. [4]In response to such arguments, climate scientists Seth Darling and Douglas Sisterson contend that "because the projected consequences of climate disruption are [5]so scary skeptics seem to find welcome ears for their claims that climate models exaggerate the threats posed by our greenhouses-gas emission."
    Even if all members of society [6]had previously and currently agreed that global temperatures are rising and humans are the cause, there is no obvious response to the challenges created by climate change. No climate model formulated by scientists to chart climate patterns has had 100 percent accuracy in predicting changes. However, scientists continue to refine their methods to produce more reliable data. [7]Much climate models failed to predict a slowdown in rising temperatures at the beginning of the twenty-first century. Some predictions have also underestimated threats. In its initial assessment of rising sea levels in 1990, the Intergovernmental Panel on Climate Change (IPCC) originally anticipated [8]a sea level rise of 1.9 millimeters per year from that year onward. However, data have revealed that sea levels have in fact risen at a rate of 3.4 millimeters per year. The science of climate change is so [9]easily misunderstood that some actions that seem helpful may actually cause damage in the long term. Some of the most potent greenhouse gases, HFCs and PFCs, are commonly used as replacements for other chemicals called chlorofluorocarbons (CFCs), which were phased out between 1989 and 1996 because they damaged the ozone layer. Consequently, the same process that solved one environmental problem—ozone damage—[10]had little to no impact on another. To avoid a similar situation, government research facilities and

policymakers have begun planning ahead and considering the possible consequences of any proposed approach to global warming.[11]

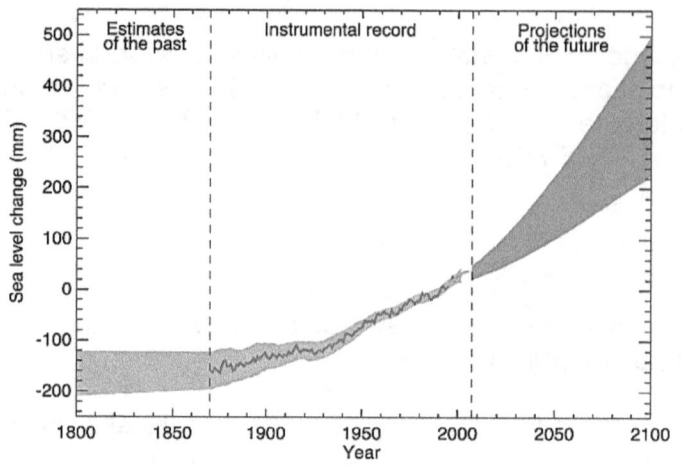

1. A. NO CHANGE   B. Consequently,
    C. In spite of,   D. Additionally,

2. A. NO CHANGE   B. including
    C. have included   D. included

3. If the author wished to be more precise in his evidence of research, which of the following details would be the BEST to add here?
    A. NO CHANGE
    B. A 2016 scientific research study
    C. A 2016 Pew Research Center study
    D. A Pew Research study, from 2016,

4. A. NO CHANGE
    B. Because of this argument
    C. Sequentially
    D. In regards to an argument such as this

5. A. NO CHANGE   B. so scary, skeptics
    C. so, scary skeptics D. so scary skeptics,

6. A. NO CHANGE   B. had agreed
    C. has agreed   D. agreed

7. A. NO CHANGE   B. Most
    C. Few   D. A ton

8. Which choice MOST effectively combines the underlined sentences?
   A. In its initial assessment of rising sea levels in 1990, the IPCC anticipated a rise of 1.9 millimeters per year, and however data have revealed that sea levels rose at a rate of 3.4 millimeters per year.
   B. In its initial assessment of rising sea levels in 1990, the IPCC predicted a rise of 1.9 millimeters per year, and yet the researched data suggests that sea levels could have possibly rose at a rate of 3.4 millimeters instead.
   C. In its initial assessment of rising sea levels in 1990, the IPCC anticipated a rise of 1.9 millimeters per year; however, data have revealed that sea levels rose at a rate of 3.4 millimeters per year.
   D. Initially, the IPCC anticipated a rise of 1.9 millimeters in rising sea levels in 1990, but data have recently revealed that sea levels have risen at a rate of 3.4 millimeters per year.

9. The author wishes to be more concise with his word choice here. Which of the following helps accomplish this goal?
   A. NO CHANGE
   B. complex
   C. hard to understand
   D. easy to misunderstand

10. A. NO CHANGE
    B. has been contributing to
    C. had minimal impact on
    D. contributed

11. The writer wants to conclude the passage with a sentence that emphasizes the importance of understanding the effects of global warming. Which choice would BEST accomplish this goal?
    A. The consequences of global warming remain an issue of great debate and uncertainty, and some researchers predict dramatic and serious problems for future generations.
    B. Global warming could also have a major impact on habitats. Some areas well suited to farming might become too dry or too wet to support agriculture.
    C. Furthermore, people would also face serious problems. Loss of farmland, for example, would cause disruptions in the food supply, bringing about famine in many areas.
    D. Regulations that place higher industry standards on performance and technology provide another way to reduce emissions.

KEY (CORRECT ANSWERS)

1. A
2. D
3. C
4. A
5. B
6. D
7. B
8. C
9. B
10. D
11. A

TEST 2

DIRECTIONS: Each question or incomplete statement is followed by several suggested answers or completions. Select the one that BEST answers the question or completes the statement. *PRINT THE LETTER OF THE CORRECT ANSWER IN THE SPACE AT THE RIGHT.*

Questions 1-11.

DIRECTIONS: Questions 1 through 11 are to be answered on the basis of the following passage and supplementary material.

 Payday [1]loan are intended to help people who want or need access to credit that banks are unwilling to provide. However, the difference between wanting credit and needing credit can be important. When high-interest credit is used for wants instead of needs, it can be a terrible idea.
 Payday loans are essentially the United States version [2]of microfinance, they have very short repayment periods, the interest rates are very high, and they target those who can't access normal credit channels. [3]Small-scale high-interest-rate loans can lead people to remain impoverished when the additional debt they accrue becomes too burdensome—a problem that often occurs in the field of microfinance and, we have found, with payday loans. That's not to say that short-term loans in the U.S. are always a bad idea. On the contrary, they fulfill a need. But what is that need, exactly?
 In the United States, the most common need is to pay for emergency expenses. Forty-seven percent of Americans say they don't have enough money saved to cover a small emergency. Unexpected medical bills, car repairs or a lower paycheck could mean a week without food. When family can't help, to whom can people turn? [4]Banks aren't interested in small, temporary loans—they don't make money that way.
 [5]But for most every other conceivable case, they are a terrible idea. They are prohibitively expensive and, perhaps more importantly, behaviorally dangerous. When easy credit is not available, people think twice before making unnecessary purchases. Payday loans allow people to make non-critical purchases at high interest rates, which means they are paying even more for things they don't really need.[6]
 [7]Short-term, high-interest loans should be available only for truly urgent needs. In a perfect world, these loans would be prohibited when people are making clearly bad choices that have long-term negative consequences for them and their families. But how? Who's to say what constitutes a family emergency or dire need? As Americans, we rely on our freedom to choose: It is up to the individual to make responsible choices.
 What the U.S. truly needs are policies that ensure that low-income people don't need payday loans to begin with. [8]You need to end the problem of hunger that leads many to look to these loans to put food on their tables when money runs low. We need to continue to reduce the burden that medical coverage places on poor families.
 Researchers have published countless articles on how to address these [9]issues. We don't have a clear solution—if it was that easy to solve poverty, it would be over by now. That said, recent solutions do show promise: guaranteed minimum income programs and cash grant programs such as Prospera (formerly Oportunidades) from Mexico, which gives families direct cash payments in exchange for school attendance and health clinic visits.

Currently, much of the United States' low-income support bureaucratically restricts individual choice. We need a system that gives options back to [10]individuals and gives them the individual power to make good long-term choices for themselves and their families. Research shows that the poor don't actually waste their money on drugs or alcohol when they receive cash programs. Instead, when given control over their own lives through policies that provide simple cash, such as Prospera, they make good choices. Sometimes it still means a high-interest short-term loan. But it's far less often.

Payday loans aren't the problem. Rather, there are a symptom of a larger epidemic. The only long-term solution is to eliminate the core problem of poverty in the United States.[11]

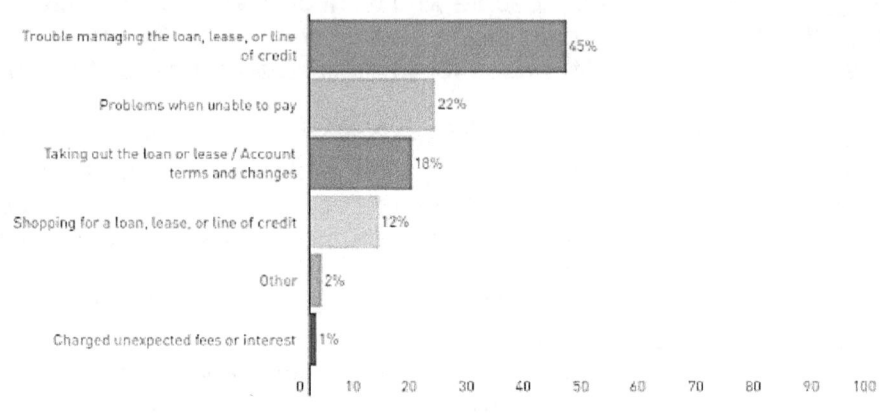

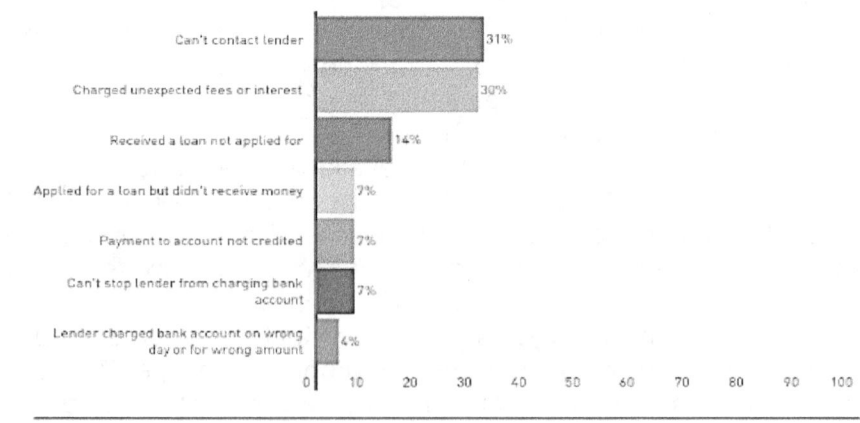

Source: Consumer Financial Protection Bureau. *Consumer Response Annual Report: January 1–December 31, 2016*, March 2017. https://s3.amazonaws.com/files.consumerfinance.gov/f/documents/201703_cfpb_Consumer-Response-Annual-Report-2016.pdf

1. A. NO CHANGE   B. loans is
   C. loans are   D. loans were

3 (#2)

2. A. NO CHANGE
    B. of microfinance; they
    C. of microfinance: they
    D. of microfinance they

    2.____

3. A. NO CHANGE
    B. Small-scale, high-interest-rate,
    B. Small-scale, high-interest-rate
    D. Small, scale high-interest-rate

    3.____

4. The writer wishes to complete the sentence with a rhetorical statement to help prove the point about when payday loans are acceptable.
    Which choice BEST accomplishes this goal?
    A. NO CHANGE
    B. When the alternative is going without food or losing your car, payday loans are the least-bad solution.
    C. If a payday loan can help you take a vacation with your kids, it might be worth the memories.
    D. A payday loan could mean paying off high-interest credit card debt, which might allow you to pay for food that week.

    4.____

5. A. NO CHANGE
    B. However
    C. Initially in
    D. Surprisingly, for

    5.____

6. At this point, the author wishes to make a more direct connection to the charts attached to the end of this article.
    Which choice MOST effectively establishes that connection?
    A. As you can see in the charts below the number one complaint people have with payday loans is their inability to keep up with the payments.
    B. The charts below reveal further danger in payday loans as they show that 61% of payday loan complaints come from inability to contact the lender and hidden interest fees.
    C. Further evidence regarding dangerous payday loans can be seen in the charts below.
    D. As shown in the charts below, many people complain about payday loans.

    6.____

7. Which choice MOST effectively establishes the main topic of the paragraph?
    A. While outlawing payday loans, except in cases of emergency, would solve this problem, the government cannot take away a person's right to choose.
    B. Americans should not be able to secure payday loans no matter the reason.
    C. If people are irresponsible with their money, then they deserve to get trapped in high-interest payday loans.
    D. The government should decide whether or not a person applying for a payday loan truly needs it.

    7.____

8. A. NO CHANGE
    B. They
    C. We
    E. US

    8.____

7

9. Which choice MOST effectively combines the sentences at the underlined portion?
   A. issues, so we
   B. issues, we
   C. issues we
   D. issues, but we

10. A. NO CHANGE
    B. individuals, yet
    C. individuals, also
    D. individuals or

11. At this point, the writer is considering adding the following sentence:
    What borrowers really need is a conventional installment loan that they can pay back over time.
    Should the writer make this addition here?
    A. Yes, because it contributes to the main point of the article, which is that payday loans are dangerous.
    B. Yes, because it shows readers that there are other ways to help pay for emergencies rather than payday loans.
    C. No, because it strays from the paragraph's overall point, which is that poverty needs to be eliminated, not payday loans.
    D. No, because it tacks on irrelevant information at the end of the passage.

KEY (CORRECT ANSWERS)

1. C
2. C
3. D
4. B
5. A
6. B
7. A
8. C
9. D
10. A
11. C

TEST 3

DIRECTIONS: Each question or incomplete statement is followed by several suggested answers or completions. Select the one that BEST answers the question or completes the statement. *PRINT THE LETTER OF THE CORRECT ANSWER IN THE SPACE AT THE RIGHT.*

Questions 1-11.

DIRECTIONS: Questions 1 through 11 are to be answered on the basis of the following passage and supplementary material.

One of the more venerable institutions that cling like barnacles to the vast bulk of Harvard University is the Signet [1]Society which fosters literary achievement and the liberal arts in general. The club occupies an eighteenth-century house at the corner of Mt. Auburn and Dunster Streets where [2]one offers lunch and conversation to members throughout the academic year. There's also a Christmas party, at which everyone gets tipsy and sings carols off key, and an annual affair called Strawberry Night, which is much too complicated to explain. There are likewise teas and receptions for various vising lions and lionesses.

When I was an undergraduate member, back in the 1950s, membership was strictly [3]male, and remained so into the 1970s, although on one occasion Adrienne Rich (invited to read) stormed out in her high feminist dudgeon at an ill-considered anecdote about a stripper. Today, the organization has achieved gender parity.

[4]By far the most gaudy Signet ritual is the Annual Dinner. The Annual Dinner is an event presided over by the Toastmaster. It includes (besides comments from various officers), a reading by The Poet, presentation of the annual Signet Medal for literary achievement to The Recipient, and a speech (or reading) by The Speaker.

In 1971, to celebrate the centenary of the society, [5]they assembled an unforgettable combination: The Toastmaster was Erich Segal, The Poet was Allen Ginsberg, The Recipient was John Updike, and The Speaker was Kurt Vonnegut.

By the 1960s, these dinners had outgrown the clubhouse, and this one was held in a banquet hall on the top floor of the Holyoke Center—recently completed—on Massachusetts Avenue. Somehow, Harvard [6]will acquire a number of immense, brooding paintings by Mark Rothko and—evidently for want of any place more appropriate to hang them—had put them into this room. The ceiling was so low (or the artwork so large) that the paintings reached almost to the floor, and there were already signs of damage from chairs rubbing against them. [They also turned out to be almost ephemeral: Rothko had used cheap enamel from Woolworth's that quickly faded. They have no lost most of their brilliance and been placed in permanent storage.] In any case, the paintings provided a remarkably gloomy backdrop for what was intended as a convivial occasion.

[7]Vonnegut, to the left, wore a respectable dinner jacket, but he had that remarkable gift of making anything he wore—no matter how fresh when he put it on—look as though he'd been wearing it for a week. Segal, to his left, was elegant in black velvet. Next to him, Ginsberg was appropriately natty, although he had forgone a tie (who could tell behind the beard?). At the right end, Updike maintained the values of an earlier day with a wing collar and brocade vest.

With dinner fished and everyone well lubricated, the speeches began; and the evening turned into a Segal roast. This raillery began with the obligatory speeches by officers and reached its climax with whoever introduced The Toastmaster. Erich himself came across as modest, earnest, and a bit chagrined at being the object of so much attention. He got a break

2 (#3)

when Ginsberg spoke, since the poet stuck to his own schtick, revved up his prayer wheel, and soon had us all changing "Om...Om...Om...."[8]

In receiving his medal, Updike was appropriately diffident and wry, but he couldn't resist pointing out that all his books to that point (respected though they were) had collectively failed to achieve the total sales of Love Story.

[9]Finally, it was Vonnegut's turn. He spoke at length about values and the human condition but somehow did so in a way that had us all laughing [10]controllably! His digression into the Segal issue put paid to all further discussion. "To shoot Erich Segal for writing Love Story would be like putting a man to death for baking a chocolate éclair."

I later learned from an acquaintance with whom Ginsberg had stated that Erich had been so nervous that Allen [11]was holding his hand throughout the whole evening to steady him. And so it goes.

1. A. NO CHANGE B. Society, which
   C. Society; which D. Society that

2. A. NO CHANGE B. they
   C. you D. it

3. A. NO CHANGE B. female
   D. unisex D. ambiguous

4. Which choice BEST combines the sentences at the underlined portion?
   A. The Annual Dinner is the most gaudy Signet ritual; because it is presided over by The Toastmaster.
   B. By far the most gaudy Signet ritual is the Annual dinner; the Annual Dinner is an event presided over by the Toastmaster.
   C. The gaudiest Signet ritual is the Annual Dinner, the Annual Dinner is an event presided over by the Toastmaster.
   D. By far the most gaudy Signet ritual is the Annual Dinner, an event presided over by The Toastmaster.

5. A. NO CHANGE B. the planners of the dinner
   C. I D. some

6. A. NO CHANGE B. acquire
   C. had acquired D. will be acquiring

7. The author wishes to find a better transition back to this memoir. Which choice BEST reintroduces the topic into this paragraph?
   A. NO CHANGE
   B. The four distinguished guests were dotted along the head table.
   C. Now back to my interesting night at a Signet Society event.
   D. As I stood entranced, I waited for the main guests to arrive, which of course they were late.

8. At this point, the writer is considering adding the following sentence:
   The burden of all these jibes was that brilliant young Harvard classicists who had rapidly achieved tenure at Yale were not expected to write overly sentimental novels, and if they do so, they should not appear on every talk show in the country and earn such large piles of money that they would never need to work again.
   Should the writer make this addition here?
   A. Yes, because it helps provide context for why everyone was roasting Erich.
   B. Yes, because it shows how angry and jealous writers can be of their successful contemporaries.
   C. No, because while it does provide context for the insults, the account has already moved on to the next part of the evening.
   D. No, because it provides no relevant information to the retelling of this story.

9. A. NO CHANGE   B. Next,
    C. Of course,   D. Naturally,

10. A. NO CHANGE   B. uncontrollably?
    C. uncontrollable.   D. uncontrollably.

11. A. NO CHANGE   B. holds
    C. held   D. will hold

KEY (CORRECT ANSWERS)

1. B   6. C   11. C
2. D   7. B
3. A   8. C
4. D   9. A
5. B   10. D

TEST 4

DIRECTIONS: Each question or incomplete statement is followed by several suggested answers or completions. Select the one that BEST answers the question or completes the statement. *PRINT THE LETTER OF THE CORRECT ANSWER IN THE SPACE AT THE RIGHT.*

Questions 1-11.

DIRECTIONS: Questions 1 through 11 are to be answered on the basis of the following passage and supplementary material.

Big Data Is Not Destiny

In the aftermath of the [1]potential Epic Big Data fail on Election Day, many Americans will judge predictions, projections and premonitions with more skepticism. They've learned an important, even comforting, lesson about the limits of polling and other measures: Big Data is not destiny.

Algorithms are formulas [2]many often times written by humans to take the guesswork out of what other human beings will do under certain circumstances. Will they buy this toothpaste? At what price?

Survey responses to pollsters, consumer buying habits, and [3]internet site visits can be plugged into computer models to suggest people's future behavior. The understandable hope is always that if you start with knowable measurements and crunch them through well-constructed formulas, you'll produce a reliable preview of what will happen.

   [4]This is not necessarily true.

Computers don't read minds [5]or do pollsters. People don't always say what they think or they change their minds. People can be convinced and unconvinced. Some people say one thing but do another. You will never write a program to take into account all those nuances and many others.

To a computer, [6]developing behavior is an efficient but wisdom-deprived matter of manipulating ones and zeros. But the real world isn't always binary.

Big Data can lead to Big Mistakes. Google Flu Trends, for instance, sought to use data from internet searches to estimate when influenza season would peak and at what level. But it drastically overestimated peak flu levels in the 2012-13 season. That failure "doesn't erase the value of big data," wrote David Lazer of Northeastern University and Ryan Kennedy of the University of Houston in Wired magazine. "What it does do is highlight a number of problematic practices in use—what we like to call "bid data hubris."[7]

We'd say that many alleged political pros suffered a serious case of that affliction before voters set them straight Nov. 8.

Should we toss out data and rely only on experience, or on anecdotes, or on what we hear (true or false) from people with whom we [8]agree!

That would be a dangerous overreaction to the election flub. If people believe the data cannot be trusted, they may turn instead to "trusting anecdotes from friends, family, and tribe," political blogger Erick Erickson [9]rites in The New York times. "Policies will be based on what people think are good ideas, not what data show. This will potentially further divide the country and further segment an already divided nation," he warms, aptly.

Humans embrace Big Data—more than they would if it were more accurately billed as Big Guesses or Big Evidence-based Hunches—because we live in an unpredictable universe that is often capricious. People feel comforted when they think they know what is going to happen. They see patterns in random chance. They purge from their thoughts the reality that a 74 percent chance of victory is a 26 percent chance of defeat. [10]However, superstition endures.

Reality is elastic. Every moment brings new possibilities. That's what makes life intriguing.[11]

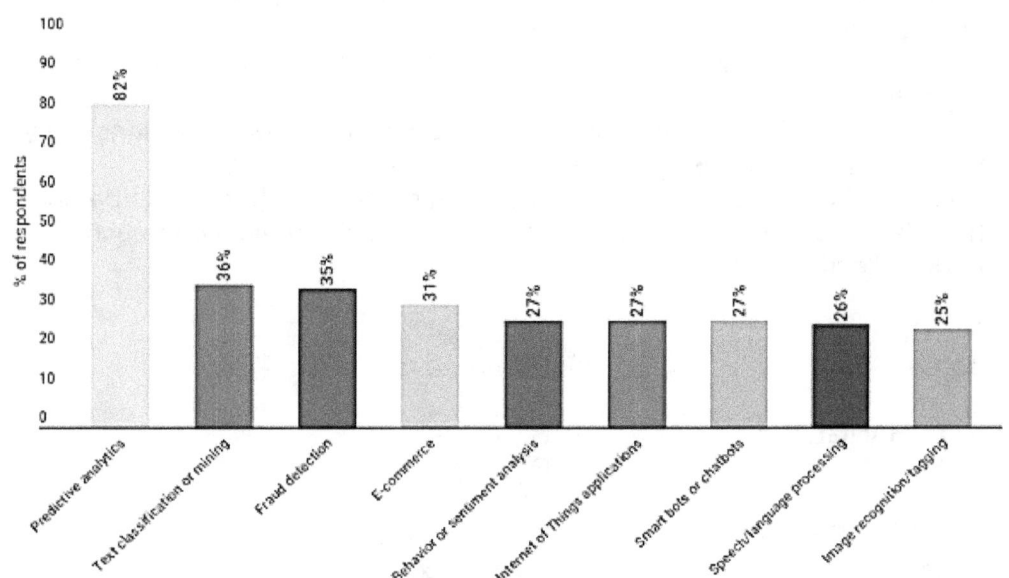

1. A. NO CHANGE B. alleged
   C. supposedly D. predicted

2. A. NO CHANGE B. oftentimes
   C. repeatedly D. delete the underlined portion

3. A. NO CHANGE B. visiting internet sites
   C. for internet site visitations D. the visitation of internet sites

4. Which choice MOST effectively sets up the list of statements that follows in the next paragraph?
   A. NO CHANGE
   B. This could possibly be the case
   C. But as we know, this is not always necessarily true
   D. However, you know, as well as I do, this is not necessarily true

5. A. NO CHANGE   B. and so
   C. nor   D. even though

6. A. NO CHANGE   B. emerging
   C. creating   D. predicting

7. The writer wishes to include a statement here that strengthens the connection between the article and the statistics provided at the end. Which choice MOST effectively accomplishes this goal?
   A. Looking at the chart below, one can easily surmise that far too many people believe in the power of big data.
   B. This hubris can be seen in the staggering amount of businesses that use big data for predictive analytics.
   C. No one knows for sure what big data is properly used for as evidenced by the different percentages of usage seen in the graph below.
   D. The chart below clearly shows how damaging big data hubris can be and how dangerous it is to make assumptions about the meaning of such a large collection of 'facts'.

8. A. NO CHANGE   B. agree
   C. agree,   D. agree?

9. A. NO CHANGE   B. rights
   C. writes   D. wrights

10. A. NO CHANGE   B. As a result,
    C. Instead,   D. For example,

11. The writer wants a conclusion that restates the main idea of the passage. Which choice MOST effectively accomplishes this goal?
    A. Ultimately, studies have shown the value of big data, but we are far from a place where they can supplant more traditional methods or theories.
    B. We can conclusively state that the majority of big data that has received attention is not the conclusion of these instruments that are designed to produce genuinely authentic data tractable for scientific analysis.
    C. In the end, practical research must stand on a foundation of measurement.
    D. Nonetheless, there are multiple challenges with improving our understanding of big data and if we don't get smarter, we'll never be able to harness it properly.

KEY (CORRECT ANSWERS)

1. B
2. D
3. A
4. A
5. C
6. D
7. B
8. D
9. C
10. B
11. A

EXAMINATION SECTION

TEST 1

DIRECTIONS: Each question or incomplete statement is followed by several suggested answers or completions. Select the one that BEST answers the question or completes the statement. *PRINT THE LETTER OF THE CORRECT ANSWER IN THE SPACE AT THE RIGHT.*

Questions 1-11.

DIRECTIONS: Questions 1 through 11 are to be answered on the basis of the following passage and supplementary material.

[1] However Zora Neale Hurston has gained considerable internet notoriety after Google dedicated a Doodle to her Tuesday in honor of her 123rd birthday, she almost didn't exist as a part of mainstream American literature.

It was an essay by another famed southern author, Alice Walker, [2] she wrote the novel "The Color Purple", that chronicled searching for Ms. Hurston's unmarked grave in the small central-Florida town that brought new critical eyes to Hurston's previously un-lauded work, and made her stories an integral part of the American anthology today.

Though she never gained widespread recognition for her work during her [3] life, it did not stop Hurston from traveling, writing, and chronicling life through [4] Harlem, the South, Haiti, the country of Jamaica, and elsewhere. She first published stories for a literary review at Howard University, in Washington, D.C., where she gained her associates degree, and at various magazines in New York City, where she studied anthropology at Barnard College. She lived in Harlem during the height of the Harlem Renaissance, where she became close with writers and artists such as Wallace Thurman and Langston Hughes with whom she wrote the play "Mule Bone."

During this time, her fellow writers found her passion for folklore, anthropology, and storytelling compelling, as well as entertaining.

"Almost nobody else could stop the average Harlemite on Lenox Avenue and measure his head with a strange-looking, anthropological device and not get bawled out for the attempt, except Zora, who used to stop anyone whose head looked interesting, and measure it," wrote Mr. Hughes in "The Big Sea."

But it was not met with the same cultural acceptance in the larger world. Many African-American authors of this time felt either ignored or pigeon-holed as a black author by the larger literary community, and Hurston (among many others) had difficulty getting work published. In the late 1950s, she wrote a hand-written letter to Harper's Brothers, asking them to publish her final work—a story of Herod the Great—an anecdote which Hurston biographer Robert Hemenway says is revealing of "how the bright promise of an earlier interest in black art—the Harlem Renaissance in the 1920s—deteriorated for many of those who had shared its exuberance."

[5] During this time, Hurston was never able to live off her writing. She took a job as a teacher. Then, she took a job as a librarian. After that, she took a job as a maid and then even a manicurist to stay afloat.

She [6] was retired to a welfare home in a town not far from Eatonville, Fla., the town where she grew up and served as inspiration for her seminal work "Their Eyes Were Watching God."

When it was originally published in 1937, "Their Eyes Were Watching God" was criticized or overlooked for its use of small town, southern vernacular (ex: "Dat wuz uh might fine thing fuh you tuh do"), and by African-American authors for playing into the confines of preconceived notions about race. Richard Wright—author of "Native Son"—wrote in his review for New Masses, "Her characters eat and laugh and cry and work and kill; they swing like a pendulum eternally in that safe and narrow orbit in which America likes to see the Negro live: between laughter and tears."

Due to this response, when she died in 1960, many of her works had gone out of print. She was buried in an unmarked grave.

[7] In the meantime, Ms. Walker began reading Hurston's works. She quickly recognized Hurston's unusual talent, and set out to find out what had become of the author. Her search culminated in an essay for Ms. Magazine titled "Searching for Zora," which followed Walker's journey to Eatonville to find Hurston's grave. There, she met several of the people who inspired Hurston's characters and got a feel for the upbringing Hurston must have had in one of the only all-black incorporated towns in Florida.

After Walker's essay and advocacy, "Their Eyes Were Watching God" was re-issued and critically re-examined to [8] lukewarm reviews. In the first month of its reissue, it sold more than 75,000 copies. More recently, it was named one of the top 100 best English language novels by Time Magazine, and Oprah became an advocate for the novel, picking it for her famous book club and producing it as a made-for-TV movie in 2005.

[9] Tom Bissell wrote "Magic Hat," a series of essays on authors who nearly disappeared after their work failed to originally take off. He says his actually speaks to the integrity of the author, and the challenge of the reader. "I like this idea because it implies that there are many wonderful artists out there, doing their thing, not particularly chasing after fame or renown, and making stuff just for the sheer job and fulfillment of it," he says in an interview with Harper's Magazine. "Also because it gives average people—you and me, in other words—an enormous amount of responsibility to go looking for stuff on our own, and champion it, and talk about it [10] ?"

Thanks to Alice Walker and other literature advocates, Hurston is a prime example among posthumous turn-around tales, and finally was given a permanent grave marker by Walker in 1973.[11]

1. A. NO CHANGE B. Even C. Though D. If   1.____

2. A. NO CHANGE   2.____
   B. (who wrote "The Color Purple")
   C. writing "The Color Purple"
   D. Alice Walker was the one who wrote "The Color Purple"

3. A. NO CHANGE B. life; it C. life. It D. life it   3.____

4. A. NO CHANGE   4.____
   B. Harlem, the South, the Republic of Haiti, the country of Jamaica, and etc.
   C. the Harlem, the South, the Haiti, the Jamaica, and elsewhere
   D. Harlem, the South, Haiti, Jamaica, and elsewhere

5. The author wishes to be more concise with his word choice here. Which of the following helps accomplish this goal?
   A. NO CHANGE
   B. During this time, Hurston was never able to live off her writing, and took side jobs as a teacher, librarian, maid, and even manicurist to stay afloat.
   C. During this time, Hurston was never able to live off her writing. She took many jobs.
   D. During this time, Hurston was never able to live off her writing. She worked as a teacher then she worked as a librarian, after that she worked as a maid, and finally she even worked as a manicurist to stay afloat.

6. A. NO CHANGE
   B. retires
   C. will have retired
   D. retired

7. A. NO CHANGE
   B. Occasionally,
   C. On the other hand,
   D. With that being said,

8. A. NO CHANGE
   B. controversial
   C. rave
   D. tantalizing

9. Which choice MOST effectively establishes the main topic of the paragraph?
   A. Some experts feel that Hurston would've been discovered eventually, even without the backing of someone like Alice Walker.
   B. Certain people feel that Zora Neale Hurston should have stayed in anonymity, never becoming a famous writer.
   C. Though her near-obscurity may seem like a disheartening close-call, some argue the opposite.
   D. While it would have been a travesty if Hurston's work were never celebrated, some experts remind us that this kind of thing happens all the time.

10. A. NO CHANGE   B. ."   C. !"   D. "?

11. The writer wants a final sentence that helps restate the main idea of the passage. Which choice MOST effectively accomplishes this goal?
    A. Ultimately, Zora Neale Hurston received her just due and while she was not alive to appreciate it, we certainly can appreciate her and her important writings.
    B. Despite this success, one cannot help but feel that genius such as hers needed to be recognized while she still lived, not 13 years after she died.
    C. There are so many undiscovered writers out there, having believed they failed as a writer as they passed on from this world, and it is our duty to make sure that never happens again.
    D. It reads: Zora Neale Hurston "A Genius of the South" 1901-1960; Novelist, Folklorist, Anthropologist

Questions 12-22.

DIRECTIONS: Questions 12 through 22 are to be answered on the basis of the following passage and supplementary material.

Air pollution [12] is referring to the release into the air of chemicals and other substances, known as pollutants, that are potentially harmful to human health and the environment. According to the World Health Organization (WHO), exposure to ambient (outdoor) air pollution causes 3 million premature deaths around the world each year, largely due to heart and lung diseases. Air pollution also contributes to such environmental threats as smog, acid rain, depletion of the ozone layer, and global climate change.

The WHO has established Air Quality Guidelines (AQGs) to identify safe levels of exposure to the emission of four harmful types of air pollution [13] pollutants worldwide: particulate matter (PM), ozone (O_3), nitrogen oxide (NO_2), and sulfur dioxide (SO_2). The US Environmental Protection Agency (EPA) sets National Ambient Air Quality Standards (NAAQS) for those four pollutants as well as carbon monoxide (CO) and lead. Since EPA criteria define the allowable concentrations of these six substances in ambient air throughout the United States, they are known as criteria air pollutants. The EPA also regulates 187 toxic air pollutants, such as asbestos, benzene, dioxin, and mercury. Finally, the EPA places limits on emissions of greenhouse gases like carbon dioxide (CO_2) and methane, which contribute to global climate change.

Air pollution is generated by many sources. More than half of US air pollution comes from mobile sources, including automobiles, trucks, and airplanes. Area sources are [14] compromised of many small emissions sources that are grouped together in a distinct area, such as furnaces in a neighborhood or methane-producing livestock in an agricultural region. Stationary or point sources emit air pollutants from a single, identifiable location, such as electrical power plants, oil refineries, and waste incinerators. Air pollution can also originate from natural resources, such as forest fires, volcanic eruptions, and blowing dust or sand. The main cause of air pollution is the burning of fossil fuels such as coal, oil, and natural gas for energy. [15]

According to the EPA, the United States sent a total of 78 million tons of pollution into the air in 2016. Ambient air quality improved steadily from 1980 to 2016. Lead emissions decreased by 99 percent during that period, largely due to the elimination of lead from gasoline, while SO_2 emissions decreased by 87 percent and CO emissions by 85 percent. [16] Moreover, 123 million Americans—or 38 percent of the population—lived in a county where air pollution levels exceeded NAAQS for one or more pollutants as of 2016. Worldwide, 92 percent of people lived in places with air pollution levels higher than recommended under WHO guidelines in 2014. Poor air quality and the associated health impacts disproportionately affect people in low- and middle-income countries (LMIC), where 87 percent of the premature deaths attributed to air pollution occurred.

Impact on Human Health

Air pollution is [17] rarely considered to be the single greatest environmental risk factor to human health. Exposure to particulate matter (PM)—tiny particles of dust, smoke, soot, chemicals, and allergens released into the air by industry, agriculture, transportation, and natural sources—is associated with a number of adverse health impacts. Breathing air containing PM less than 10 microns in diameter, for instance, increases the risk of cardiovascular disease as well as respiratory illnesses and lung cancer. PM less than 2.5 microns in diameter has the capacity to penetrate lung tissue and enter the bloodstream, where

[18] they increase the risk of kidney disease. A study of US military veterans, published in 2017, found that environmental exposure to elevated levels of PM 2.5 led to an annual increase of nearly 45,000 cases of chronic kidney disease and 2,500 cases of end-stage kidney disease.

[19] Ground-level ozone is produced when pollutants from burning fossil fuels react with UV radiation to create smog. Exposure to high levels of O_3 can cause eye and throat irritation, decrease lung function, and increase the severity of symptoms for people with allergies or asthma. Pollutants that deplete the protective ozone layer in the atmosphere, meanwhile, increase human exposure to UV radiation, which can increase the risk of skin cancer, cataracts, and immune system disorders.

Exposure to airborne toxic chemicals is also associated with serious human health [20] affects, including cancer, reproductive issues, and birth defects. Benzene, for instance, causes eye, skin, and lung irritation as well as blood disorders and cancers. Dioxins have been linked to immune and nervous system disorders, and liver and other cancers. Mercury causes damage to the central nervous system. Studies have shown that exposure to lead causes damage to a child's developing brain, increasing the risk of low IQ, learning difficulties, and behavioral issues. [21] The EPA-mandated removal of lead from gasoline beginning in 1975 resulted in health improvements, reducing the blood concentration of lead in the US population by 90 percent and increasing the average IQ of children born since 1980 by 2 to 5 points.

According to the WHO, 94 percent of the premature deaths attributed to ambient (outdoor) air pollution worldwide are due to noncommunicable diseases, with 36 percent related to ischemic heart disease, 36 percent to stroke, 14 percent to lung cancer, and 8 percent to chronic obstructive pulmonary disease (COPD). Acute lower respiratory infections in children under the age of five account for the remaining 6 percent of premature deaths. As emission of greenhouse gases continue to drive global climate change, however, the threats to public health and welfare are likely to evolve. [22]

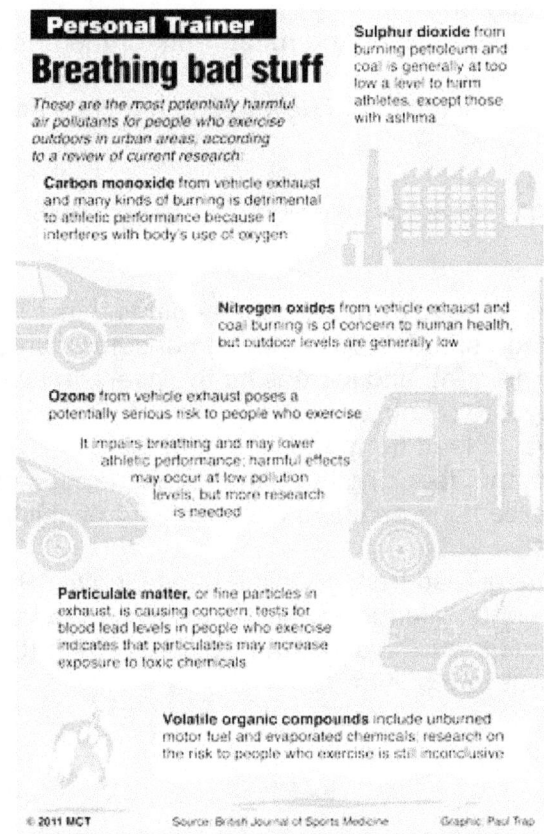

12. A. NO CHANGE B. will refer C. referred D. refers 12._____

13. A. NO CHANGE B. pollutants worldwide: particulate 13._____
    C. pollutants worldwide; particulate D. pollutants worldwide, particulate

14. A. NO CHANGE B. compromising 14._____
    C. composing D. comprised

15. To make this paragraph most logical, sentence 5 should be placed 15._____
    A. where it is now B. before sentence 1
    C. after sentence 2 D. after sentence 3

16. A. NO CHANGE B. Additionally 16._____
    C. Nevertheless D. Initially

17. A. NO CHANGE B. scarcely considered 17._____
    C. widely considered D. largely in consideration of

18. A. NO CHANGE B. he C. she D. it 18._____

19. The writer is considering deleting the underlined sentence. Should the 19._____
    writer do this?
    A. Yes, because it does not provide a transition from the previous paragraph.
    B. Yes, because it fails to support the main argument of the passage as introduced in the first paragraph.
    C. No, because it sets up the argument in the paragraph for the benefits of O_3.
    D. No, because it sets up the explanation of how ozone affects a person's health.

20. A. NO CHANGE B. effects C. accepts D. excepts 20._____

21. A. NO CHANGE 21._____
    B. The EPA-mandated removal of lead from gasoline beginning in 1975 resulted in health improvements; reducing the blood concentration of lead in the US population by 90 percent; and increasing the average IQ of children born since 1980 by 2 to 5 points.
    C. The EPA-mandated removal of lead from gasoline beginning in 1975 resulted in health improvements reducing the blood concentration of lead in the US population by 90 percent increasing the average IQ of children born since 1980 by 2 to 5 points.
    D. The EPA-mandated removal of lead from gasoline beginning in 1975 resulted in health improvements. Reducing the blood concentration of lead in the US population by 90 percent. And increasing the average IQ of children born since 1980 by 2 to 5 points.

22. The writer wishes to reinforce the danger of air pollution with the final sentence of the conclusion. Which choice MOST effectively accomplishes this goal?
    A. Experts predict an increase in deaths related to extreme heat and drought, severe weather events and flooding, transmission of waterborne and pest-related infectious diseases, and food scarcity due to disruption of agriculture and ocean acidification.
    B. Many researchers believe that we need to take drastic action to prevent severe weather events, transmission of infectious diseases, and food scarcity issues.
    C. Experts believe there is still time to pass measures at the federal and local levels before air pollution truly reaches catastrophic levels, because while the threat is not too late to fix, it is imminent.
    D. The good news, according to many scientists, is that air pollution seems to cause no lasting damage to a person's lungs and other vital organs, which means as long as people strive to clean up the air, children should not have to worry about how their organs will function when they are older.

22.____

Questions 23-33.

DIRECTIONS: Questions 23 through 33 are to be answered on the basis of the following passage and supplementary material.

[23] Outdated research has shown that children's risk for learning and behavior problems and obesity rises in correlation to their level of trauma exposure, says the psychiatrist at the Stanford University School of Medicine and Lucile Packard Children's Hospital who oversaw the study. The findings could encourage physicians to consider diagnosing post-traumatic stress disorder (PTSD) rather than attention-deficit/hyperactivity disorder (ADHD), which has similar symptoms to PTSD but very different treatment.

The study examined children living in a [24] violent: low income neighborhood and documented an unexpectedly strong link between abuse, trauma and neglect and the children's mental and physical health. It reported, for instance, that children experiencing four types of trauma were 30 times more likely to have behavior and learning problems than those not exposed to trauma.

"In communities where there is violence, where children are exposed to events such as shootings in their neighborhoods, kids experience a constant environmental threat," said senior author Victor Carrion, MD, associate professor of psychiatry and behavioral sciences at Stanford. [25] "In accordance to some people's belief, these children don't get used to trauma. These events remain stressful and impact children's physiology.

The new study is being published online today in Child Abuse & Neglect: The International Journal. Carrion collaborated on the research with scientists at the University of New Orleans and the Bayview Child Health Center, part of San Francisco's California Pacific Medical Center.

The findings provide compelling evidence [26] it pediatricians should routinely screen children for trauma exposures, said Carrion, who is also a child psychiatrist at Packard Children's.

"As simple as it may seem, physicians do not ask about trauma," he said. "And kids get the wrong diagnoses."

The study builds on earlier work that linked worsening health in adults with their dose of exposure to nine types of adverse childhood events, including being subject to various kinds of abuse or neglect; having a household member who abused alcohol or drugs, was incarcerated or was mentally ill; having a mother who was treated violently; and not living in a two-parent household. Middle-class men exposed to more of these events had more chronic diseases in adulthood, the prior research found. The results of the current study highlight the need for early identification of such adversity-associated health problems and early intervention. Obesity, for example, may act as a mediator to other health problems such as diabetes, cardiac risk and inflammatory illness. [27]

To perform the study, [28] the correspondent evaluated medical records from 701 children treated at a primary care clinic in Bayview-Hunters Point, a San Francisco neighborhood with high rates of poverty and violence. About half the children were African-American; the rest came from other ethnic backgrounds. Each child's exposure to adverse events was scored on a scale from 0 to 9, with one point given for each type of adversity. The researchers also evaluated the medical records for evidence of obesity and learning or behavior problems.

Two-thirds of the children in the study had experienced at least one category of adversity, and 12 percent experienced four or more categories. An adversity score of 4 or higher left kids 30 times as likely to show learning and behavior problems and twice as likely to be obese as those with a score of 0. Children with an adversity score of 1 were 10 times as likely to have [29] learned and behavior problems as those not exposed to trauma.

Prior research has shown that about 30 percent of children in violent communities have symptoms of post-traumatic stress disorder, which can include the learning and behavior problems detected in the current study, Carrion noted. [30] Surprisingly, a physician unaware of the fact that a child experienced trauma, and noting the child's physiological hyper-arousability and cognitive difficulties, may diagnose ADHD instead of PTSD. That's a problem because the two disorders have opposite treatments, he said. Kids with PTSD need psychotherapy, not the stimulant medications given for ADHD.

"Children can recover from PTSD with the appropriate treatment, which is one of approach and not avoidance," Carrion said. "By not asking about trauma, we're utilizing avoidance. We're perpetuating PTSD."

[31] As part of their efforts to address the long-term health problems that stem from childhood trauma, Carrion, his collaborators and several San Francisco community partners are working to launch the Center for Youth Wellness. This center would be a one-stop health and wellness center for urban children and families in San Francisco. The Center for Youth Wellness will combine pediatrics with mental health services, educational support, family support, research and best practices in child-abuse response under one roof. With both public and private support, the center will coordinate the services of multiple agencies to give children a safe and accessible place to increase their resilience to adverse life experiences and improve their well-being.

The center…is a partnership between California Pacific Medical Center's Bayview Child Health Center, San Francisco Child Abuses Prevention Center, San Francisco district attorney's office, Stanford's Early Life Stress [and Pediatric Anxiety] Research Program at Lucile Packard Children's Hospital and Tipping Point Community. [32] Nadine Burke; MD; director of the Bayview center, is also a coauthor of the study.

"We need to create trauma-informed systems," Carrion [33] began, adding that the Center for Youth Wellness hopes to function as a model for such systems across the nation. People working for the welfare of children need to be on the lookout for trauma and know how to intervene, and how to work with the family and with schools, he said. "If trauma goes untreated, it's very costly for the individuals involved and for society in general."

Understanding Causes

NATIONAL STATISTICS

1 IN 6 BOYS / 1 IN 4 GIRLS WILL HAVE EXPERIENCED AN EPISODE OF SEXUAL ABUSE BY AGE 18

1 OF 3 ABUSED AND NEGLECTED CHILDREN MAY LATER ABUSE THEIR OWN CHILDREN

A REPORT OF CHILD ABUSE IS MADE EVERY 10 SECONDS

Rate of victimization of youth (per 1000 youth)	
National rate	9.5

23. A. NO CHANGE B. Outdated C. New D. Current

24. A. NO CHANGE B. violent, low-income C. violent. Low-income D. violent low-income

25. A. NO CHANGE B. In spite of C. Contrary to D. With regards to

26. A. NO CHANGE B. that C. which D. if

27. The author wishes to add a sentence at the end of this paragraph in an attempt to strengthen the connection between the article and statistics found at the end of the article. Which choice MOST effectively accomplishes this goal?
    A. If one connects these links of worsening health to adverse childhood experiences to the statistics at the end of the article, it reveals nothing short of an epidemic, especially in girls who have a 25% chance to be physically abused.
    B. This information, combined with the statistics found at the end of this article, yield a terrifying result.
    C. One can conclude, upon looking at these links and the statistics at the end of this article, that lifelong obesity can directly result from adverse situations as a child.
    D. The most shocking of all of this information comes when one looks at the statistics found at the end of the article, where they can see just how many men and women are exposed to these mental health risks.

28. A. NO CHANGE B. the correspondents C. a researcher D. the researchers

29. A. NO CHANGE B. learn C. learns D. learning

30. A. NO CHANGE B. However, 30._____
    C. Shockingly, D. Nevertheless

31. Which choice MOST effectively combines the underlined sentences? 31._____
    A. As part of their efforts to address the long-term health problems that stem from childhood trauma, Carrion, his collaborators and several San Francisco community partners are working to launch the Center for Youth Wellness, a one-stop health and wellness center for urban children and families in San Francisco.
    B. As part of their efforts to address the long-term health problems that stem from childhood trauma, Carrion, his collaborators and several San Francisco community partners are working to launch the Center for Youth Wellness, and this is center will be a one-stop health and wellness center for urban children and families in San Francisco.
    C. As part of their efforts to address the long-term health problems that stem from childhood trauma, Carrion, his collaborators and several San Francisco community partners are working to launch the Center for Youth Wellness.
    D. As part of their efforts to address the long-term health problems that stem from childhood trauma: Carrion, his collaborators and several San Francisco community partners are working to launch the Center for Youth Wellness; a one-stop health and wellness center for urban children and families in San Francisco.

32. A. NO CHANGE B. Nadine Burke MD 32._____
    C. Nadine Burke, MD, D. Nadine Burke, MD

33. A. NO CHANGE B. concluded C. admitted D. realized 33._____

Questions 34-44.

DIRECTIONS: Questions 34 through 44 are to be answered on the basis of the following passage and supplementary material.

The national policy that set a minimum legal drinking age of 21 is being questioned by a group of 135 college and university presidents through an effort called the Amethyst Initiative. In a September 15 (2009) commentary on CNN.com, [34] Amethyst Initiative leader John McCardell, a former president of Middlebury College, proposed lowering the drinking age, which he suggests will lead to less drinking and related problems among college students.

History and a comprehensive review of the research tell a much different story. The evidence is clear, consistent and compelling: A drinking age of 21 has led to less drinking, fewer injuries, and fewer deaths.

In the [35] 1970's when many states reduced their drinking ages, drinking-related deaths among young people increased. When the drinking age of 21 was restored, deaths declined. This effect is not simply a historical artifact explained by advances in safety technology and other policies.

New Zealand recently lowered the drinking age based on many of the same arguments advanced by the Amethyst Initiative. The result was more alcohol-involved traffic crashes and emergency room visits among 15- to 19-year-olds. New Zealand is now considering raising its drinking age. The National Highway Traffic Safety Administration estimates that setting the drinking age at 21 saves the lives of 900 young people each year and has saved more than 25,000 lives since 1975.

It was on the basis of compelling research evidence about its [36] life-saving benefits that a bipartisan effort created Public Law 98-363, "The National Minimum Legal Drinking Age Act" in the first place. Subsequent research has strengthened the evidence. College students who are underage, for example, binge drink less than students aged 21-23.

Underage students who attend colleges that rigorously enforce the drinking age, and who reside in states that have more laws restricting access to alcohol for those under the legal age, are less likely to binge drink. Another myth promulgated by the Amethyst Initiative is that European young people are taught by families to drink responsibly because of the typically lower legal drinking ages there. The reverse is the case. [37] Surveys of youth in multiple European countries show that rates of frequent being drinking among adolescents are higher in Europe than in the United States.

Panels of experts, convened separately by the National Institute on Alcohol Abuse and Alcoholism, the Substance Abuse and Mental Health Services Administration, the National Academy of Sciences Institute of Medicine and the Centers for Disease Control and Prevention have studied the evidence on the age-21 law and concluded that it is effective public policy. [38] Rather than lowering the drinking age, they recommended bolstering the law by closing loopholes in state law and strengthening enforcement.

There is a silver lining to the call for reopening discussion on the minimum legal drinking age. While some college presidents have signed on to the Amethyst Initiative, most have not. College presidents [39] acquiesce that a serious problem exists on their campuses and that something needs to be done. Working effectively with their communities and states to address student drinking is the place to start, not with a discussion about lowering the drinking age.

College presidents must show leadership by promoting solutions recommended by a report from the National Institute on Alcohol Abuse and Alcoholism Collect Drinking Task Force released in 2002.

These recommendations for college and community leaders included creating systems for reaching individual students with effective interventions, implementing, publicizing, and enforcing laws to prevent alcohol-impaired driving and underage drinking, restrictions on alcohol retail outlets, increasing prices and excise taxes on alcoholic beverages, and responsible beverage service policies at on-and-off-campus venues. [40] Seldom colleges and their communities have even begun the steps needed to enact these efforts.

These recommendations will be difficult to implement and significant barriers [41] exist, which includes, but is not limited to resistance from the industries that profit from selling alcohol. College presidents cannot accomplish this alone. They need the support of students, regents, parents, alumni, and their communities.

State and local legislators [42] have needed to pass tougher restrictions and provide resources for enforcement. Lobbying legislators to dismantle the effective drinking age law is a step in the wrong direction.

So rather than try the approaches advocated by the Amethyst Initiative that have no foundation in research, let's be clear about the issues.

College student drinking is a serious problem. Each year more young people are injured, sexually assaulted, and die as the result of drinking. These statistics would be even worse without the age-21 law. [43]

Lowering the drinking age will not save lives or make our campuses and communities better places to live. It will increase heavy drinking and the problems that accompany it in college communities and push the problem back into high schools. [44] Taking on real prevention requires constant vigilance, dedication, and the courage to implement difficult solutions.

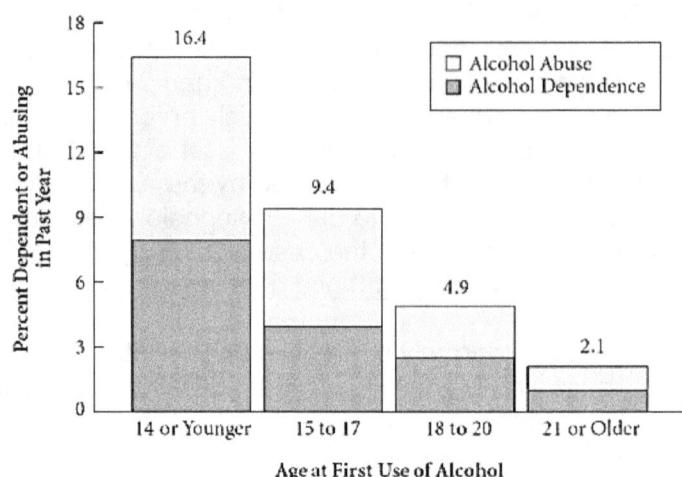

Age of First Alcohol Use and Later Dependence or Abuse

*Alcohol dependence or abuse in the past year among adults aged twenty-one or older, by age of first use of alcohol.

34. A. NO CHANGE B. their C. its D. one's

35. A. NO CHANGE B. Nineteen Seventies
    C. 1970;s D. 1970s

36. A. NO CHANGE B. lifesaving C. life saving D. live-saving

37. The writer is considering deleting the underlined sentence. Should the sentence be kept or deleted?
    A. Kept, because it introduces the idea that underage drinking is worse in Europe than in the United States because of the lower drinking age.
    B. Kept, beause it supports the main idea of the paragraph that binge drinking is lowered by laws that make it difficult to obtain alcohol as a minor, not through European parents teaching their kids how to drink in moderation.
    C. Deleted, because it blurs the focus of the paragraph by introducing loosely related information.
    D. Deleted, because it contains information that undermines the main claim of the passage.

38. A. NO CHANGE B. In addition to
    C. Starting by D. With regards to

39. A. NO CHANGE B. believe C. deny D. acknowledge 39.____

40. A. NO CHANGE B. Many C. Few D. Often 40.____

41. A. NO CHANGE
    C. exist. Resistance
    B. exist, which does include resistance
    D. exist, including resistance
    41.____

42. A. NO CHANGE
    C. need
    B. will have needed
    D. will need
    42.____

43. At this point, the writer is considering adding the following sentence:
    Moreover, when you add in the statistics concerning the likelihood of lifelong alcoholism, shown at the end of the article, the very last idea lawmakers should be entertaining is lowering or abolishing the drinking age.
    Should the writer make this addition here?
    43.____
    A. Yes, because the statistic strengthens the author's claim that the drinking age should not be lowered.
    B. Yes, because it reinforces the writer's point about the need for new, stricter laws concerning underaged drinking.
    C. No, because it fails to take into account the importance of mental development tied into underaged drinking.
    D. No, because it blurs the focus of the paragraph by introducing a poorly integrated piece of information.

44. A. NO CHANGE
    C. Overtaking
    B. Undertaken in
    D. Taking off from
    44.____

KEY (CORRECT ANSWERS)

1. C	11. A	21. A	31. A	41. D
2. B	12. D	22. A	32. C	42. C
3. A	13. A	23. C	33. B	43. A
4. D	14. D	24. B	34. C	44. A
5. B	15. B	25. C	35. D	
6. D	16. C	26. B	36. A	
7. A	17. C	27. A	37. B	
8. C	18. D	28. D	38. A	
9. C	19. D	29. D	39. D	
10. B	20. B	30. B	40. C	

EXAMINATION SECTION
TEST 1

DIRECTIONS: Each question or incomplete statement is followed by several suggested answers or completions. Select the one that BEST answers the question or completes the statement. *PRINT THE LETTER OF THE CORRECT ANSWER IN THE SPACE AT THE RIGHT.*

Questions 1-11.

DIRECTIONS: Questions 1 through 11 are to be answered on the basis of the following passage.

The Rise of Cloud Computing Systems

{1} In addition to touching a relatively simple computer, a connected smartphone, laptop, car, or sensor in some way touches a big cloud computing system. These include Amazon Web Services, Microsoft Azure, or my employer, Google.

Over the [2] century since they started coming online, these big public clouds have moved from selling storage, network, and computing at commodity prices to also offering higher-value applications. They host Artificial Intelligence software for companies that could never build their own and enable large-scale software development and management systems, such as Docker and Kubernetes. From anywhere, it's also possible to reach and maintain the software on millions of devices at once.

For consumers, this isn't too [3] divisible. They see an app update or a real-time map that shows traffic congestion based on reports from other phones. It might be a change in the way a thermostat heats a house or in a new layout on an auto dashboard. It doesn't upend life.

For companies, though, this is an entirely new information loop, gathering and analyzing data and deploying its learning at [4] increasing scale and sophistication.

Sometimes the information flows in one direction, from a sensor in the Internet of Things. More often, it's an interactive exchange: connected devices at the edge of the system send information upstream, where it is merged in clouds with more data and analyzed. [5] This process then repeats, with businesses adjusting based on new insights.

Creating New Business Models

This cloud-based loop amounts to a new industrial model, according to Andrew McAfee, a professor at M.I.T. and, with Eric Brynjolfsson, co-author of Machine, Platform, Crowd, a new book on the rise of Artificial Intelligence. A.I. is an [6] increasing important part of the analysis. Seeing the dynamic as simply more computers in the world, McAfee says, is making the same kind of mistake industrialists made with the first electric [7] motors:

"They thought an electric engine was more efficient, but basically like a steam engine. Then they put smaller engines around and created conveyor belts, overhead cranes—they rethought what a factory was about, what the new routines were. Eventually, it didn't matter what other strengths you had, you couldn't compete if you didn't figure that out."

It is already changing how new companies operate. Startups like Snap, Spotify, or Uber create business models that assume high levels of connectivity, data ingestion, and analysis—a combination of tools at hand from a single source rather than discrete functions. [8] One assume their product will change rapidly in look, feel, and function, based on new data. The same dynamic is happening in industrial businesses that previously didn't need lots of software.

Tech in the Physical Business World

Take Carbon, a Redwood City, Calif. maker of industrial 3D printers. Over 100 of its cloud-connected products are with customers, making resin-based items for sneakers, helmets, [9] and cloud computing parts, among other things.

Rather than sell machines, Carbon offers them like subscriptions. That way it can observe what all of its machines are doing under different uses, derive conclusions from all of them on a continuous basis, and upgrade the printers with monthly software downloads. A screen in the company's front lobby shows total consumption of resins being collected on AWS, the basis for Carbon's collective learning. [10]

"The same way Google gets information to make searches better, we get millions of data points a day from what our machines are doing. We can see what one industry does with the machine, and share that with another."

One recent improvement involved changing the mix of oxygen in a Carbon printer's manufacturing chamber. That [11] approved printing time by 20 percent. Building sneakers for Adidas, they were able to design and manufacture 50 prototype shoes faster than it used to take to do half a dozen test models. It also manufactures novel designs that were previously theoretical.

1. A. NO CHANGE   B. Instead of   C. Despite   D. Additionally,   1.____

2. A. NO CHANGE   B. ten year span   2.____
   C. epoch   D. decade

3. A. NO CHANGE   B. invisible   C. visible   D. indivisible   3.____

4. A. NO CHANGE   B. decreasing   C. ascendant   D. transcendent   4.____

5. At this point, the writer is considering adding the following sentence.
   The results may be used for over-the-air software upgrades that substantially change the edge device.
   Should the writer make this addition here?
   A. Yes, because it reinforces the important of having smart devices in homes.
   B. Yes, it helps explain the significance of the previous sentences.
   C. No, because it blurs the paragraph's focus on the far-reaching effects the cloud has on consumers.
   D. No, because it undermines the idea that the paragraph is trying to prove.

5.____

6. A. NO CHANGE   B. decrease
   C. increasingly   D. nonlinear

6.____

7. A. NO CHANGE   B. motors,   C. motors.   D. motors;

7.____

8. A. NO CHANGE   B. one assumes
   C. you assume   D. they assume

8.____

9. A. NO CHANGE
   B. and they also make cloud computing parts
   C. and if you can believe it they also make cloud computing parts
   D. and parts for cloud computers

9.____

10. Which choice MOST effectively sets up the quote that follows in this sentence?
    A. NO CHANGE
    B. The CEO of Carbon likens it to Google in the way the company gathers data points.
    C. Joe DeSimone has a more relevant way of explaining it.
    D. Their founder and CEO, Joe DeSimone, explains it another way.

10.____

11. A. NO CHANGE   B. improved   C. proofed   D. provided

11.____

Questions 12-22.

DIRECTIONS: Questions 12 through 22 are to be answered on the basis of the following passage and supplementary material.

[12] A paradigm shift needs to occur in the way we view and treat behavioral health conditions so that we can improve clinical outcomes and recovery of patients seeking mental health or addiction treatment. Instead of treating addiction and mental illness with episodic care, as if they are acute conditions, we should be treating these illnesses in the same way that we treat asthma, diabetes, chronic obstructive pulmonary disease and other chronic [13] conditions. With a continuum of care.

A patient [14] whose been diagnosed with diabetes requires the same long-term follow-up, monitoring and support, as patients with mental illness or [15] addiction; shouldn't stop after they complete a treatment program. Like the medical treatment that is provided to patients who have other chronic and pervasive diseases, behavioral health treatment should also focus on the management and long-term monitoring of mental and substance use disorders, not solely on their stabilization.

[16] Patients who are treated for any chronic illness are vulnerable to relapse, and recurrence is very much a part of the disease. It is the responsibility of treatment providers to teach patients how to manage their symptoms and make healthy choices that support their overall health and wellbeing.

In behavioral health, recovery management is provided to patients after they complete formal treatment; it may consist of education, motivational interviewing and cognitive behavior strategies. [17] However, these strategies aim to help patients make progress toward their goals in recovery (McKay, 2009). Within a recovery management framework, professionals must help patients learn how to manage and take responsibility for their condition (Kushner, Dennis, & McKay, 2013).

Recovery management is [18] the hot button component of the treatment and recovery processes because it empowers patients to understand their condition, and teaches them how to cope with triggers and stress and manage their symptoms in times of crisis and distress. In addition to these benefits, continuing care services, also referred to as aftercare, can be provided [19] to, patients to reduce, their risk of relapse and rehospitalization after they [20] receive treatment.

Sovereign Health, a leading national behavioral health treatment [21] provider, offers recovery management services to patients for extended period through our comprehensive Continuing Care Program. The Continuing Care Program includes ongoing monitoring, process groups, community activities and continuing education to teach patients' important life skills to help patients continue to make progress in their recovery after their treatment. Continuing care services provide follow-up, support and monitoring to patients long after their treatment has been completed to help them manage their recovery from mental and substance use disorders, so they can go on to live happy and healthy lives. [22]

Substance addiction and treatment

In 2009, 20.9 million people needed treatment for a substance addiction, but only 5.1% perceived this need and fewer still (1.8%) actually pursued treatment.

Dependence on specific drugs included:

Marijuana	4.2 million users
Pain relievers	1.8 million
Cocaine	1.1 million
Tranquilizers	481,000
Heroin	399,000
Stimulants	371,000
Hallucinogens	371,000
Inhalants	164,000
Sedatives	147,000

SOURCE: Substance Abuse and Mental Health Services Administration, Office of Applied Studies. *Results from the 2009 National Survey on Drug Use and Health: Volume 1 Summary of National Findings* (September 2010).

12. Which choice is the BEST introduction to the paragraph?
    A. NO CHANGE
    B. The way that we view and treat behavioral health conditions so that we can improve clinical outcomes and recovery of patients seeking mental health or addiction treatment needs to change.
    C. Recovery of patients and their clinical outcomes regarding addiction treatment needs to change so that we can improve them.
    D. Many addicts need to have better addiction treatment which means we need a paradigm shift in the way we view and treat behavioral health conditions.

13. A. NO CHANGE
    B. conditions, with a continuity of caring
    C. conditions—with a continuum of care
    D. conditions: with a continuing of care

14. A. NO CHANGE   B. who's   C. hews   D. who is

15. A. NO CHANGE   B. addiction, shouldn't
    C. addiction, they shouldn't   D. addiction; they shouldn't

16. At this point, the writer is considering adding the following sentence.
    Similarly, just as patients who have diabetes can have symptoms of their disease recur after a period of improvement, a person with an addiction or mental health condition shouldn't be viewed any differently for having a relapse.
    Should the writer make this addition here?
    A. Yes, because it acts as the topic sentence and leads into the rest of the paragraph.
    B. Yes, because it inserts the author's opinion as a turning point in the article.
    C. No, because it does not adequately cite the range of issues at stake in the paragraph.
    D. No, because it does not specifically define how addictions are treated differently from diseases.

17. A. NO CHANGE   B. Conversely,
    C. To clarify,   D. Subsequently,

18. A. NO CHANGE
    B. an important
    C. a colossal
    D. an incredibly important and significant

19. A. NO CHANGE   B. to, patients to reduce their
    C. to patients to reduce their,   D. to patients to reduce their

20. A. NO CHANGE B. will have received 20.____
    C. may or may not receive D. have received in the past

21. A. NO CHANGE B. provider offers 21.____
    C. provider; offers D. provider: offers

22. Suppose the writer's goal had been to write an article that criticizes 22.____
    healthcare professionals and their treatment of drug addicts.
    Would this article fulfill that goal?
    A. Yes, because it refers to much of what ails healthcare professionals and their lack of effective treatment of addicts.
    B. Yes, because it shows that the U.S. healthcare system has some problems.
    C. No, because it tells the story of diabetes patients and their treatments.
    D. No, because its focus is on the public view of addiction in an attempt to change public perception about treatment.

Questions 23-33.

DIRECTIONS: Questions 23 through 33 are to be answered on the basis of the following passage and supplementary material.

If you had a magic wand, would you ban your child from social media for as long as possible? If you [23] says yes, you're not alone. Glennon Doyle, author of "Love Warrior" and a mom of three, recently tweeted that her kids aren't allowed on social media. And I've been hearing more about this approach as I work with schools across the country as the founder of the Social Institute, which promotes the positive use of social platforms. The effects of screen time and the risks associated with social media, whether bullying or meeting strangers, are serious enough for some parents to forbid it outright.

I understand that parents know their kids best and want the best for their kids. But beware of making social media a forbidden fruit. Here's why it's a bad idea to ban [24] it – and what to do instead.

I speak with thousands of students across the country about social media, and they describe how ahead of the game they are compared with parents: "All my friends talk about Fortnite at our school lunch table, but my parents don't know much about the game."

"My sister is up to a 350-day Snap streak, and my dad is clueless [25] about the reason for that being so very cool."

"My mom gave me permission to use Instagram, but [26] my mom has no idea about my finsta." (A finsta is a second Instagram account teens use to hide from parents and share more honest photos and captions.)

"My parents regularly search my phone, but they [27] are lacking in the knowledge of an application that acts as a decoy." (Kids download "decoy apps" like Calculator% and Audio Manager, neither of which calculates or controls volume. After entering a code, kids can hide their photos and videos, make secret calls and message people – all within the app.)

The lesson? Kids will never stop migrating to new apps that are foreign to parents. Banning social media just isn't realistic.

Headlines often focus on the pitfalls of social media, so benefits such as building relationships with friends and future employers, supporting causes, and joining movements are easy to overlook. Not only can students use social media to fuel their success, but they will be increasingly expected to do so. According to a 2017 study by CareerBuilder with more than 2,300 hiring managers, more than half won't interview someone they can't find online. [28]

[29] By teaching kids to use social media in a healthy way, parents can help them take charge of their online reputation and follow positive role models who can push them toward their goals.

Unlike rules, which restrict negative behaviors, standards [30] also discourage positive behaviors and open, trusting relationships. Living up to high standards takes practice, and when a group of people – a family – agrees to live by the same standards, they keep each other accountable.

Take screen time. Adults often complain that teens look at their devices [31] to much. In reality, according to a 2017 study by Common Sense Media, adults spend 26 minutes longer each day "with screen media" than children ages 8-18 (and more than 80 percent of it is "devoted to personal screen media"). Kids can't be what they can't see.

How to Help

[32] These days: even elementary kids can join apps like YouTube Kids or Facebook Kids Messenger or play Fortnite (on multiplayer mode). Apps and multiplayer games are becoming a part of their childhood. And children of different ages need different amounts – and types – of guidance. With younger kids, you might use tools like Net Nanny or Bark to monitor their every move. But all kids benefit far more from a two-way conversation because it promotes an atmosphere of openness and trust.

When you huddle, discuss the "do's" of social media, not just the "don'ts." [33] Replacing do not post anything you wouldn't want your grandmother to see with post what represents your character and values. Let's empower our kids to fuel their potential by using social media. Yes, banning social media altogether would be easier – for you. Your child, however, would miss out.

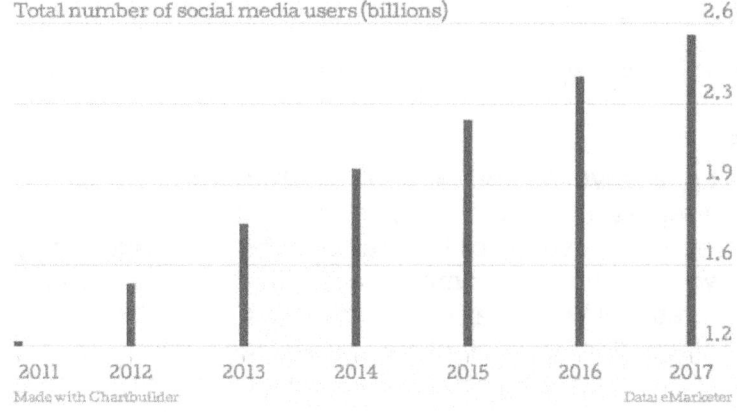

23. A. NO CHANGE   B. said   C. have said   D. will say   23.____

24. A. NO CHANGE   B. if. And what to do instead   24.____
    C. it, and what to do instead   D. it: and what to do instead

25. A. NO CHANGE   25.____
    B. about the reason for that coolness
    C. about why that's cool
    D. about that

26. A. NO CHANGE   B. her   C. one   D. she   26.____

27. A. NO CHANGE   27.____
    B. don't know about my decoy app.
    C. don't know anything.
    D. do not have knowledge about my decoy application that runs interference.

28. The author wishes to make a strong connection between the article and the   28.____
    graph that follows at this point. Which choice BEST accomplishes that goal?
    A. To further this point, in 2017, the amount of social media users numbered in the 2 billion range, which might cause concern for potential employers if they cannot find someone's online presence
    B. With that said, social media use has increased every year since 2011, which means the likelihood of an employer not finding someone online rather small.
    C. What strengthens this point is the fact that those who choose not to join social media are often left behind and do not succeed in life.
    D. This study is further bolstered by the fact that in 2017 almost a third of the world's population has some kind of social media presence.

29. A. NO CHANGE   B. By forcing pupils   29.____
    C. By patronizing children   D. Attempting to teach students

30. A. NO CHANGE   B. discourages   30.____
    C. encourage   D. may encourage or may discourage

31. A. NO CHANGE   B. too   C. two   D. tew   31.____

32. A. NO CHANGE   B. These days   C. These days;   D. These days,   32.____

33. A. NO CHANGE   33.____
    B. Replace "don't post anything you wouldn't want your grandmother to see" with "post what represents your character and values."
    C. One has the need and responsibility to replace the old adage "don't post anything you wouldn't want grandma to see" with the updated saying "post what clearly represents your character and values."
    D. You should replace "don't post anything you wouldn't want your grandmother to see" with "post what represents your character and values."

Questions 34-44.

DIRECTIONS: Questions 34 through 44 are to be answered on the basis of the following passage and supplementary material.

Once I [34] am talking with a friend when he remarked that in rugby, there are fewer injuries per player than in the football. This seemed spurious to me, because football players have helmets and padding while rugby players have none. Wouldn't more protective gear reduce the likelihood of injury especially when compared to the unprotected rugby players?

What I was not considering was how football players' safety gear actually affects their behavior [35] on the field? In Chapter One of The Armchair Economist, "The Power of Incentives, How Seat Belts Kill," Professor of Economics Steven E. Landsburg summarizes economics by saying, "People respond to incentives." More specifically, reducing the price of a certain behavior will increase that behavior. As a corollary, increasing the price of a certain behavior will decrease that behavior. I agree with this theory (technically, it is an economic law) and it is best illustrated through several case studies.

The Peltzman Effect
In the 1960s, [36] a federal Government—in it infinite wisdom—thought that cars were too unsafe for the general public. In response, [37] it passed automobile safety legislation, requiring that seat belts, padded dashboards, and other safety measures be put in every automobile. although well-intended, auto accidents actually increased after the legislation was passed and enforced. Why? As Landsburg explains, "the threat of being killed in an accident is a powerful incentive to drive carefully."

[38] The benefit of the policy was that it reduced the number of deaths per accident. The cost of the policy was that it increased the number of accidents, thus canceling the benefit. Or at least, that is the conclusion of University of Chicago's Sam Peltzman, who found the two effects canceled each other. His work has led to a theory called "The Peltzman Effect," also known as risk compensation. Risk compensation says that safety requirements incentivize people to increase risky behavior in response to the lower price of that behavior.

Are Helmets Really Protecting Cyclists?
In 1990, the Australian state of Victoria made safety helmets mandatory for all bicycle riders. Although this change resulted in fewer injuries overall, the number of injuries per biker increased.

[39] The best explanation for this is that the requirement of wearing a helmet increased the cost of cycling, so the number of bikers was reduced, further, many bikers wearing helmets were more likely to engage in unsafe biking (risk compensation), personally, I wear a helmet when I bike and, in my opinion, I am a safe biker. But that doesn't mean that the introduction of mandatory helmets doesn't affect our behavior.

We are always at risk whenever we get on a bike or sit behind the wheel, so a biker or a driver may be willing to conduct these activities more recklessly in exchange for getting to his destination more quickly. [40] Landsburg say that a baby-on-board sign may induce other drivers to drive more carefully.

Are Humans Rational?
Other times, a change in the cost of an activity can make the difference as to whether or not an individual engages in that activity at all. Economists assume humans are rational an engage in a cost-and-benefit analysis in nearly every activity. After all, resources are limited, so we must make choices on how we will use our time and money. [41] Most economy experts agree that asset scarcity means each individual needs to decide how to spend capital and energy.

In the 1970s, the Federal government controlled gasoline's value, holding it at [42] a very lowest price. This sparked widespread oil shortages, which in turn led to very long lines at gas stations, among other factors. When President Reagan lifted the price controls upon reaching office, prices increased, and the lines disappeared. Clearly, a small difference in the price of gasoline (or any other product) makes the difference for some people, in the question of whether or not to buy gasoline.

[43] Now can you guess why football is a relatively more dangerous sport than rugby! Economics tells us that it is because the padding and helmets lead football players to play rougher, increasing the likelihood of injury. According to the magazine American Heritage, the introduction of helmets in the 1950s "reduced some head damage but was held responsible for a tripling of neck injuries and a doubling of deaths from cervical spine injuries." The same is true for hockey players.

The fact that incentives reduce or increase behavior is an economic law. Landsburg posits that "the literature of economics contains tens of thousands of empirical studies verifying this proposition and not one that convincingly refutes it." Incentives change the [44] effect of government policy and shape day-to-day life.

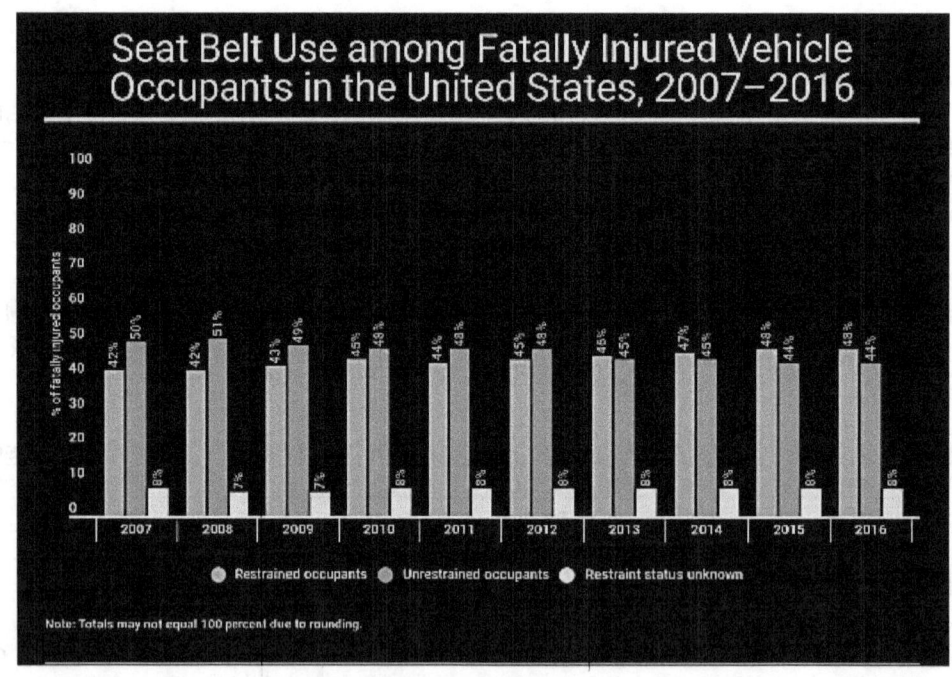

34. A. NO CHANGE   B. talk   C. was talking   D. were talking   34.____

35. A. NO CHANGE   B. on the field!   C. on the field,   D. on the field.   35.____

36. A. NO CHANGE   B. the federal government   36.____
    C. the Federal Government   D. an Federal Government

37. A. NO CHANGE   B. they   C. we   D. he   37.____

38. At this point, the writer is considering adding the following paragraph before   38.____
    this one.
    > In other words, the high price (certain death from an accident) of an activity (reckless driving) reduced the likelihood of that activity. The safety features reduced the price of reckless driving by making cars safer. For example, seat belts reduced the likelihood of a driver being hurt if he drove recklessly and got into an accident. Because of this, drivers were more likely to drive recklessly.

    Should the writer make this addition here?
    A. Yes, because it provides analysis for why adding safety measures actually made people worse drivers.
    B. Yes, because it provides a counter argument for the paragraph that follows it.
    C. No, because it interrupts the flow of the article by supplying irrelevant information.
    D. No, because it weakens the focus of the passage by discussing a subject other than reckless drivers.

39. A. NO CHANGE   39.____
    B. The best explanation for this is that the requirement of wearing a helmet increased the cost of cycling, so the number of bikers was reduced. Further, many bikers wearing helmets were more likely to engage in unsafe biking (risk compensation). Personally, I wear a helmet when I bike and, in my opinion, I am a safe biker.
    C. The best explanation for this is that the requirement of wearing a helmet increased the cost of cycling, which the number of bikers was reduced. Further many bikers wearing helmets were more likely to engage in unsafe biking (risk compensation). Personally, I wear a helmet when I bike and, in my opinion, I am a safe biker.
    D. The best explanation for this is that the requiring of the wearing of a helmet increased the cost of cycling, so the number of bikers was reduced. Further, many bikers wearing helmets were more likely to engage in unsafe biking (risk compensation). I wear a helmet when I bike and, in my opinion, I am a safe biker.

40. A. NO CHANGE   B. Landsburg has said   40.____
    C. Landsburg stated   D. Landsburg says

41. The writer is considering deleting the underlined sentence. Should the sentence be kept or deleted?
    A. Kept, because it further explains how cost benefit analysis works for each person.
    B. Kept, because it provides details to illustrate how a person arrives at a decision.
    C. Deleted, because it is redundant and adds nothing new to the paragraph.
    D. Deleted, because it creates confusion about how economists know about cost-benefit analysis.

41.____

42. A. NO CHANGE   B. a very lower price
    C. the lowest price   D. a very low price

42.____

43. A. NO CHANGE
    B. Now can you guess why football is a relatively more dangerous sport than rugby?
    C. Now you can guess why football is a relatively more dangerous sport than rugby?
    D. Now can you guess why football is a relatively more dangerous sport than rugby.

43.____

44. A. NO CHANGE   B. affect   C. expect   D. defect

44.____

KEY (CORRECT ANSWERS)

1. B	11. B	21. A	31. B	41. C
2. D	12. A	22. D	32. D	42. D
3. C	13. C	23. B	33. B	43. B
4. A	14. B	24. C	34. C	44. A
5. B	15. D	25. C	35. D	
6. C	16. A	26. D	36. C	
7. A	17. C	27. B	37. A	
8. D	18. B	28. A	38. A	
9. A	19. D	29. A	39. B	
10. D	20. A	30. C	40. D	

EXAMINATION SECTION
TEST 1

DIRECTIONS: Each question or incomplete statement is followed by several suggested answers or completions. Select the one that BEST answers the question or completes the statement. *PRINT THE LETTER OF THE CORRECT ANSWER IN THE SPACE AT THE RIGHT.*

Questions 1-15.

DIRECTIONS: Questions 1 through 15 are to be answered on the basis of the following passage. (This passage is excerpted from a publication by a contemporary education specialist.)

1   An anti-racist framework offers much to music education...I explore three areas of music education, where people can mobilize such a framework to push toward counter-hegemonic change. The first area speaks directly to positionality and recognition. Employing an anti-racist orientation allows teachers to understand where students are
5   situated in the matrix of domination (Collins 2000) and adjust their teaching and their teaching relationships accordingly. Secondly, anti-racism encourages multi-centricity and readily allows for multiple epistemologies or ways of knowing the world, in a manner quite contrary to some of the more dominant ensemble-based paradigms of music education. Finally, this critical theoretical orientation enables the pursuit of an equity agenda in the
10 actual practice of teaching. Using such an orientation allows teachers to pursue "courageous conversations" (Singleton and Linton 2006) in the classroom and seize the opportunities that arise to have these difficult conversations. I begin with an exploration of anti-racism as a theoretical framework, followed by a theoretical examination of three possible ways this framework may function in music education to interrupt the logic of
15 white supremacy. Finally, I employ the findings of a multiple case study to illustrate with practical examples the theoretical facets.

The Importance of Positionality: Locating Myself

In Rebollo-Gil and Moras' (2006) work, Amanda Moras, a white anti-racist scholar, critiques her positionality and states why she believes it is so important to situate herself in the research and in her classroom. She remarks that "[i]n any classroom, beginning a
20 dialogue about race or opening an anti-racist agenda must be pre-empted by these introspective assessments of our own social locations as educators" (391). She finds that such introspections facilitate the opening of a dialogue within spaces where such conversation is typically shut down. As a white, middle class academic and teacher, my positionality is certainly relevant to this work. I have received unearned privileges at times
25 due to my race. Further, as a white scholar doing anti-racist work, there is actually a paradox hidden in my ability to start these conversations about race and white privilege. In situations where a person of color Hess, Juliet. 2015. Upping the "anti-": The value of an anti-racist theoretical framework in music education. In situations where a person of color may be shut down for being "angry" or "having an agenda," my own positionality is
30 often read as "neutral," allowing me to start a discussion – a terrible irony in the work of anti-racism.

Why Anti-racism?

When we consider Dei's (2000) definition in more depth, it becomes clear that this focus on power and dominance allows for a powerful critique of whiteness and dominant positionality with an orientation toward change. This critique is important because
35 unfortunately, the structures of domination that anti-racist orientation target did not disappear with the election of Obama. They are all too apparent in high-profile cases in the United States, including those of Michael Brown, Eric Garner, Trayvon Martin, and Jordan Davis, a well as in the less blatant, but insidious reinscriptions of white supremacy as the prevalent operating structure in the world today.

40 Within the field of music education, Butler, Lind, and McKoy (2007) help us understand the effect of race, ethnicity, and culture on music education through grounded theory. They put forward a conceptual framework to understand how these factors affect music teaching and learning and explore "educational equity in relationship to music education" (241). They examine five factors: the teacher, the student, the content, the instruction, and the
45 classroom context. Butler, Lind, and McKoy consider the influence of race, culture, and ethnicity on the student, the teacher, and the interactions between them. The model then illustrates the ways in which these relationships (which are affected by race, culture, and ethnicity) mediate content, instruction, and context, and ultimately influence music learning. The quantity of literature they explore in the music education context may
50 indicate a recognition of the significance of positionality to teaching and learning. However, the presence of such literature indicates a need in music education for a theoretical framework that acknowledges positionality in a manner that emphasizes these factors and works against white supremacy as an operating structure.

1. The primary purpose of the first paragraph (Lines 1-16) is to
   A. inspire students to be open-minded
   B. argue that music education aids in anti-racism pursuits
   C. encourage people to join anti-racism efforts in the field of music education
   D. outline the potential benefits towards an anti-racist framework in music education
   E. impress upon the reader the importance of acceptance in diverse educational environments

2. The author uses the word "counter-hegemonic" in Line 2 to mean
   A. revolutionary   B. predominant   C. rebellious
   D. authoritative   E. confident

3. The series of phrases in Lines 17-21 ("In Rebollo-Gil...as educators") PRIMARILY conveys the
   A. importance of positionality in music education
   B. significance of reflecting on one's own standing in society
   C. author's attempt to add credibility by referencing experts
   D. value of having anti-racial discussions within a classroom
   E. necessitation of implementing an "anti-white privilege" campaign

4. When the author mentions "Michael Brown...Trayvon Martin", the implied connection between each person is they
   A. were all enrolled in a music education program
   B. all advocated for an anti-racist outlook in education
   C. all attempted to diversify their educational approach to the classroom with mixed results
   D. worked to ensure white privilege stay a part of music education
   E. were all victims of a system that promotes white supremacy

5. Which of the following BEST describes the relationship between the first and second paragraphs and the third paragraph?
   A. The third paragraph illustrates the reasons for the focus on anti-racial work mentioned in the first and second paragraphs.
   B. The third paragraph questions the logic of an idea expressed in the first and second paragraphs.
   C. The third paragraph describes the effects of an issue raised in the first and second paragraphs.
   D. The third paragraph lists the justification of a theory proposed in the first and second paragraphs.
   E. There is no correlation between the first two paragraphs and the third.

6. The author paraphrases Butler, Lind, and McCoy (Lines 40-46) to emphasize the
   A. intricacy of the relationship between music education and the underprivileged
   B. fact that this theory has been researched and justified by experts in music education
   C. necessity of using scientific knowledge in a worthwhile manner
   D. amount of evidence in support of considering one's positionality when planning a diverse educational environment
   E. danger of postponing a framework for combating racism in education

7. The author uses the word "paradox" in Line 26 to mean
   A. puzzle   B. inconsistency   C. oddity
   D. enigma   E. contradiction

8. The third paragraph (Lines 32-54) serves which of the following functions?
   A. It presents evidence in support of the previously stated argument.
   B. It explains the results of a controversial study.
   C. It speculates about a potential improvement within education.
   D. It serves to strengthen the belief that white supremacy is rampant in education and society.
   E. It presents the opposing viewpoint.

9. Which of the following is TRUE of the position presented in Lines 51-54 ("However, the presence...structure")?
   A. It is based on information given at the start of the excerpt.
   B. It takes issue with the argument made in the previous paragraphs.
   C. It summarizes the main thesis of the excerpt.

D. It emphasizes the importance of understanding the main concept presented in the paragraph.
E. It suggests that a supposition held by many experts may be misunderstood.

10. One important purpose of the passage is to
    A. urge the public to change educators' minds regarding anti-racist frameworks as it pertains to standards that promote white privilege
    B. suggest that music education is beneficial to putting an end to white supremacist viewpoints
    C. question why some educators promote music education frameworks that allow for a focus away from positionality within anti-racist programs
    D. argue that educators need to change how they approach anti-racist frameworks specifically regarding positionality
    E. reveal the hypocrisy of educational theorists who clamor for equality but shy away from anti-racism frameworks

11. The PRIMARY rhetorical strategy in the passage is the
    A. illustration of significant concepts and theories
    B. relation of anecdotes and use of personal examples
    C. comparison and contrast of differing viewpoints
    D. reassessment of traditional concepts of cause and effect
    E. repeated questions with answers that end up as questions themselves

12. The author's tone is BEST described as
    A. civil but patronizing
    B. concerned though hopeful
    C. enthusiastic and surprised
    D. cynical and disheartened
    E. supercilious and benevolent

13. The passage is MOST likely excerpted from a(n)
    A. academic essay authenticating the reliability of a recent educational study
    B. research report reprimanding the conduct of both sides of an issue
    C. scientific article endorsing attentiveness to a critical educational issue
    D. newspaper article bemoaning the inequality of the educational system
    E. scholarly brochure aimed at discussing upcoming educational seminar topics

14. It can be inferred from the passage that the author assumes the reader is a(n)
    A. expert examining every part of the author's dispute
    B. generalist who needs clarification of specific concepts
    C. student seeking facts in order to formulate his or her own teaching concepts
    D. educational theorist seeking more information for a scholastic conference
    E. colleague evaluating the need to change methods of instruction

15. The organization of the passage can BEST be described as
    A. analysis preceded by individual account
    B. criticism of current practice succeeded by new theory

C. expressive exploration followed by final judgment
D. observational data followed by speculation
E. chronological argument followed by expert testimony

Questions 16-28.

DIRECTIONS: Questions 16 through 28 are to be answered on the basis of the following passage. (This passage is from a contemporary essay.)

1 Nigeria was a former colony of the British Government and the origin of governance and administration of state can be traced to the administration of Lord Lugard who was the Governor-General of the amalgamated Administration of the Northern and Southern Nigeria. The objective of the colonial bureaucracy is basically to maintain law and order
5 (Akinboye & Anifowose, 1999).

This is tagged as "Minimal Administration". The rudimentary administration was guided by indirect political system just like that of the French Assimilation and Portuguese Assimilados. The scope of bureaucracy was limited owing to paucity of financial and human resources. For instance, in 1913, the Nigerian Government total revenue stood at
10 3.4 million pounds and total expenditure was 2.9 million pounds (Imahoro, 2006).

In spite of its political shortcomings, the colonial bureaucracy was able to be financially self-sustaining for its maintenance of law and order. Its little performances were far reaching. For instance, the following performances were noted.

a. Construction of Western Railway line between Iddo, South and Nguru North, 847
15 miles (1,365.2km);
b. The first motor road in Nigeria was constructed in 1905 which connected Ibadan with Oyo;
c. 3,700 miles of roads were constructed as far back as 1930;
d. Public Works Department replaced the traditional hammock and timber bridges with
20 steel and concrete structures.
e. Medical facilities were spread to the rural areas in spite of the conservative beliefs of the people in traditional medicine.
f. In 1931, 83 dispensaries were opened in Nigeria (Balogun, 1983). We now consider the performance of Bureaucracy under Representative Government in Nigeria
25 (Umahoro, 2006).

Bureaucracy Under Representative Government

With the advent of politics and representative government, the bureaucracy underwent some changes which had both negative and positive effect on the performance of the Institution it was working for. The first change was that of new Cabinet government and its attendant problems. Then it was a problem to situate administration vis-à-vis politics
30 (Olowu, 1995). Due to differences in orientation, the political class viewed that entire administration process from the political perspectives only, whereas the career officials by their training examined issues from the professional and administrative angle.

In line with the conventional West Minister model, the political leaders were expected to initiate policies while the civil servants were expected to carry out the decisions and remained impartial, politically neutral and anonymous. The relevance of change lied in the fact that the political class viewed administrative processes from political and ethnic perspectives.

Obviously, this was the commencement of ailment attack on Nigeria as a nation. This problem greatly contributed to the limited contribution of civil servants to socio-economic development of Nigeria during the period under review.

Another problem handicapping the bureaucracy's performance was the sharp conflict between the generalists Administrators and the Professionals. The professionals were of the view that the generalists lacked skill, knowledge, and professional competence in the process of policy formulation (Olowu, 1995).

At the end of the day, it was resolved that professional skill and competence alone should not be the only overriding criterion for leadership in Ministries. Instead, the holders of the highest career of Permanent Secretary ought to have proven administrative experience.

The implication of this decision of the generalist Administrator being appointed Chief Executive of Ministries is that of perennial frictions within the system. The conflict generated lack of mutual trust, inferiority complex, power tussle and suspicion among the bureaucrats/technocrats in Nigeria. At the end of the day, it was administrative stalemate, jeopardy, and delay in policy implementation that ensued.

The gradual decay of political values and institutions in Nigeria and in particular in Western region led to a wave of violence in the House of Assembly, which spread to the rest of Nigeria (Omoleke, 2004). The house then was turned into pandemonium where chairs, mace, etc. were used as weapons of battle in the House of Assembly. This situation worsened the ailment that attacked Nigeria as a nation newly independent. Consequently in 1962, Mr. Majekodunmi was appointed as a Sole Administrator to govern the Western Region of Nigeria.

The persistence of the anarchic situation dented the image of the politicians, created political and administrative decay, hence it generated disillusion with politics and politicians. Thus, the political turmoil in the West became a chronic social ailment.

Coupled with the controversial census as well as charges of corruption and "operation wet", i.e., burning of political party opponents houses eventually prepared ground for the military cabal to intervene in the governance of Nigeria and, of course, by January 15, 1966, the soldiers observed some political dislocation and fermented ground for intervention, hence the decayed system collapsed and the military stepped in to manage the government bureaucracy (Omoleke, 2008).

What is important to us here is the impact of the political functionaries on the performance of the government bureaucracy in the Nigerian State. The implication of the political trend discussed lies in the fact that the political pandemonium pushed the career bureaucrats into performing the role of political functionaries. This is also a misnomer ailment.

Consequently, the administrative process was colored with bias, political sentiment, primordial considerations, hence the institution of bureaucracy was infected with corruption
75 both at the political and administrative levels of the State Administration. This situation gave way to Administocracy which enables us to assess the strength of government bureaucracy to cope with an extraordinary situation.

16. The author's purpose in including the list in Lines 14-25 is to
    A. demonstrate the scope of failure from occupying forces
    B. validate the existence of occupying forces in Nigeria
    C. accumulate reasons for optimistic feelings towards British occupied Nigeria
    D. predict future positive outcomes for countries currently under Imperial rule
    E. establish the fact that occupation was not as one-sided and negative as it originally appears

17. The first paragraph (Lines 1-25) serves to
    A. explain why Nigeria was a successful colony for the British Empire
    B. describe the reasons why imperialism was good for Nigeria despite British occupation
    C. make generalizations that will be developed later
    D. detail the power of British government and mass effect of imperialism in Nigeria
    E. explore ways in which Nigerian people can cope with British imperialism

18. The author used the portmanteau word "Administocracy" in Line 76 to mean a government
    A. that forms when officials make decisions based on policy
    B. that is created when officials make decisions that allow them to simultaneously formulate and implement policy
    C. where entities with private components control the direction and governance of a country
    D. where representatives of a particular ethnic group hold a number of government posts disproportionate to the percentage of total population
    E. that extends personal wealth and political power of government officials at the expense of the population

19. The last two paragraphs (Lines 69-77) marks a shift from
    A. neutral to negative characterization of British colonialism
    B. popular to academic contexts
    C. supported to unsound generalizations
    D. impersonal to personal examples
    E. generalized evidence and facts to specific conclusions about the meaning of those generalizations

8 (#1)

20. The author's attitude toward British occupation of Nigeria can BEST be described as
    A. sympathetic and admiring
    B. curious yet skeptical
    C. unbiased and dispassionate
    D. unrepentant and condescending
    E. mollifying and tolerant

    20.____

21. Which of the following BEST represents the author's intended audience?
    A. Individuals who are fairly familiar with Nigerian history
    B. Readers who have trouble understanding British colonialism
    C. Writers who hope to write about British occupation of Nigeria
    D. Instructors looking for different ways of understanding colonialism in Nigeria
    E. Scholars seeking information about the author's personal connection to Nigerian history

    21.____

22. Given the context of the rest of the sentence, paucity (Line 8) can BEST be defined as
    A. famine
    B. scarcity
    C. abundance
    D. rarity
    E. scope

    22.____

23. Which of the following statements is BEST supported by information given in the passage?
    A. While colonialism is highly negative and base, there were positive aspects of it for Nigeria.
    B. The economic influence and elevated Nigerian infrastructure collapsed once they sought independence.
    C. Because the Nigerian government was filled with British Administers, Administocracy dominated Nigerian politics.
    D. Nigeria was limited in its development because there was a schism between British political leaders and ethnic civil servants.
    E. Geriatric policies failed to cope with the realities of a modernized developing country.

    23.____

24. The word "Institution" as used in Line 28 refers to which of the following?
    A. Nigerian civil servants
    B. British Empire officials in Nigeria
    C. Nigerian citizens
    D. Hegemonic Colonialism
    E. Great Britain

    24.____

25. The final sentence (Lines 75-77) serves to
    A. conclude an argument begun in the first paragraph
    B. argue that historians need to pay more attention to the effects of colonialism
    C. suggest a probable cause for an ongoing issue
    D. offer a final analysis of the issue described in the first two paragraphs
    E. explain why the author has chosen to study this particular era of Nigerian history

    25.____

26. Which of the following stylistic features is used MOST extensively throughout the piece?
    A. Inverting standard subject/verb/object order
    B. Repeating sentence structure
    C. Sporadic and inconsistent sentence structure
    D. Sentence errors (fragments, run-ons) for effect
    E. Use of connotative meanings that add text complexity

27. The author develops this passage PRIMARILY through
    A. accumulation of detail
    B. cause-and-effect argument
    C. claim followed by evidence
    D. assertion support by qualification
    E. analysis of the ideas of others

28. Based on the excerpt, the author could BEST be described as a(n)
    A. enquiring individual who pursues varied information from multiple sources
    B. serious historian who is determined to learn more about the causes and effects of British occupation in Nigeria
    C. confused novice who is unable to decide which claims are accurate
    D. ironic historian who comments on the failures and follies of British occupation
    E. thoughtful scholar who attempts to explain the positives and negatives of colonial Nigeria

Questions 29-40.

DIRECTIONS: Questions 29 through 40 are to be answered on the basis of the following passage. (This passage is excerpted from a contemporary essay.)

1. INTRODUCTION

1   The study of Heritage in local context values History as a learning living source, facilitates the understanding of historical concepts and helps to understand the world in which we live, contributing to the multiple understanding of history and to the building of the three pillars of history education: History, Memory, Identity. Cultural assets and heritage are,
5   therefore, pedagogically important as they are significant consolidation and implementation learning means that make teaching less bookish and more alive, giving meaning to learning too (Mendes, 2009).

    Studying heritage and local and/or regional history is central to history learning and to the introduction to students to the discipline methodology and specific language – it is
10. motivating, increasing the interest in history learning, integrator, because it contributes to the placement of the students in the environment they live in and, in that sense, reinforces aspects of identity building, and it facilitates the understanding of history as a dynamic process in which knowledge appears not as being imposed, but making sense in a network of connections that are established between information, sources, testimonials,
15 and a narrative.

On the other side of the question, combining history teaching with technological tools and multimedia runs into the motivation of the majority of the "digital-born" for whom the screen is the most natural way to learn, communicate, play and interact (Moura, 2008, p. 142), taking advantage of students' potential and approaching the school and the teaching practice to the daily practice of this generation, familiar with the Internet and the constantly updating of technology. Simultaneously, it is a way to provide the same opportunities to all students and fight the digital divide.

"It is the quality of teacher education programs that is the key issue to a successful integration of ICT into the classroom and depends on the ability of teachers to structure the learning environment in non-traditional ways, to merge new technology with new pedagogy, to develop socially active classrooms, encouraging cooperative interaction, collaborative learning, and group work." (UNESCO, 2010)

The main aim of this work was to develop a way that prioritizes research methods, discovery learning and problem solving, motivating students to the understanding of the local environment and valuing them as active learners, showing also the possibilities and pedagogical advantages of approaching seventh grade History contents in conjunction with Heritage and Local History and using innovative and recent tools and technological applications in the areas of e-learning, Digital Culture and Historical and Geographical Information Systems.

2. MOBILE DEVICES AND GEOREFERENCED APPROACHES IN EDUCATION/HISTORY

Mobile technology is a resource with great potential to be used both in teaching and learning. Its characteristics of mobility, portability and interactivity, ease of use, low cost, multiple and varied functions (like communication, taking pictures, recording, geographical orientation, etc.) bring great advantages (and challenges) to the process of teaching and learning: it eases experimental learning, it enhances collaborative work and makes knowledge more accessible, personalized and adapted to each one's rhythm.

Also the use of mobile technology with activities of georeferencing (Global Positioning System (GPS) and mobile phones/smartphones) has been done in education. Among the many experiences we can find, we can refer the "Projecto GO: Mobility in education," in the areas of History and of Heritage and Natural History contemplates the "development of historical, cultural and environmental pathways for Web global positioning systems" and the sharing of "information in the Internet as part of promotional activities of the local environment (in cooperation with the surrounding community) and national and international exchange projects" (CCEMS, 2008).

Also, the project SchoolSenses@Internet uses geo-referenced multisensory applications developed by and for Portuguese students and teachers from the first cycle of education, as a strategy to improve the quality of elementary school education (Marcelino, et al, 2007). Through active practices that enable the analysis of complex dynamical systems, as well as the acquisition and sharing of knowledge, skills such as understanding, reasoning, reflection and creativity are developed with very positive results on the cognitive development of children.

These and similar applications enable interaction and the introduction of multimedia content, along with georeferencing, and that became pedagogical tools with unquestionable advantages: they allow the accomplishment of tasks through physical actions in the local environment, they encourage a greater participation and reflection
60 ("enable children to reflect on what they are currently engaged in," Druin, 2009), and they favor the development of diverse, but efficient, forms of management and sharing of information. The ease of use and the friendly interface stimulate students' performance, capturing their attention and developing their autonomy, as they can be used in the construction of new knowledge, in the perspective of a collaborative and interactive
65 learning.

Some other experiences of m-leaning corroborate the mentioned potential, namely:
- A greater collaboration among peers;
- Better results were achieved, but above all the quality of learning was considered better: the learning process was more attractive, students felt more motivated and active
70   participants in the construction of learning;
- Also the sense of belonging and identification were increased by the participation in "virtual communities" that overcomes age and cultural barriers" (Moura, 2008).

In conclusion, with Druin – "bridges can be built with mobile technologies that transcend differences in age, race, religion, nationality and culture which are worth significant
75 investment" (Druin, 2009, p. 331).

29. The author's attitude toward the main subject of the passage can BEST be described as:
    A. awe and fascination
    B. disbelief and cynicism
    C. amusement and nostalgia
    D. certainty and significance
    E. boredom and indifference

29.____

30. What is the effect of the syntax of the first sentence (Lines 1-4)?
    A. It suggests that history without heritage makes for an incomplete comprehension of the subject.
    B. It emphasizes the importance of history as a personal connection, not just something read in a book.
    C. It conveys that without the three pillars history cannot be fully appreciated or grasped.
    D. It stresses a top down approach as a successful means of connecting more fully to history.
    E. It cautions against an impending indifference with regards to history, unless personal investments can be made.

30.____

31. As it is used in this passage, the phrase "digital divide" MOST NEARLY refers to the
    A. separation between children who have access to technology and children who do not
    B. gap between a child's digital knowledge and the digital knowledge of instructors/parents
    C. division between teachers who grew up using technology and those who did not

31.____

D. disparity in technology access between affluent families and impoverished ones
E. inconsistency in usage of digital media between wealthier school districts and less well funded districts

32. Which of the following would the author be LEAST likely to encourage?
    A. A lesson in which students use tablets to hear first person accounts of an historical event
    B. A field trip to a local site where students interview persons in historically accurate costumes
    C. A project that had students use a form of digital media to "bring in" an expert on their historical assignment
    D. A homework assignment that asked students to put themselves in the shoes of ancestors in their hometown to see how they would react to an event/situation
    E. An interactive online assessment testing what students learned in a given lesson

33. The sentence that BEST expresses the essence of the message of the essay is:
    A. Simultaneously, it is a way to provide the same opportunities to all students and fight the digital divide.
    B. Mobile technology is a resource with great potential to be used both in teaching and learning.
    C. ..."bridges can be built with mobile technologies that transcend differences in age, race, religion, nationality, and culture which are worth significant investment"
    D. The main aim of this work was to develop a way that prioritizes research methods, discovery learning and problem solving, motivating students to the understanding of the local environment and valuing them as active learners...
    E. The study of Heritage in local context values History as a learning living source facilitates the understanding of historical concepts and helps to understand the world in which we live, contributing to the multiple understanding of history and to the building of the three pillars of history education

34. In Lines 8-12, the pronoun "it" refers to
    A. technology in history classes
    B. studying heritage and local history
    C. quality teacher education programs
    D. georeferencing used in education programs
    E. collaborative work between students

35. Throughout this essay, the author's main rhetorical approach uses
    A. pathos
    B. deductive reasoning
    C. ethos
    D. logic
    E. definition

13 (#1)

36. In Paragraphs 3, 4, and 5, the author makes all of the following points EXCEPT: 36.____
    A. Teacher education programs largely influence a teacher's successful integration of technology into a classroom
    B. Technology used in cell phones is a valuable resource that should be explored
    C. The reason for writing this article was to look at ways to increase focus on motivating students through heritage, local history, and mobile technology
    D. There are numerous student-centered advantages to prioritizing heritage and local history combined with mobile technology usage
    E. without technology, motivation for the digital age students drops significantly

37. In Paragraph 9 (Lines 56-65), the author is MOST concerned that 37.____
    A. multimedia content focused lessons can lead to a technology dependency
    B. students that do not use multimedia content are at a significant disadvantage from those who are exposed to it
    C. teachers will avoid using multimedia content because it will make their students more autonomous and less dependent on the instructor
    D. m-learning gives students numerous advantages such as greater collaborative skills and a curiosity for learning
    E. poorer communities will not be able to raise students that are more well-rounded and independent as those communities that have access to technology

38. Lines 1-34 utilize all of the following types of sentences EXCEPT 38.____
    A. compound-complex   B. declarative
    C. rhetorical question   D. loose
    E. cumulative

39. Paragraph 7 contains an example of 39.____
    A. understatement   B. analogy   C. allusion
    D. sarcasm   E. logical fallacy

40. To illustrate the importance of mobile technology, the author uses all of the following EXCEPT: 40.____
    A. "the quality of teacher education programs that is the key issue to a successful integration of ICT into the classroom"
    B. "the introduction of multimedia content, along with georeferencing, and that became pedagogical tools with unquestionable advantages"
    C. "Through active practices that enable the analysis of complex dynamical systems, as well as the acquisition and sharing of knowledge, skills such as understanding, reasoning, reflection and creativity are developed"
    D. "it eases experimental learning, it enhances collaborative work and makes knowledge more accessible"
    E. "Its characteristics of mobility, portability and interactivity, ease of use, low cost, multiple and varied functions (like communication, taking pictures, recording, geographical orientation, etc.) bring great advantages"

Questions 41-55.

DIRECTIONS: Questions 41 through 55 are to be answered on the basis of the following passage. (This passage is excerpted from a 19th century novel about Charles Darwin and the Galapogos.)

1   Charles Darwin came to the Galapagos in 1835, on the Beagle; he was twenty-six. He threw the marine iguanas as far as he could into the water; he rode the tortoises and sampled their meat. He noticed that the tortoise's carapaces varied wildly from island to island; so also did the forms of various mockingbirds. He made collections. Nine years
5   later he wrote in a letter, "I am almost convinced (quite contrary to the opinion I started with) that species are not (it is like confessing a murder) immutable." In 1859 he published On the Origin of Species, and in 1871 The Descent of Man. It is fashionable now to disparage Darwin's originality; not even the surliest of his detractors, however, faults his painstaking methods or denies his impact.

10   Darwinism today is more properly called neo-Darwinism. It is organic evolutionary theory informed by the spate of new data from modern genetics, molecular biology, paleobiology - from the new wave of the biologic revolution which spread after Darwin's announcement like a tsunami. The data are not all in. Crucial first appearances of major invertebrate groups are missing from the fossil record-but these early fOnDS,
15   sometimes modified larvae, tended to be fragile either by virtue of their actual malleability or by virtue of their scarcity and rapid variation into "hardened," successful forms. Lack of proof in this direction doesn't worry scientists. What neo-Darwinism seriously lacks, however, is a precise description of the actual mechanism of mutation in the chromosomal nucleotides. In the larger sense, neo-Darwinism also lacks, for many,
20   sheer plausibility. The triplet splendors of random mutation, natural selection, and Mendelian inheritance are neither energies nor gods; the words merely describe a gibbering tumult of materials. Many things are unexplained, many discrepancies unaccounted for.

     It all began in the Galapagos, with these finches. The finches in the Galapagos are
25   called Darwin's finches; they are everywhere in the islands, sparrowlike, and almost identical but for their differing beaks. At first, Darwin scarcely noticed their importance. But by 1839, when he revised his journal of the Beagle voyage, he added a crucial sentence about the finches' beaks: "Seeing this gradation and diversity of structure in one small, intimately related group of birds, one might really fancy that from an original
30   paucity of birds in this archipelago, one species had been taken and modified for different ends." And so it was.

     The finches come when called. I don't know why it works, but it does. Scientists in the Galapagos have passed down the call: you say pssssh pssssh pssssh pssssh psssssh until you run out of breath; then you say it again until the island runs out of
35   birds. You stand on a flat of sand by a shallow lagoon rimmed in mangrove thickets and call the birds right out of the sky. It works anywhere, from island to island.

     Some wield chunky parrot beaks modified for cracking seeds. Some have slender warbler beaks, short for nabbing insects, long for probing plants. One sports the long chisel beak of a woodpecker; it bores wood for insect grubs and often uses a twig or cactus spine, like a pickle fork, when the grub won't dislodge. They have all evolved, fanwise, from one ancestral population.

The finches evolved in isolation. So did everything else on earth. With the finches, you can see how it happened. The Galapagos Islands are near enough to the mainland that some strays could hazard there; they are far enough away that those strays could evolve in isolation from parent species. And the separate islands are near enough to each other for further dispersal, further isolation, and the eventual reassembling of distinct species. (In other words, finches blew to the Galapagos, blew to various islands, evolved into differing species, and blew back together again.) The tree finches and the ground finches, the woodpecker finch and the warbler finch, veered into being on isolated rocks. The witless green sea shaped those beaks as surely as it shaped the beaches. Now on the finches in the palo santo tree you see adaptive radiation's results, a fluorescent splay of horn. It is as though an archipelago were an arpeggio, a rapid series of distinct but related notes. If the Galapagos had been one unified island, there would be one dull note, one super-dull finch.

They circled and homed to a vortex, like a whirlwind of chips, like draining water. The tree on which I leaned was the vortex. A dry series of puffs hit my cheeks. Then a rough pulse from the tree's thin trunk met my palm and rang up my arm – and another, and another...

Geography is life's limiting factor. Speciation - life itself - is ultimately a matter of warm and cool currents, rich and hare soils, deserts and forests, fresh and salt waters, deltas and jungles and plains. Species arise in isolation. A plaster cast is as intricate as its mold; life is a gloss on geography. And if you dig your fists into the earth and crumble geography, you strike geology. Climate is the wind of the mineral earth's rondure, tilt, and orbit modified by local geological conditions. The Pacific Ocean, the Negev Desert, and the rain forest of Brazil are local geological conditions. So are the slow carp pools and splashing trout riffles of any backyard creek. It is all, God help us, a matter of rocks. The rocks shape life like hands around swelling dough. In Virginia, the salamanders vary from mountain ridge to mountain ridge; so do the fiddle tunes the old men play. These are not merely anomalous details. This is what life is all about: salamanders, fiddle tunes, you and me and things, the split and burr of it all, the fizz into particulars. No mountains and one salamander, one fiddle tune, would be a lesser world. No continents, no fiddlers. The earth, without form, is void.

41. The author shows in the first paragraph Darwin's sense of   41.____
    A. meticulous research   B. instantaneous work ethic
    C. inability for innovative philosophy   D. youthful playfulness
    E. steadiness of purpose

42. From Lines 3-6, one can conclude that Darwin initially thought of species as   42.____
    A. unique   B. indistinct   C. evolutionary
    D. indistinguishable   E. invariable

43. The author leads with the line "finches evolved in isolation" in Paragraph 6 to stress that
    A. finches are solitary creatures
    B. some finches were separated from the mainland and thus evolved separately
    C. finches helped demonstrate environmental evolution
    D. species growing up detached from other species are socially inept
    E. finches had to leave the main land to avoid predatory animals

44. The author writes in Line 24 that "It all began in the Galapagos." In this line, "It" refers to
    A. the origins of sentient life
    B. the author's interest in nature
    C. the birth of Darwin's theory of evolution
    D. measured research
    E. unique species of creatures

45. In Line 31, "ends" MOST likely means
    A. borders   B. extremities   C. limits
    D. purposes   E. deaths

46. When the author uses the words "run out" twice in three lines (Lines 32-35), it stresses
    A. the waste of time in the activity
    B. the difference between human actions and bird actions
    C. irritation of scientists calling to the birds
    D. anxiety of the author when confronted by odd situations
    E. the awe-inspiring response by the birds

47. The author's description of the finches (Lines 37-39) PRIMARILY serves to
    A. provide a distinction between their overall drabness with their variety in one specific aspect
    B. illustrate the dominance of tree finches over their cousins the ground finch
    C. emphasize the use of memorable names to distinguish different species
    D. convey a sense of possibilities for further evolution in the finch family
    E. distinguish them from the warblers and mockingbirds found in the islands

48. Lines 37-41 insinuate the evolution of the finches' beaks served to
    A. imitate an s-like shape
    B. enable them to reach nourishment
    C. shelter them from predatory attacks
    D. interest Darwin greatly
    E. enhance the male's attractiveness to females

17 (#1)

49. The "fluorescent splay of horn" referred to by the author in Lines 51-52 is MOST likely
    A. a series of musical notes
    B. a flock of birds
    C. the birds' shiny beaks
    D. branches of the palo santo tree
    E. a primitive musical instrument

49.____

50. The passage's tone is BEST described as
    A. analytical   B. defensive   C. sardonic
    D. lighthearted   E. bitter

50.____

51. In the final paragraph, the author does all of the following EXCEPT
    A. restate an assertion   B. make a comparison
    C. refute an argument   D. define a term
    E. describe a sequence of events

51.____

52. The word "hazard" in Line 44 means
    A. venture   B. speculate   C. develop
    D. contemplate   E. illuminating

52.____

53. Based on the passage as a whole, the MAIN reason finches are so vital to Darwin is because they
    A. were easy to call, making them easier to study
    B. were the most numerous animal on the island
    C. were distinct enough to separate into different types
    D. were common so no one missed them if they were dissected for further study
    E. help prove his theory of evolution

53.____

54. The pulse that the author feels (Lines 55-58) is MOST likely
    A. her heart beating wildly in her chest
    B. the rhythmic landing of the finches
    C. insects leaping against the tree
    D. the wind of birds passing
    E. an agonizing pain in her upper appendage

54.____

55. The author's intended audience for this section of book would likely be
    A. individuals who are fairly familiar with Darwin and his theories
    B. evolutional theorists who hope to comment on Darwin's initial findings
    C. people who have trouble understanding practical applications of Darwin's evolutional theories
    D. instructors looking for different ways of understanding Darwin's theory of evolution
    E. scholars seeking information about the author's personal connection to Darwin

55.____

KEY (CORRECT ANSWERS)

1. D	11. A	21. D	31. A	41. A	51. D
2. A	12. B	22. B	32. E	42. E	52. A
3. B	13. C	23. A	33. D	43. B	53. E
4. E	14. E	24. E	34. B	44. C	54. B
5. C	15. D	25. C	35. C	45. D	55. C
6. B	16. E	26. B	36. E	46. E	
7. E	17. D	27. C	37. D	47. D	
8. A	18. B	28. E	38. C	48. B	
9. C	19. A	29. D	39. A	49. C	
10. D	20. C	30. A	40. B	50. A	

TEST 2

DIRECTIONS: Each question or incomplete statement is followed by several suggested answers or completions. Select the one that BEST answers the question or completes the statement. *PRINT THE LETTER OF THE CORRECT ANSWER IN THE SPACE AT THE RIGHT.*

Questions 1-11.

DIRECTIONS: Questions 1 through 11 are to be answered on the basis of the following passage.

1   Every explorer names his island Formosa, beautiful. To him it is beautiful because, being first, he has access to it and can see it for what it is. But to no one else is *it* ever as beautiful – except the rare man who manages to recover it, who knows that it has to be recovered. Garcia Lopez de Cardenas discovered the Grand Canyon and
5   was amazed at the sight. It can be imagined: One crosses miles of desert, breaks through the mesquite, and there it is at one's feet. Later the government set the place aside as a national park, hoping to pass along to millions the experience of Cardenas. Does not one see the same sight from the Bright Angel Lodge that Cardenas saw?

    The assumption is that the Grand Canyon is a remarkably interesting and beautiful place
10 and that if it had a certain value P for Cardenas, the same value P may be transmitted to any number of sightseers - just as Banting's discovery of insulin can be transmitted to any number of diabetics. A counterinfluence is at work, however, and it would be nearer the truth to say that if the place is seen by a million sightseers, a single sightseer does not receive value p but a millionth part of value P.

15 It is assumed that since the Grand Canyon has the fixed interest value P, tours can be organized for any number of people. A man in Boston decides to spend his vacation at the Grand Canyon. He visits his travel bureau, looks at the folder, signs up for a two-week tour. He and his family take the tour, see the Grand Canyon, and return to Boston. May we say that this man has seen the Grand Canyon? Possibly he has. But it is more
20 likely that what he has done is the one sure way not to see the canyon.

    Why is it almost impossible to gaze directly at the Grand Canyon, under these circumstances and see it for what it is - as one picks up a strange object from one's back yard and gazes directly at it? It is almost impossible because the Grand Canyon, the thing as it is, has been appropriated by the symbolic complex which has already been
25 formed in the sightseer's mind. Seeing the canyon under approved circumstances is seeing be symbolic complex, head on. The thing is no longer the thing as it confronted the Spaniard; it is rather 'that which has already been formulated-by picture postcard, geography book, tourist folders, and the words *Grand Canyon.* As a result of this preformulation, the source of the sightseer's pleasure undergoes a shift. Where the
30 wonder and delight of the Spaniard arose - from his penetration of the thing itself, from a progressive discovery of depths, patterns, colors, shadows, etc., now the sightseer measures his satisfaction *by the degree to which the canyon conforms* to *the preformed complex.* If it does so, if it looks just like the postcard, he is pleased; he might even say, "Why it is every bit as beautiful as a picture postcard!" He feels he has not been

cheated. But if it does not conform, if the colors are somber, he will not be able to see it directly; he will only be conscious of the disparity between what it is and what it is supposed to be. He will say later that he was unlucky in not being there at the right time. The highest point, the term of the sightseer's satisfaction, is not the sovereign discovery of the thing before him; it is rather the measuring up of the thing to the criterion of the preformed symbolic complex.

Seeing the canyon is made even more difficult by what the sightseer does when the moment arrives, when sovereign knower confronts the thing to be known. Instead of looking at it, he photographs it. There is no confrontation at all. At the end of forty years of preformulation and with the Grand Canyon yawning at his feet, what does he do? He waives his right of seeing and knowing and records symbols for the next forty years. For him there is no present; there is only the past of what has been formulated and seen and the future of what has been formulated and not seen. The present is surrendered to the past and the future.

The sightseer may be aware that something is wrong. He may simply be bored; or he may be conscious of the difficulty: that the great thing yawning at his feet somehow eludes him. The harder he looks at it, the less he can see. It eludes everybody. The tourist cannot see it; the bellboy at the Bright Angel Lodge cannot see it: for him it is only one side of the space he lives in, like one wall of a room; to the ranger it is a tissue of everyday signs relevant to his own prospects blue haze down there means that he will probably get rained on during the donkey ride.

How can the sightseer recover the Grand Canyon? He can recover it in any number of ways, all sharing in common the stratagem of avoiding the approved confrontation of the tour and the Park Service. It may be recovered by leaving the beaten track. The tourist leaves the tour, camps in the backcountry. He arises before dawn and approaches the South Rim through a wild terrain where there are no trails and no railed-in lookout points. In other words, he lees the canyon by avoiding all the facilities for seeing the canyon. If the benevolent Park Service hears about this fellow and thinks he has a good idea and places the following notice in the Bright Angel Lodge: *Consult ranger for information on getting off the beaten track* - the end result will only be the closing of another access to the canyon.

1. According to the author in Lines 6-7 (Later...Cardenas), the government's reason for making the Grand Canyon a national park was to
    A. inhibit restaurants and hotel construction
    B. memorialize the achievements of de Cardenas as a pioneer
    C. stylize it as the foundation of the national park system
    D. promote it so as to increase funding from the millions of annual visitors
    E. allow people to share in de Cardenas' sense of discovery

2. When the author uses the word *counterinfluence*, which MOST accurately encapsulates the result (Line 12)?
    A. As many sightseers as there are, there are at least that many different ways of seeing the Grand Canyon.
    B. The ability to see the Grand Canyon as de Cardenas saw it is about a one in a million chance.

C. The value of seeing the Grand Canyon is reduced by the number of tourists who visit it.
D. The value of the Grand Canyon as a sightseeing attraction has become difficult to determine over the years.
E. The value of viewing the Grand Canyon is heightened by its historical importance.

3. The author's purpose for the second paragraph's (Lines 9-14) organization can BEST be described as
   A. a supposition is set forth and conclusively proven
   B. a comparison is measured, then shown false
   C. two opposite perspectives are discussed and a compromise follows
   D. an equation is formulated then solved
   E. a theory is stated and then supporting evidence is proffered

4. In Line 15, the author uses the word "fixed" to MOST NEARLY mean
   A. unchanging   B. adjusted   C. restored
   D. prearranged   E. motionless

5. When the author brings up the "man in Boston" (Line 16), his MAIN reason for doing so is to
   A. demonstrate that traveling to the Grand Canyon is unlike traveling to any other destination
   B. imply that de Cardenas did not have a unique experience
   C. illustrate that holidays are more enticing and heartening when planned out meticulously
   D. depict a typical experience emblematic of all tourists when seeing the Grand Canyon
   E. indicate the immense popularity of the Grand Canyon amongst tourists

6. The author uses the word "see" multiple times (Line 18 and Line 20) in his "man from Boston" paragraph. Which of the following BEST reflects the different meanings of the word?
   A. Watching opposed to genuine encounter
   B. Skimming opposed to meticulous scrutiny
   C. Searching opposed to passive observation
   D. Gaping opposed to unobtrusive examination
   E. Gazing opposed to creatively visualizing

7. In Lines 29-33 (Where...complex), the implication is that de Cardenas reacted the way he did due to
   A. his seeing the canyon after a long and painstaking voyage
   B. a lack of tourists interrupting his gratification
   C. the canyon being geographically reminiscent of his native Spain
   D. the canyon far exceeding in exceptionality than he expected
   E. his lack of preconceived notions about what he was going to see

8. The author suggests in Lines 29-37 (Where...right time) that the Bostonian visitor will feel "cheated" if
   A. the travel agency does not fulfill its commitments
   B. the Grand Canyon does not look exactly as he expects
   C. he does not see the Canyon in the exact same fashion as de Cardenas
   D. he does not understand the history of de Cardenas' voyage and examination of the Canyon
   E. he is not able to take photos of the Grand Canyon

9. The experience described in Lines 35-37 (But...supposed to be) draws the BEST comparison to someone who
   A. is negatively surprised by a movie's ending
   B. learns that an excursion has been cancelled due to poor weather
   C. is disenchanted by a few songs on an audio recording that sound different live in concert
   D. is relieved to discover that a difficult task is not as hard as predicted
   E. finds the thematic colors of a food establishment to be disheartening

10. Overall, the author's purpose in writing this excerpt is to
    A. amuse readers with tales of how it was better to explore the Grand Canyon in Cardenas' lifetime
    B. present an edict on the only true way to enjoy the Grand Canyon
    C. explain that just because it is not perfect when a person goes, they should not be disappointed by the Grand Canyon
    D. convince the reader to discover the Grand Canyon for themselves instead of comparing it to what the commercialized version of it "should be"
    E. recite the all-too-common story of families who take tours of the Grand Canyon instead of backpacking it themselves and going off the beaten path

11. The author's tone in the passage can BEST be described as
    A. evasive   B. solemn   C. apathetic
    D. compassionate   E. indignant

Questions 12-19.

DIRECTIONS: Questions 12 through 19 are to be answered on the basis of the following passage.

1   Back in 2000, Randy Jirtle, a professor of radiation oncology at Duke University, and his postdoctoral student Robert Waterland designed a groundbreaking genetic experiment that was simplicity itself. They started with pairs of fat yellow mice known to scientists as agouti mice, so called because they carry a particular gene — the agouti gene — that in
5   addition to making the rodents ravenous and yellow renders them prone to cancer and diabetes. Jirtle and Waterland set about to see if they could change the unfortunate genetic legacy of these little creatures.

Typically, when agouti mice breed, most of the offspring are identical to the parents: just as yellow, fat as pincushions, and susceptible to life-shortening disease. The parent mice in Jirtle and Waterland's experiment, however, produced a majority of offspring that looked altogether different. These young mice were slender and mousy brown. Moreover, they did not display their parents' susceptibility to cancer and diabetes and lived to a spry old age. The effects of the agouti gene had been virtually erased.

Remarkably, the researchers effected this transformation without altering a single letter of the mouse's DNA. Their approach instead was radically straightforward — they changed the moms' diet. Starting just before conception, Jirtle and Waterland fed a test group of mother mice a diet rich in methyl donors, small chemical clusters that can attach to a gene and turn it off. These molecules are common in the environment and are found in many foods, including onions, garlic, beets, and in the food supplements often given to pregnant women. After being consumed by the mothers, the methyl donors worked their way into the developing embryos' chromosomes and onto the critical agouti gene. The mothers passed along the agouti gene to their children intact, but thanks to their methyl-rich pregnancy diet, they had added to the gene a chemical switch that dimmed the gene's deleterious effects.

"It was a little eerie and a little scary to see how something as subtle as a nutritional change in the pregnant mother rat could have such a dramatic impact on the gene expression of the baby," Jirtle says. "The results showed how important epigenetic changes could be."

Our DNA — specifically the 25,000 genes identified by the Human Genome Project — is now widely regarded as the instruction book for the human body. But genes themselves need instructions for what to do, and where and when to do it. A human liver cell contains the same DNA as a brain cell, yet somehow it knows to code only those proteins needed for the functioning of the liver. Those instructions are found not in the letters of the DNA itself but on it, in an array of chemical markers and switches, known collectively as the epigenome, that lie along the length of the double helix. These epigenetic switches and markers in turn help switch on or off the expression of particular genes. Think of the epigenome as a complex software code, capable of inducing the DNA hardware to manufacture an impressive variety of proteins, cell types, and individuals.

The even greater surprise is the recent discovery that epigenetic signals from the environment can be passed on from one generation to the next, sometimes for several generations, without changing a single gene sequence. It's well established, of course, that environmental effects like radiation, which alter the genetic sequences in a sex cell's DNA, can leave a mark on subsequent generations. Likewise, it's known that the environment in a mother's womb can alter the development of a fetus. What's eye-opening is a growing body of evidence suggesting that the epigenetic changes wrought by one's diet, behavior, or surroundings can work their way into the germ line and echo far into the future. Put simply, and as bizarre as it may sound, what you eat or smoke today could affect the health and behavior of your great-grandchildren. In recent years, epigenetics researchers have made great strides in understanding the many molecular sequences and patterns that determine which genes can be turned on and off. Their work has made it increasingly clear that for all the popular attention devoted to genome-sequencing projects, the epigenome is just as critical as DNA to the healthy development of organisms, humans included. Jirtle and Waterland's experiment was a benchmark demonstration that the epigenome is sensitive to cues from the environment. More and more, researchers are finding that an extra bit of a vitamin, a brief exposure to a toxin, even an added dose of mothering can tweak the epigenome — and thereby alter the software of our genes — in ways that affect an individual's body and brain for life.

All of these discoveries are shaking the modern biological and social certainties about genetics and identity. We commonly accept the notion that through our DNA we are destined to have particular body shapes, personalities, and diseases. Some scholars even contend that the genetic code predetermines intelligence and is the root cause of many social ills, including poverty, crime, and violence. "Gene as fate" has become conventional wisdom. Through the study of epigenetics, that notion at last may be proved outdated. Suddenly, for better or worse, we appear to have a measure of control over our genetic legacy.

12. This passage is BEST described as an example of
    A. analysis of a process
    B. cause-and-effect analysis
    C. evaluative argument
    D. anecdotal narrative
    E. classification and comparison

13. The author's PRIMARY purpose in the first paragraph is to
    A. establish the framework for research that could lead to a scientific breakthrough in genetics
    B. strengthen his argument through ethos
    C. evaluate the agouti mouse as the control for a genetic experiment
    D. introduce the importance of genetic research in modern science
    E. initiate the exploration of a study in changing genetic hereditary markers

14. The last sentence in the third paragraph (The mothers passed…) is characterized by
    A. parallel syntax
    B. subtle irony
    C. an elaborate metaphor
    D. metonymy
    E. complex structure

15. In Line 24, "deleterious" is BEST understood to mean
    A. beneficial
    B. hardy
    C. harmful
    D. brilliant
    E. passive

16. The author's rhetorical strategy in this passage is to
    A. discredit invalid views on the topic
    B. propagate newer research about genetic heredity
    C. challenge the reader to disbelieve the research presented
    D. alarm the reader about the controversy surrounding genetic research
    E. broaden the reader's awareness of advancement in genetic research

17. In the section of the essay that immediately follows this excerpt, the author MOST likely does which of the following?
    A. Gives an example of another researcher that strengthens the evidence for the newer genetic theories
    B. Urges readers to change their own genetic heredity
    C. Shows oppositional researchers' opinions and evidence
    D. Discusses the researchers' next steps after concluding their current experiment
    E. Explains his own belief in the ability to change one's genomes

18. The MAIN idea of this essay is to
    A. demonstrate that agouti mice make great test subjects
    B. argue that people should avoid harmful addictions because the effects could be passed down to their children
    C. claim that genetic factors once thought to be set in stone can be changed through simple means such as diet and environment
    D. protest those that oppose new evidence that genetic coding can change through each generation
    E. argue for continued research into the different ways people can change the genetic markers passed down to their offspring

19. In the context of this passage, the last sentence is BEST viewed as
    A. hypothetical   B. ironic   C. metaphoric
    D. understated   E. redundant

Questions 20-30.

DIRECTIONS: Questions 20 through 30 are to be answered on the basis of the following passage, which is an excerpt from a 19th century essay written by Ralph Waldo Emerson.

1   There is a time in every man's education when he arrives at the conviction that envy is ignorance; that imitation is suicide; that he must take himself for better, for worse, as his portion; that though the wide universe is full of good, no kernel of nourishing corn can come to him but through his toil bestowed on that plot of ground which is given to him to
5   till. The power which resides in him is new in nature, and none but he knows what that is which he can do, nor does he know until he has tried. Not for nothing one face, one character, one fact, makes much impression on him, and another none. This sculpture in the memory is not without pre-established harmony. The eye was placed where one ray should fall, that it might testify of that particular ray. We but half express ourselves,
10 and are ashamed of that divine idea which each of us represents. It may be safely trusted as proportionate and of good issues, so it be faithfully imparted, but God will not have his work made manifest by cowards. A man is relieved and gay when he has put his heart into his work and done his best; but what he has said or done otherwise, shall give him no peace. It is a deliverance which does not deliver. In the attempt his genius
15 deserts him; no muse befriends; no invention, no hope.

Trust thyself: every heart vibrates to that iron string. Accept the place the divine providence has found for you, the society of your contemporaries, the connection of events. Great men have always done so, and confided themselves childlike to the genius of their age, betraying their perception that the absolutely trustworthy was seated at their heart, working through their hands, predominating in all their being. And we are now men, and must accept in the highest mind the same transcendent destiny; and not minors and invalids in a protected corner, not cowards fleeing before a revolution, but guides, redeemers, and benefactors, obeying the Almighty effort, and advancing on Chaos and the Dark.

The nonchalance of boys who are sure of a dinner, and would disdain as much as a lord to do or say aught to conciliate one, is the healthy attitude of human nature. A boy is in the parlour what the pit is in the playhouse; independent, irresponsible, looking out from his corner on such people and facts as pass by, he tries and sentences them on their merits, in the swift, summary way of boys, as good, bad, interesting, silly, eloquent, troublesome. He cumbers himself never about consequences, about interests: he gives an independent, genuine verdict. You must court him: he does not court you. But the man is, as it were, clapped into jail by his consciousness. As soon as he has once acted or spoken with eclat, he is a committed person, watched by the sympathy or the hatred of hundreds, whose affections must now enter into his account. There is no Lethe for this. Ah, that he could pass again into his neutrality! Who can thus avoid all pledges, and having observed, observe again from the same unaffected, unbiased, unbribable, unaffrighted innocence, must always be formidable. He would utter opinions on all passing affairs, which being seen to be not private, but necessary, would sink like darts into the ear of men, and put them in fear.

For nonconformity the world whips you with its displeasure. And therefore a man must know how to estimate a sour face. The by-standers look askance on him in the public street or in the friend's parlor. If this aversion had its origin in contempt and resistance like his own, he might well go home with a sad countenance; but the sour faces of the multitude, like their sweet faces, have no deep cause, disguise no god, but are put on and off as the wind blows, and a newspaper directs. Yet is the discontent of the multitude more formidable than that of the senate and the college. It is easy enough for a firm man who knows the world to brook the rage of the cultivated classes. Their rage is decorous and prudent, for they are timid as being very vulnerable themselves. But when to their feminine rage the indignation of the people is added, when the ignorant and the poor are aroused, when the unintelligent brute force that lies at the bottom of society is made to growl and mow, it needs the habit of magnanimity and religion to treat it godlike as a trifle of no concernment.

20. The comparison made in Line 3 (no kernel of nourishing corn...) is made to prove what point?
   A. One must work diligently to make corn grow just as they must work hard to achieve their own potential.
   B. Society cannot survive without food, so all need to work with ardor.
   C. A kernel of corn is tiny and difficult to see. Our prospects are similarly hidden and hard to see

9 (#2)

    D. As corn grows slowly, so it takes a long time for people to realize their own potential.
    E. If left untouched and unhandled, corn will grow wild and noxious as will a man's spirit.

21. The first paragraph (Lines 1-15) contain each of the following features of syntax EXCEPT
    A. asyndeton
    B. periodic sentence
    C. compound sentence
    D. parallelism
    E. cumulative sentence

21.____

22. The speaker's tone in the first sentence of Paragraph 2 (Trust thyself...) might be BEST described as
    A. pensive and reflective
    B. critical and indignant
    C. exhortative and lofty
    D. reproachful and compelling
    E. detached and haughty

22.____

23. Paragraph 3 contains an example of each of the following EXCEPT
    A. personification
    B. simile
    C. metaphor
    D. synecdoche
    E. allusion

23.____

24. What is the MOST likely purpose for the analogy at the beginning of Paragraph 3?
    A. To reveal the grating nature of the pit of the ancient playhouse
    B. To heap praise on the honesty and indomitable excitement of youth
    C. To elucidate divisions of class as related to dramatic interpretations
    D. To condemn the unrefined and wild conduct to which youth is prone
    E. To hyperbolize the bold and naïve responsibility of youth

24.____

25. Line 40-47 suggest that individuals should ignore others' irritation at his own nonconformity because
    A. the scorn shown from others resembles a weak personal feeling
    B. people change their attitudes constantly
    C. people guise their prejudice as religious beliefs and godly inspiration
    D. the individual is always strong within himself
    E. the hypocrites are limited to public streets and friends' living rooms

25.____

26. In this context, the word "feminine" in Line 49 MOST NEARLY means
    A. weak
    B. peculiarly disarming
    C. thoughtless
    D. nurturing
    E. spirited

26.____

27. The tone of the whole passage might BEST be described as
    A. instructive and motivating
    B. mournful
    C. optimistic and joyous
    D. pessimistic and cynical
    E. doubtful yet desirous

27.____

28. This selection is an example of which mode of writing? 28._____
    A. Descriptive   B. Argument   C. Narrative
    D. Expository   E. Critique

29. Which of the following statements about society would the author MOST 29._____
    likely agree with?
    A. It helps its members achieve to their fullest potential by challenging them.
    B. Even if one disagrees with society, everyone must accept the rules set forth.
    C. One should look to oppose society through violent means to bring about its destruction.
    D. Society conspires to deny people their freedom.
    E. Our joined grouping is all that keeps the forces of chaos at bay.

30. The author's likely purpose in writing this essay is to 30._____
    A. express his dissatisfaction with the society of the time
    B. warn against the dangers of following the rules and regulations of society
    C. explain and analyze the nature of individuals willing to believe in themselves
    D. describe a profound way of seeing oneself in relation to society
    E. argue that individuals should not concern themselves with what others think, they should be self-sufficient and honest with themselves

Questions 31-39.

DIRECTIONS: Questions 31 through 39 are to be answered on the basis of the following passage, which is an excerpt from Martin Luther King's "Letter From Birmingham Jail".

1   Let us consider a more concrete example of just and unjust laws. An unjust law is a code that a numerical or power majority group compels a minority group to obey but does not make binding on itself. This is difference made legal. By the same token, a just law is a code that a majority compels a minority to follow and that it is willing to
5   follow itself. This is sameness made legal.

       Let me give another explanation. A law is unjust if it is inflicted on a minority that, as a result of being denied the right to vote, had no part in enacting or devising the law. Who can say that the legislature of Alabama which set up that state's segregation laws was democratically elected? Throughout Alabama all sorts of devious methods are used to
10   prevent Negroes from becoming 10 registered voters, and there are some counties in which, even though Negroes constitute a majority of the population, not a single Negro is registered. Can any law enacted under such circumstances be considered democratically structured?

       Sometimes a law is just on its face and unjust in its application. For instance, I have
15   been arrested on a charge of parading without a permit. Now, there is nothing wrong in having an ordinance which requires a permit for a parade. But such an ordinance becomes unjust when it is used to maintain segregation and to deny citizens the First Amendment privilege of peaceful assembly and protest.

I hope you are able to ace the distinction I am trying to point out. In no sense do I advocate evading or defying the law, as would the rabid segregationist. That would lead to anarchy. One who breaks an unjust law must do so openly, lovingly, and with a willingness to accept the penalty. I submit that an individual who breaks a law that conscience tells him is unjust and who willingly accepts the penalty of imprisonment in order to arouse the conscience of the community over its injustice, is in reality expressing the highest respect for law.

Of course, there is nothing new about this kind of civil disobedience. It was evidenced sublimely in the refusal of Shadrach, Meshach and Abednego to obey the laws of Nebuchadnezzar, on the ground that a higher moral law was at stake. It was practiced superbly by the early Christians, who were willing to face hungry lions and the excruciating pain of chopping blocks rather than submit to certain unjust laws of the Roman Empire. To a degree, academic freedom is a reality today because Socrates practiced civil disobedience. In our own nation, the Boston Tea Party represented a massive act of civil disobedience.

We should never forget that everything Adolf Hitler did in Germany was "legal" and everything the Hungarian freedom fighters did in Hungary was "illegal." It was "illegal" to aid and comfort a Jew in Hitler's Germany. Even so, I am sure that, had I lived in Germany at the time, I would have aided and comforted my Jewish brothers. If today I lived in a Communist country where certain principles dear to the Christian faith are suppressed, I would openly advocate disobeying that country's antireligious laws.

I must make two honest confessions to you, my Christian and Jewish brothers. First, I must confess that over the past few years I have been gravely disappointed with the white moderate. I have almost reached the regrettable conclusion that the Negro's great stumbling block in his stride toward freedom is not the White Citizen's Counciler or the Ku Klux Klanner, but the white moderate, who is more devoted to "order" than to justice; who prefers a negative peace which is the absence of tension to a positive peace which is the presence of justice; who constantly says: "I agree with you in the goal you seek, but I cannot agree with your methods of direct action"; who paternalistically believes he can set the timetable for another man's freedom; who lives by a mythical concept of time and who constantly advises the Negro to wait for a "more convenient season." Shallow understanding from people of good will is more frustrating than absolute misunderstanding from people of ill will. Lukewarm acceptance is much more bewildering than outright rejection.

31. All of the following devices can be found in Paragraphs 1 and 2 EXCEPT
    A. antithesis
    B. rhetorical question
    C. metaphor
    D. compound-complex sentence
    E. imperative sentence

32. What is the author's PRIMARY purpose in writing Paragraph 3?
    A. To challenge a point made in the previous paragraph
    B. To introduce a concept that he will argue against later
    C. To reinforce his own personal experience
    D. To show a distinction between theory and practice
    E. To sum up points made in Paragraphs 1 and 2

33. What rhetorical device is used in Paragraph 4 (Lines 19-25)?
    A. Oxymoron
    B. Paradox
    C. Hyperbole
    D. Parallelism
    E. Repetition

34. The author's tone in Paragraph 6 can BEST be described as
    A. angry
    B. bitter
    C. respectful
    D. sympathetic
    E. cynical

35. The author's purpose in denouncing the evasion and defiance of the law (Lines 19-20) can BEST be described as an effort to
    A. underscore a supposition of his argument
    B. indicate a change in attitude
    C. allow and repudiate a counterargument
    D. offer a detailed instance of a point he makes earlier
    E. to qualify his claim and overall argument

36. When the author mentions Adolf Hitler and Nazi Germany (Lines 34-39), he is appealing to the audience through which of the following?
    A. Pathos
    B. Logos
    C. Paradox
    D. Hyperbole
    E. Complex Symbolism

37. In the context which it is used, the author uses the phrase "negative peace" (Line 45) in reference to
    A. conservatives who do not want real justice, only a lack of violence
    B. protesters who refuse to use violence of any kind in public
    C. moderate white people who seek true justice for all races
    D. violent members of the KKK who intimidate moderates who want true justice
    E. legislators who say they want change, but do not enact laws that would promote it

38. This style of passage as a whole would BEST be characterized as
    A. unceremonious yet evocative
    B. unbiased and formal
    C. emotional yet detailed
    D. theoretical and indirect
    E. intricate and rational

39. Looking at the passage as a whole, which of the following organization patterns BEST describes it?
    I. Cause-and-effect
    II. Compare and contrast
    III. Definition
    The CORRECT answer is:
    A. I and II only
    B. II only
    C. I and III only
    D. III only
    E. I, II, and III

Questions 40-47.

DIRECTIONS: Questions 40 through 47 are to be answered on the basis of the following passage, which is excerpt from an essay written in 2009.

1   The bank called today, and I told them my deposit was in the mail, even though I hadn't written a check yet. It'd been a rough day. The baby I'm pregnant with decided to do aerobics on my lungs for two hours, our three-year-old daughter painted the living-room couch with lipstick, the IRS put me on hold for an hour, and I was late to a business
5   meeting because I was tired. I told my client that traffic had been bad. When my partner came home, his haggard face told me his day hadn't gone any better than mine, so when he asked, "How was your day?" I said, "Oh, fine," knowing that one more straw might break his back. A friend called and wanted to take me to lunch. I said I was busy. Four lies in the course of a day, none of which I felt the least bit guilty about.

10   We lie. We all do. We exaggerate, we minimize, we avoid confrontation, we spare people's feelings, we conveniently forget, we keep secrets, we justify lying to the big-guy institutions. Like most people, I indulge in small falsehoods and still think of myself as an honest person. Sure I lie, but it doesn't hurt anything. Or does it?

     I once tried going a whole week without telling a lie, and it was paralyzing. I discovered
15   that telling the truth all the time is nearly impossible. It means living with some serious consequences: The bank charges me $60 in overdraft fees, my partner keels over when I tell him about my travails, my client fires me for telling her I didn't feel like being on time, and my friend takes it personally when I say I'm not hungry. There must be some merit to lying.

20   But if I justify lying, what makes me any different from slick politicians or the corporate robbers who raided the S&L industry? Saying it's okay to lie one way and not another is hedging. I cannot seem to escape the voice deep inside me that tells me: When someone lies, someone loses.

     What far-reaching consequences will I, or others, pay as a result of my lie? Will
25   someone's trust be destroyed? Will someone else pay my penance because I ducked out? We must consider the meaning of our actions. Deception, lies, capital crimes, and misdemeanors all carry meanings. Webster's definition of lie is specific: 1.: a false statement or action especially made with the intent to deceive; 2.: anything that gives or is meant to give a false impression. A definition like this implies that there are many, many
30   ways to tell a lie. Here are just a few.

     The White Lie

     A man who won't lie to a woman has very little consideration for her feelings. — Bergen Evans. The white lie assumes that the truth will cause more damage than a simple, harmless untruth. Telling a friend he looks great when he looks like hell can be based on a decision that the friend needs a compliment more than a frank opinion. But, in effect, it
35   is the liar deciding what is best for the lied to. Ultimately, it is a vote of no confidence. It is an act of subtle arrogance for anyone to decide what is best for someone else. Yet not all

circumstances are quite so cut-and-dried. Take, for instance, the sergeant in Vietnam who knew one of his men was killed in action but listed him as missing so that the man's family would receive indefinite compensation instead of the lump-sum pittance the military gives widows and children. His intent was honorable. Yet for twenty years this family kept their hopes alive, unable to move on to a new life.

Ignoring the Plain Facts

Well, you must understand that Father Porter is only human. A Massachusetts priest in the '60s, the Catholic Church in Massachusetts began hearing complaints that Father James Porter was sexually molesting children. Rather than relieving him of his duties, the ecclesiastical authorities simply moved him from one parish to another between 1960 and 1967, actually providing him with a fresh supply of unsuspecting families and innocent children to abuse. After treatment in 1967 for pedophilia, he went back to work, this time in Minnesota. The new diocese was aware of Father Porter's obsession with children, but they needed priests and recklessly believed treatment had cured him. More children were abused until he was relieved of his duties a year later. By his own admission, Porter may have abused as many as a hundred children. Ignoring the facts may not in and of itself be a form of lying, but consider the context of this situation. If a lie is a false action done with the intent to deceive, then the Catholic Church's conscious covering for Porter created irreparable consequences. The church became a co-perpetrator with Porter.

How much do we tolerate before we become sick and tired of being sick and tired? When will we stand up and declare our right to trust? When do we stop accepting that the real truth is in the fine print? Whose lips do we read this year when we vote for president? When will we stop being so reticent about making judgments? When do we stop turning over our personal power and responsibility to liars?

Maybe if I don't tell the bank the check's in the mail I'll be less tolerant of the lies told me every day. A country song I once heard said it all for me: "You've got to stand for something or you'll fall for anything."

40. The PRIMARY rhetorical function of Lines 10-13 is to
    A. introduce an idea that will be discussed later in the passage
    B. question the authenticity and acceptability of a concept
    C. provide a transition between Paragraphs 1 and 3
    D. reiterate the main idea of the passage
    E. illustrate a concept presented in the previous paragraph

41. The mood of the fourth paragraph of the passage would BEST be described as
    A. anxious   B. sentimental   C. humorous
    D. suspenseful   E. sarcastic

42. Based on the author's explanations and examples, one can conclude that she believes individuals
    A. lack awareness in how many different ways they lie
    B. cannot distinguish between lies of functionality and lies that are harmful
    C. unsuccessfully understand the real consequences of falsehoods
    D. condone lying as a necessary part of contemporary life
    E. inadvertently lie more than lying on purpose

43. Lines 10-11 (We exaggerate, we minimize...to the big-guy institutions) is a clear example of
    A. run-on
    B. complex sentence
    C. polysyndeton
    D. cumulative sentence
    E. asyndeton

44. In Paragraph 7, the author characterizes the Catholic Church's stance as
    A. a deceitful inaction that was just as culpable as the priest's actions
    B. a form of lying that is usually acceptable, but in this case had disastrous consequences
    C. the worst form of deceit imaginable and worse than the priest's original actions
    D. the type of lie one can expect from larger institutions such as a government or religious organization
    E. a deliberate act against families that shows the hypocrisy of large-scale moral institutions

45. Which of the following BEST describes the tone of the essay?
    A. Sardonic and caustic
    B. Confrontational and instructive
    C. Spirited and stimulating
    D. Indifferent and unceremonious
    E. Educational and high-minded

46. All of the following words or phrases are examples of the author's use of colloquialism EXCEPT
    A. "a rough day" (Line 2)
    B. "decided to do aerobics in my lungs" (Lines 2-3)
    C. "one more straw might break his back" (Lines 7-8)
    D. "ducked out" (Lines 25-26)
    E. "cut-and-dried" (Line 37)

47. The effect of the last sentence of the passage (Lines 61-62) can BEST be described as a(n)
    A. symbolic metaphor
    B. deliberate understatement
    C. comic anticlimax
    D. allegorical conclusion
    E. resolution of an argument

Questions 48-55.

DIRECTIONS: Questions 48 through 55 are to be answered on the basis of the following passage, which is an excerpt from a contemporary essay arguing the drawbacks of television consumption.

1   Not much more than fifty years after the introduction of television into American society, the medium has become so deeply ingrained in daily life that in many states the TV set has attained the rank of a legal necessity, safe from the repossession in case of debt along with clothes and cooking utensils. Only in the early years after television's
5   introduction did writers and commentators have sufficient perspective to separate the activity of watching television from the actual content it offers the viewer. In those days writers frequently discussed the effects of television on a family life. However, a curious myopia afflicted those first observers: almost without exception they regarded television as a favorable, beneficial, indeed, wondrous influence upon the family.

10   "Television is going to be a real asset in every home where there are children," predicted a writer in 1949.

"Television will take over your way of living and change your children's habits, but this change can be a wonderful improvement," claimed another commentator.

"No survey's needed, of course, to establish that television has brought the family
15   together in one room," wrote the New York Time's television critic in 1949.

The early articles about television were almost invariably accompanied by a photograph or illustration showing a family cozily sitting together before the television set, Sis on Mom's lap. Buddy perched on the arm of Dad's chair, Dad with his arm around Mom's shoulder. Who could have guessed that twenty or so years later Mom would be
20   watching a drama in the kitchen, the kids would be looking at cartoons in their room, while Dad would be taking in the ball game in the living room?

But television did not merely influence the child: it deeply influenced that "pattern of influences" everyone hoped would ameliorate the new medium's effects. Home and family life have changed in important ways since the advent of television. The peer
25   group has become television-oriented, and much of the time children spend together is occupied by television viewing. Culture generally has been transformed by television. Participation in church and community activities has diminished, with television a primary cause of this change. Therefore, it is improper to assign to television the subsidiary role with its many apologists insist it plays. Television is not merely one of a number of
30   important influences upon today's child. Through the changes it has made in family life, television emerges as the important influence in children's lives today.

Without conjuring up fantasies of bygone eras with family games and long, leisurely meals, the question arises: Isn't there a better family life available than this dismal, mechanized arrangement of children watching television for however long is allowed
35   them, evening after evening?

Of course, families today still do things together at times: go camping in the summer, go to the zoo on a nice Sunday, take various trips and expeditions. But their ordinary daily life together is diminished - those hours of sitting around at the dinner table, the spontaneous taking up of an activity, the little games invented by children on the spur of the moment when there is nothing else to do, the scribbling, the chatting, and even the quarreling, all the things that form the fabric of a family, that define a childhood. Instead, the children have their regular schedule of television programs and bedtime, and the parents have their peaceful dinner together.

As families have come to spend more and more of their time together engaged in the single activity of television watching, those rituals and pastimes that once gave family life its special quality have become more and more uncommon. Not since prehistoric times, when cave families hunted, gathered, ate, and slept, with little time remaining to accumulate a culture of any significance, have families been reduced to such a sameness.

Studies show the importance of eye-to-eye contact, for instance, in real-life relationships, and indicate that the nature of one's eye-contact patterns, whether one looked another squarely in the eye or looks to the side or shifts one's gaze from side to side, may play a significant role in one's success or failure in human relationships. But no eye contact is possible in the child television relationship, although in certain children's programs people purport to speak directly to the child and the camera fosters this illusion by focusing directly upon the person being filmed. How much might such a distortion affect a child's development of trust, of openness, of an ability to relate well to real people?

One research study alone seems to contradict the idea that television has a negative impact on family life. In their important book Television and the Quality of Life, sociologists Robert Kubey and Mihaly Csikszentmihalyi observe that the heaviest viewers of TV among their subjects were "no less likely to spend time with their families" than the lightest viewers. Moreover, those heavy viewers reported feeling happier, more relaxed, and satisfied when watching TV with their families than light viewers did. Based on these reports, the researchers reached the conclusion that "television viewing harmonizes with family life."

Using the same data, however, the researchers made another observation about the heavy and light viewers: "families that spend substantial portions of their time together watching television are likely to experience greater percentages of their family time feeling relatively passive and unchallenged compared with families who spend small proportions of their time watching TV."

In spite of everything, the American family muddles on, dimly aware that something is amiss but distracted from an understanding of its plight by an endless stream of television images. As family ties grow weaker and vaguer, as children's lives become more separate from their parents', as parents' educational role in their children's lives is taken over by the media, the school, and the peer group, family life becomes increasingly more unsatisfying for both parents and children. All that seems to be left is love, an abstraction that family members know is necessary but find great difficulty giving it to each other since the traditional opportunities for expressing it within the family that have been reduced or eliminated.

18 (#2)

48. In Lines 1-10, which of the following does the author NOT do?
    I. State the claim of the essay
    II. Place television in an historical context
    III. Imply a critical attitude toward television
    The CORRECT answer is:
    A. I only
    B. II only
    C. III only
    D. I and II only
    E. I and III only

49. The author presents three separate quotes in Paragraphs 2, 3, and 4, respectively, as a means to
    A. suggest that early critics were mistaken in their valuation of the television
    B. reveal the dissonance between programming in early and current television broadcasting
    C. show the foresight of early critics of the TV
    D. disclose the valuable influence of early era broadcasting
    E. institute influential support for her argument

50. In the excerpt, the author uses all of the following EXCEPT
    A. authenticated evidence
    B. an appeal to credibility
    C. rhetorical questions
    D. qualifications and reservations
    E. arguments of policy

51. With Lines 22-41 (But the television did not merely…), the author indicates a(n)
    A. extension and verification of ideas from previous parts of the essay
    B. change in rhetoric from confirmation toward a claim statement
    C. shifting from opinion to fact
    D. swing toward offering allowances to previously stated arguments
    E. movement toward the confirmation of previously stated claims

52. The author references a study throughout Lines 58-65 to suggest an association between which of the following?
    A. Fulfillment and inactiveness
    B. Happiness and passivity
    C. Activity and dissatisfaction
    D. Contentment and chance
    E. Satisfaction and activity

53. Throughout the entire excerpt, the author is MOST critical of regarding television and its
    A. stimulating effect
    B. glamorous content
    C. convenience
    D. harmful attraction
    E. commercial appeal

54. The author's tone throughout the essay can BEST be described as
    A. frustrated
    B. serious
    C. biased
    D. surprised
    E. analytical

55. Paragraph 10 includes an example of
    A. metaphor
    B. direct address
    C. periodic sentence
    D. personification
    E. cumulative sentence

KEY (CORRECT ANSWERS)

1.	E	11.	D	21.	A	31.	C	41.	D
2.	C	12.	B	22.	C	32.	D	42.	C
3.	B	13.	A	23.	D	33.	B	43.	E
4.	A	14.	E	24.	E	34.	A	44.	A
5.	D	15.	C	25.	B	35.	E	45.	B
6.	A	16.	E	26.	C	36.	D	46.	B
7.	E	17.	B	27.	A	37.	A	47.	D
8.	B	18.	C	28.	B	38.	C	48.	C
9.	C	19.	A	29.	D	39.	E	49.	A
10.	D	20.	D	30.	E	40.	B	50.	E

51.	C
52.	B
53.	C
54.	A
55.	E

EXAMINATION SECTION
TEST 1

DIRECTIONS: Each question or incomplete statement is followed by several suggested answers or completions. Select the one that BEST answers the question or completes the statement. *PRINT THE LETTER OF THE CORRECT ANSWER IN THE SPACE AT THE RIGHT.*

1. *After completing fighter pilot training, women's access to battle has often been denied.*
   The above sentence contains
   A. a dangling modifier
   B. a euphemism
   C. problems with parallel construction
   D. a split infinitive

   1.____

2. *That is a strange type of a bird.*
   The above sentence contains problems with
   A. split infinitives   B. idiom
   C. parallel construction   D. subject-verb agreement

   2.____

3. *Native Americans are often portrayed or stereotyped as lazy, despite overwhelming evidence to the contrary.*
   The above sentence contains
   A. a dangling modifier   B. a split infinitive
   C. redundancy   D. no errors

   3.____

4. *After the initial excitement had worn off, Jessica decided to carefully weigh her options.*
   The above sentence contains
   A. a dangling modifier   B. an inconsistent verb tense
   C. faulty apposition   D. a split infinitive

   4.____

5. Despite our efforts to rid ourselves of them, the fats in our bodies serve a purpose. Fat cells never die, which is why exercising is better than dieting. Few people understand that almost three-quarters of our calories are burned while we rest.
   Based on the above information, which of the following represents a correct logical inference?
   A. Fat is increasingly harmful to our bodies as we age.
   B. Understanding the way our bodies function is central to good health.
   C. The more a person rests, the more weight he or she will lose.
   D. Dieting is useless.

   5.____

6. How to Get Out of a Locked Trunk, Philip Weiss: *Every culture comes up with tests of a person's ability to get out of a _____ situation.*
   Which of the following words provides the appropriate connotation to complete the above sentence?
   A. death-defying   B. sticky   C. flavorful   D. hopeful

7. *Carol has a habit of jumping out of the frying pan and into deep water.*
   The above sentence contains problems with
   A. split infinitives   B. mixed metaphors
   C. idiom   D. jargon

8. *When I go skiing I like to purchase a lift ticket. Otherwise you spend all your time walking uphill.*
   The above passage contains
   A. a dangling modifier   B. problems with parallel construction
   C. a shifting point of view D. a split infinitive

9. *Her hopes rise as they draw near to the animal store, and then fell when her parents drove past it.*
   The above sentence contains
   A. a dangling modifier
   B. an inconsistent verb tense
   C. a shifting point of view
   D. problems with subject-verb agreement

10. *The doctor, a very lucrative profession, requires a great deal of education and training.*
    The above sentence contains
    A. a dangling modifier   B. a shifting point of view
    C. faulty apposition   D. an inconsistent verb tense

11. *Tony and Kim were devastated to learn that their dog, Sentinel, would have to be put to sleep.*
    The above sentence contains
    A. jargon   B. slang   C. a metaphor   D. a euphemism

12. Which of the following is the CLEAREST description of a particular scene?
    A. A Canadian bridge building official on a windy day in 1886 on a bridge high above the St. Lawrence river saw a group of Caughnawaga Mohawk Indians playing.
    B. On a bridge high above the St. Lawrence river a Canadian bridge-building official saw a group of Caughnawaga Indians playing on a windy day in 1886.
    C. On a windy day in 1886, a Canadian bridge-building official saw a group of Caughnawaga Mohawk Indians playing on a bridge high above the St. Lawrence river.
    D. A group of Caughnawaga Mohawk Indians playing on a windy day in 1886 were seen by a Canadian bridge-building official high above the St. Lawrence river.

13. Which of the following provides the MOST objective point of view on the part of the writer?
    A. A student protest group blocked the entry to the graduate library for 2 hours today.
    B. A group of left-wing radicals blocked our way into the study carrels this afternoon.
    C. Students blocked the entrance to the graduate library that sits like an eyesore on the campus.
    D. These student groups rarely seem to understand what it is they're protesting.

13.____

14. *When I saw Gabriel Samuels in the county courthouse, I knew he must have been arrested.*
    The above statement is an example of
    A. a faulty use of cause and effect
    B. an ad hominem attack
    C. circular reasoning
    D. a hasty generalization

14.____

15. *The wise politician promises the possible and accepts the inevitable.*
    The above statement contains
    A. elliptical phrases
    B. parallel construction
    C. a shift in point of view
    D. euphemisms

15.____

16. *The actor Brad Pitt is so handsome that I know he must be smart.*
    The above statement is an example of
    A. a faulty use of cause and effect
    B. a non sequitur
    C. circular reasoning
    D. a hasty generalization

16.____

Questions 17-18.

DIRECTIONS: Questions 17 and 18 are to be answered on the basis of the following passage.

Kill 'Em! Crush 'Em! Eat 'Em Raw!, John McCurty:

The family resemblance between football and war is, indeed striking. Their languages are similar: "field general," "long bomb," "blitz," "take a shot," "front line," "pursuit," "good hit," "the draft," and so on. Their principles and practices are alike: mass hysteria, the art of intimidation, absolute command and total obedience, territorial aggression, censorship, inflated insignia and propaganda, blackboard maneuvers and strategies, drills, uniforms, formations, marching bands and training camps.

17. The diction in the above passage is BEST characterized as
    A. formal, with slang terms
    B. colloquial with slang terms
    C. formal
    D. colloquial

17.____

18. The above passage depends MOST upon
    A. imagery
    B. metaphor
    C. comparison
    D. contrast

18.____

Questions 19-25.

DIRECTIONS: Questions 19 through 25 are to be answered on the basis of the following passage.

The Awakening, Kate Chopin

A certain light was beginning to dawn dimly within her—the light which, showing the way, forbids it.(1)
At that early period it served but to bewilder her.(2) It moved her to dreams, to thoughtfulness, to the shadowy anguish which had overcome her the midnight when she had abandoned herself to tears.(3)
In short, Mrs. Pontellier was beginning to realize her position in the universe as a human being, and to recognize her relations as an individual to the world within and about her.(4) This may seem like a ponderous weight of wisdom to descend upon the soul of a young woman of twenty-eight—perhaps more wisdom than the Holy Ghost is usually pleased to vouchsafe to any woman.(5)
But the beginning of things, of a world especially, is necessarily vague, tangled, chaotic, and exceedingly disturbing.(6) How few of us ever emerge from such beginning!(7) How many souls perish in its tumult!(8)
The voice of the sea is seductive; never ceasing, whispering, clamoring, murmuring, inviting the soul to wander for a spell in abysses of solitude; to lose itself in mazes of inward contemplation.(9)
The voice of the sea speaks to the soul.(10) The touch of the sea is sensuous, enfolding the boy in its soft, close embrace.(11)

19. This passage is BEST characterized as a(n)
    A. concrete description of the sea and its dangers
    B. descriptive narrative about Mrs. Pontellier's depression
    C. descriptive narrative about Mrs. Pontellier's soul
    D. account of Mrs. Pontellier's fear of swimming

20. In this passage, the sea is BEST characterized as a(n)
    A. element of nature that encourages deep reflection
    B. dangerous and unpredictable body of water that threatens human life
    C. mysterious force that entices people to abandon their loved ones
    D. element of nature that causes people to reflect upon their childhoods

21. In line 5, the word *ponderous* is used to mean
    A. surprising   B. unexpected   C. thoughtful   D. heavy

22. Lines 6-8 provide a(n)
    A. description of the dangers of the sea
    B. explanation of the causes of Mrs. Pontellier's depression
    C. description of the transformation of Mrs. Pontellier's soul
    D. argument for greater understanding of those suffering from depression

23. Mrs. Pontellier is BEST characterized as a
    A. middle-aged woman overcome with sadness
    B. young woman just beginning to discover herself
    C. middle-aged women who has discovered a new sense of power
    D. young woman in love with the sea

24. Which of the following words BEST describes Mrs. Pontellier's reaction to this experience?
    A. Confusion   B. Sorrow   C. Ecstasy   D. Happiness

25. The MAIN implication of this passage is that
    A. Mrs. Pontellier is a very religious woman
    B. Mrs. Pontellier needs help for her debilitating depression
    C. the sea is a mesmerizing, overwhelming element of nature
    D. the discovery of self is a bewildering and sometimes dangerous process

KEY (CORRECT ANSWERS)

1.	A	11.	D
2.	B	12.	C
3.	C	13.	A
4.	D	14.	A
5.	B	15.	B
6.	B	16.	B
7.	B	17.	A
8.	C	18.	C
9.	B	19.	C
10.	C	20.	A

21. D
22. C
23. B
24. A
25. D

TEST 2

DIRECTIONS: Each question or incomplete statement is followed by several suggested answers or completions. Select the one that BEST answers the question or completes the statement. *PRINT THE LETTER OF THE CORRECT ANSWER IN THE SPACE AT THE RIGHT.*

1. *For a successful stockbroker, Adam is remarkably ingenuous.*
   Which of the following BEST captures the meaning of the word *ingenuous* as used in the above sentence?
   A. Ignorant
   B. Terse
   C. Straightforward, frank
   D. Duplicitous

   1.____

2. *I had every intention of complying to the rules.*
   The above sentence contains problems with
   A. split infinitives
   B. mixed metaphors
   C. idiom
   D. jargon

   2.____

3. The Ring of Time, E.B. White:
   The enchantment grew not out of anything that happened or was performed but out of something that seemed to go round and around and around with the girl, attending her, a steady gleam in the shape of a circle—a ring of ambition, of happiness, of youth.
   The above passage depends MOST heavily on
   A. irony
   B. parallel construction
   C. correlative conjunctions
   D. elliptical phrases

   3.____

4. Which of the following titles utilizes a slang tone?
   A. Just How Do You Suppose That Alice Knows?
   B. Leisure Will Kill You
   C. Gotta Dance
   D. When I Heard the Learn'd Astronomer

   4.____

5. Which of the following presents the BEST sequence of the following sentences to make a coherent paragraph?
   I. One of the most important of these nutrients is nitrogen, derived from the decomposing organic matter—material from living things—in the soil.
   II. If these plants did not have a source for nitrogen, they would not be able to produce their own food, and would quickly die.
   III. Nearly all the world's green plants make their own food using sunlight, water, and nutrients that are drawn from the soil through their roots.
   IV. However, some plants live in wet, marshy areas where much of this organic material, including nitrogen, is washed out of the soil.
   The CORRECT answer is:
   A. I, II, IV, III
   B. II, III, I, IV
   C. III, I, IV, II
   D. III, IV, I, II

   5.____

6. *On his new mountain bike, Justin flew over the hills at a full head of steam.*
   The above sentence contains problems with
   A. split infinitives B. mixed metaphors
   C. idiom D. jargon

7. *Prior than yesterday, we had never seen such a thing.*
   The above sentence contains problems with
   A. split infinitives B. mixed metaphors
   C. idiom D. jargon

8. *I _____ under this pressure. Unable to compete, yet unwilling to shut down, I simply stumbled onward.*
   Which of the following words provides the appropriate connotation to complete the above passage?
   A. diminished B. shriveled C. suffered D. thrived

9. *In his lecture on twentieth century art, the professor alluded to Andy Warhol.*
   Which of the following BEST captures the meaning of the word *alluded* as it is used in the above sentence?
   A. Indirectly referred B. Directly referred
   C. Footnoted D. Introduced

10. Which of the following is the CLEAREST description of a particular scene?
    A. During the dance, which is beautiful to watch, these tin cones strike one another to produce a soft, rhythmic sound.
    B. During the dance these tin cones strike one another to produce a soft, rhythmic sound, which is beautiful to watch.
    C. During the dance these tin cones strike one another to produce a sound that is soft, rhythmic and beautiful to watch.
    D. During this beautiful dance, these tin cones strike one another to produce a soft, rhythmic sound.

11. *Throughout her life, Martina Navratilova has used her differences creating a career marked by determination, skill, and discipline to her advantage.*
    The above sentence contains
    A. redundancy B. a faulty modifier
    C. improper punctuation D. mixed metaphors

12. *Journalists are trained to approach stories with an amoral perspective.*
    Which of the following BEST captures the meaning of the word *amoral* as it is used in the above sentence?
    A. Subjective B. Emotional C. Judgmental D. Non-judgmental

13. On Going Home, Joan Didion:
    I would like to promise her that she will grow up with a sense of her cousins and of rivers and of great-grandmother's teacups, would like to pledge her a picnic on a river with friend chicken and her hair uncombed, would like to give her home for her birthday, but we live differently now and I can promise her nothing like that.

The above passage depends MOST heavily on
A. parallel construction
B. metaphor
C. analogy
D. coordination

14. *A few countries produce most of the world's toxins, but pollution affected many countries.*
The above sentence contains
A. a false analogy
B. faulty parallel construction
C. a shift in point of view
D. a shift in verb tense

15. *I glanced quickly through the pages of the old family album, unable to believe my eyes.*
The above sentence contains
A. improper punctuation
B. faulty subordination
C. redundancy
D. no errors

16. *Called Skywalkers, they have helped them find a modern expression for old Mohawk traditions of bravery, courage, and endurance.*
The above sentence contains
A. an ambiguous pronoun reference
B. faulty subordination
C. a dangling modifier
D. no errors

17. *One can become rich if you practice frugality.*
The above sentence contains
A. a shift in verb tense
B. a shift in point of view
C. faulty parallel construction
D. a dangling modifier

18. *While English is both a written and an oral language, the Navajo language is almost entirely oral.*
The above sentence contains
A. faulty subordination
B. a misplaced modifier
C. faulty parallel structure
D. no errors

19. *She is different than you.*
The above sentence contains problems with
A. split infinitives
B. mixed metaphors
C. idiom
D. jargon

20. *After starting at the bottom of the ladder, Samson had made it to CEO of the company.*
The above sentence contains
A. jargon
B. a cliché
C. an idiom
D. slang

21. *The representative's remarks were vigorously censured by his colleagues.*
Which of the following BEST captures the meaning of the word *censured* as it is used in the above sentence?
A. Severely criticized
B. Edited or suppressed
C. Applauded
D. Silenced

22. Whenever she had to warn us about life, my mother told fantastic stories with complicated morals. She tested our ability to _____ realities.
 Which of the following words provides the appropriate connotation to complete the above sentence?
 A. figure out   B. establish   C. make up   D. discern

23. In a dictionary, this label is applied to terms that were once common but are now rare.
 A. Formal   B. Informal   C. Nonstandard   D. Archaic

24. *Her skills are weak and her performance only average.*
 The above sentence contains
 A. ambiguous modifiers
 B. subject-verb agreement
 C. parallel construction
 D. elliptical phrasing

25. *The graduate student cited Freud in her dissertation.*
 Which of the following BEST captures the meaning of the word *cited* as it is used in the above sentence?
 A. Thanked
 B. Quoted as an authority
 C. Acknowledged
 B. Located

KEY (CORRECT ANSWERS)

1.	C		11.	B
2.	C		12.	D
3.	B		13.	A
4.	C		14.	D
5.	C		15.	C
6.	B		16.	A
7.	C		17.	B
8.	B		18.	D
9.	A		19.	C
10.	D		20.	B

21. A
22. B
23. D
24. D
25. B

TEST 3

DIRECTIONS: Each question or incomplete statement is followed by several suggested answers or completions. Select the one that BEST answers the question or completes the statement. *PRINT THE LETTER OF THE CORRECT ANSWER IN THE SPACE AT THE RIGHT.*

Questions 1-3.

DIRECTIONS: Questions 1 through 3 are to be answered on the basis of the following excerpts.

A. As Henry David Thoreau famously declared, *In Wilderness is the preservation of the World*. But is it? The more one knows of its peculiar history, the more one realizes that wilderness is not quite what it seems.

B. For whatever else a prison does, it demands that one confront it. If you are a prisoner, it might take you a dozen years to realize that the life you hope to create requires, above all else, that it be lived within these walls, for these walls do not go away. Here, of all the world's places, there is everything to accept.

C. I've been around and seen the Taj Mahal and the Grand Canyon and Marilyn Monroe's footprints outside Grauman's Chinese Theater, but I've never seen my mother wash her own hair. Upon matrimony, she began weekly treks to the beauty salon where Julie washed and styled her hair. Her appointment on Fridays at two o'clock was never canceled or rescheduled.

D. The ongoing loss will not be replaced by evolution in any period of time that has meaning for humanity. Extinction is now proceeding thousands of times faster than the production of new species.

1. In which excerpt is the tone meant to be humorous?
    A. A B. B C. C D. D

2. Which excerpt relies MOST heavily on imagery?
    A. A B. B C. C D. D

3. In which excerpt is the writing style MOST colloquial?
    A. A B. B C. C D. D

4. *Just try and do it anyway.*
    The above sentence contains problems with
    A. idiom
    B. mixed metaphors
    C. a split infinitive
    D. jargon

5. *At three or four o'clock in the afternoon, my mother's friends would _____ in her kitchen to tell the story of their days, their small triumphs, and struggles.*
    Which of the following words provides the appropriate connotation to complete the above sentence?
    A. gossip   B. circle up   C. gather   D. collect

6. Which of the following presents the BEST sequence of the following sentences to make a coherent paragraph?
   I. The Portuguese navy was then considered by the Western world to be the most formidable on earth.
   II. Unlike the Portuguese, this fleet had already sailed beyond the China Sea and the Indian Ocean, reaching all the way to the tip of the African continent.
   III. However, on the other side of the world, Chinese navigators were in possession of a navy that was unequaled in numbers, skills, and technology.
   IV. In the early fifteenth century, Portugal's naval ships were inching their way down the west coast of Africa, searching for an ocean passage to India and Asia.
   The CORRECT answer is:
   A. IV, I, III, II   B. IV, II, I, III   C. I, IV, III, II   D. I, III, II, IV

7. The world's various industries produce an estimated 400 million tons of waste each year. The majority of this waste comes from the United States. Ironically, many citizens of the United States refuse to allow waste dumps in their communities and even in their country. As a result, much of this waste is diverted to poorer countries who are in no position to refuse it.
   Based on the above information, which of the following is a CORRECT logical inference?
   A. Other countries find it economically beneficial to dispose of the waste from the United States.
   B. Poor countries have found an economic opportunity in the disposal of waste from richer countries.
   C. It is better for the United States to dump its waste in other countries than its own.
   D. Poor countries are forced to act as dumping grounds for the world's richest countries.

8. The Stunt Pilot, Annie Dillard:
   Nothing on earth is more _____ than knowing we must roll up our sleeves and move back the boundaries of the humanly possible once more.
   Which of the following words provides the appropriate connotation to complete the above sentence?
   A. heart-rending   B gladdening   C. saddening   D. lovely

9. *The climactic moment of the hike came at the top of Long's Peak.*
   Which of the following BEST captures the meaning of the word *climactic* as it is used in the above sentence?
   A. Traumatic   B. Geographical height
   C. Climate of greatest intensity   D. Point of greatest intensity

10. The issue of child care represents an ongoing crisis in this country. Families are forced to make profound decisions with lifelong effects regarding the care of their children. Many families do not believe it is possible to live adequately on only one salary. Not that conservatives care. If they had their way, women would be back in the kitchen, baking cookies for junior.
    The above passage contains
    A. a shifting point of view
    B. an inconsistent tone
    C. ad hominem attacks
    D. false analogies

11. *That ruler belonged to Mr. Abel as though it grew out of his right hand, as wings grow out of an angel, or a tail out of a devil.*
    The above sentence contains
    A. a false analogy
    B. a euphemism
    C. parallel construction
    D. an elliptical phrase

12. *The diplomat returned to the clinic where he underwent lung surgery in 1991 in a limousine provided by his embassy.*
    The above sentence contains
    A. an inconsistent tone
    B. faulty parallel construction
    C. a misplaced modifier
    D. a dangling modifier

13. Maintenance, Naomi Shihab Nye:
    Somewhere close behind me the outline of Thoreau's small cabin plods along ghost set on _____. It even has the same rueful eyes Henry David had in his book.
    Which of the following words provides the appropriate connotation to complete the above sentence?
    A. haunting   B. terrifying   C. startling   D. scolding

14. *The coarse language of the instructor was a shock to everyone.*
    Which of the following BEST captures the meaning of the word *coarse* as it is used in the above sentence?
    A. Related to a unit of study
    B. Crude
    C. Technical
    D. Emotional

15. *Recuperation is like spring.*
    The above sentence is an example of a(n)
    A. allegory   B. metaphor   C. euphemism   D. analogy

Questions 16-22.

DIRECTIONS: Questions 16 through 22 are to be answered on the basis of the following passage.

Sonny's Blues, James Baldwin

But houses exactly like the houses of our past yet dominated the landscape, boys exactly like the boys we once had been found themselves smothering in these houses, came down into the streets for light and air and found themselves encircled by disaster.(1) Some escaped the trap, most didn't.(2) Those who got out always left something of themselves behind, as some animals amputate a leg and leave it in the trap.(3) It might be said, perhaps, that I had escaped. after all, I was a school teacher; or that Sonny had, he hadn't lived in Harlem for years.(4) Yet, as the cab moved uptown through streets which seemed, with a rush, to darken with dark people, and as I covertly studied Sonny's face, it came to me that what we both were seeking was that part of ourselves which had been left behind.(5) It's always at the hour of trouble and confrontation that the missing member aches.(6)

16. What is the point of view of this passage?
    A. First person singular
    B. Second person
    C. Third person singular
    D. Third person plural

17. This passage is BEST characterized as a
    A. concrete description of Harlem
    B. descriptive narrative about a traumatic event in the narrator's childhood
    C. concrete explanation of how the narrator escaped from Harlem
    D. descriptive narrative about the narrator's troubled childhood

18. The narrator relies MOST heavily on which of the following to dramatize the emotional experience of leaving and then returning to Harlem?
    A. Metaphor   B. Analogy   C. Imagery   D. Emotional appeal

19. In line 6, the author is speaking of his need to
    A. ease his own suffering over the loss of Sonny
    B. find Sonny
    C. discover his roots
    D. recover that part of himself left behind in Harlem

20. This passage is a description of a
    A. cab ride the author and his brother took to Harlem when they were young boys
    B. cab ride the author took to Harlem when he was a young boy
    C. cab ride to Harlem
    D. train ride to Harlem

21. The descriptive details given in line 1 provide a(n)
    A. precise visual of Harlem
    B. emotional image linking past to present
    C. precise visual image of the narrator's house and neighborhood
    D. distorted emotional image from the narrator's childhood

22. In line 5, the word *covertly* is used to mean
    A. secretly   B. openly   C. fearfully   D. knowingly

23. *Rebecca hurriedly glanced through the contract before signing it.* 23._____
    The above sentence contains
    A. redundancy
    B. faulty parallel construction
    C. faulty subordination
    D. no errors

24. *There are many pictures of celebrities who have dined at Sal's Diner on the walls.* 24._____
    The above sentence contains
    A. faulty parallel construction
    B. a misplaced modifier
    C. a dangling modifier
    D. no errors

25. *Susanna took great care to ensure her dinner guest complemented one another in education and background.* 25._____
    Which of the following BEST captures the meaning of the word *complemented* as it is used in the above sentence?
    A. Balanced
    B. Flattered
    C. Contrasted with
    D. Competed against

KEY (CORRECT ANSWERS)

1.	C		11.	D
2.	B		12.	C
3.	C		13.	A
4.	A		14.	B
5.	C		15.	D
6.	A		16.	A
7.	D		17.	D
8.	B		18.	A
9.	D		19.	D
10.	B		20.	C

21.	B
22.	A
23.	A
24.	B
25.	A

TEST 4

DIRECTIONS: Each question or incomplete statement is followed by several suggested answers or completions. Select the one that BEST answers the question or completes the statement. *PRINT THE LETTER OF THE CORRECT ANSWER IN THE SPACE AT THE RIGHT.*

1. *After seeing the empty coffin, Edward turned white as a sheet.*
   The above sentence contains a(n)
   A. metaphor   B. idiom   C. cliché   D. euphemism

   1.____

2. Which of the following presents the BEST sequence of the following sentences to make a coherent paragraph?
   I. At that time, the American South was an agricultural region that relied on African-American slaves to work plantations where cotton, tobacco, sugar, and other crops were grown.
   II. Most of them promptly tried to secede, or withdraw, from the United States to form their own country, the Confederate States of America.
   III. The United States elections of 1860 brought to power a president, Abraham Lincoln, and a congressional majority who were against the practice of slavery.
   IV. Lincoln's election made it possible that slavery would eventually be outlawed in the United States, and Southern states saw this as a threat to their way of life.

   The CORRECT answer is:
   A. IV, III, I, II   B. I, III, IV, II   C. III, II, IV, I   D. III, I, IV, II

   2.____

3. *The informant was unable to elicit any useful information for his contact.*
   Which of the following BEST captures the meaning of the word *elicit* as it is used in the above sentence?
   A. Reject   B. Discuss   C. Draw out   D. Illegal

   3.____

4. *Though Mildred still drove, she admitted to being blind as a bat.*
   The above sentence contains a(n)
   A. metaphor   B. idiom   C. cliché   D. euphemism

   4.____

5. *Only a single parent can understand the plight of single parents.*
   The above statement is an example of
   A. a faulty use of cause and effect   B. an ad hominem attack
   C. circular reasoning   D. a hasty generalization

   5.____

Questions 6-9.

DIRECTIONS: Questions 6 through 9 are to be answered on the basis of the following passage.

What We Talk About When We Talk About Love, Raymond Carver

> Outside in the backyard, one of the dogs began to bark.(1) The leaves of the aspen that leaned past the window ticked against the glass.(2) The afternoon sun was like a presence in this room, the spacious light of ease and generosity.(3) We could have been anywhere, somewhere enchanted. (4) We raised our glasses again and grinned at each other like children who had agreed on something forbidden.(5)

6. In line 3, the phrase *spacious light of ease and generosity* mainly implies
    A. charitable feeling
    B. joy
    C. contentment
    D. enlightenment

7. What is the point of view of this passage?
    A. First person singular
    B. First person plural
    C. Second person
    D. Third person plural

8. The descriptive details in this passage provide a
    A. view of the room from a child's perspective
    B. sentimental tone
    C. concrete image of the room
    D. visual image and an emotional tone

9. The tone of this passage is BEST characterized as
    A. sentimental   B. nostalgic   C. humorous   D. solemn

10. Which of the following titles is MOST colloquial?
    A. Casa: A Partial Remembrance of A Puerto Rican Childhood
    B. Borges and Myself
    C. Anarchy in the Tenth Grade
    D. How It Feels to Be Colored Me

11. *In 1941, Edward emigrated to avoid persecution.*
    Which of the following BEST captures the meaning of the word *emigrated* as it is used in the above sentence?
    A. Entered   B. Left   C. Returned   D. Challenged

12. Which of the following presents the BEST sequence of the following sentences to make a coherent paragraph?
    I. Cornbread is a food that originated during the settlement of the American Midwest, and is still popular in both urban and rural sections of the country's interior.
    II. Ashcake was mixed from cornmeal and water, made into thick cakes, and baked directly on the cinders and ashes of prairie camp fires.
    III. For many years this method of baking cornbread remained unchanged by people who settled the frontier.

IV. Unlike most American foods, which were variations of dishes that pioneers brought from their home countries, cornbread originated on this continent, in the Kansas Territory, as a direct descendant of the "ashcake" of the Kansas Indians.

The CORRECT answer is:
A. IV, I, II, III B. I, IV, II, III C. IV, I, III, II D. I, IV, III, II

13. When you significantly shorten a passage, restating the MOST important points in your own words, you have _____ the passage.
    A. plagiarized   B. paraphrased   C. summarized   D. quoted

14. *The driver awaited his eminent passenger.*
    Which of the following BEST captures the meaning of the word *eminent* as it is used in the above sentence?
    A. Impending   B. Inevitable   C. Anonymous   D. Distinguished

15. *The culprit was described as a 5 foot, tall female with a mole weighing approximately 120 pounds.*
    The above sentence contains which of the following mistakes?
    A. Faulty parallel construction   B. Faulty coordination
    C. Misplaced modifier   D. Dangling modifier

16. *Harry says he is failing Economics 101 because his teaching assistant doesn't speak English well.*
    The above statement is an example of
    A. a faulty use of cause and effect   B. an ad hominem attack
    C. circular reasoning   D. a hasty generalization

17. *Opening the lens to take the picture, the camera fell.*
    The above sentence contains which of the following mistakes?
    A. Faulty parallel construction   B. Faulty coordination
    C. Misplaced modifier   D. Dangling modifier

18. *A car driving on the highway has an auto-rental sticker on its bumper.*
    Based on the above information, which of the following is a CORRECT logical inference?
    A. The car is probably a rental car.
    B. The driver is returning the rental car.
    C. The driver doesn't know the area freeways very well.
    D. A tourist is driving the car.

19. A book's glossary contains
    A. the page numbers where key terms and ideas are discussed
    B. an author's acknowledgments
    C. definitions of unfamiliar words used in the book
    D. a list of the texts the author referred to in the book

Questions 20-24.

DIRECTIONS: Questions 20 through 24 are to be answered on the basis of the following excerpts.

A. It was the book that moved me to the sort of angelic devotion to the female, which is finally a form of exclusion, a tyrannical boundary (albeit usually unwitting) between the real world of men and the dream world of women, a world which was of course dreamed by men, not by the women who were held in deleterious yet tender captivity there.

B. Long before studying geometry, I learned there is a mystical virtue in right angles. There is an unspoken morality in seeking the level and the plumb. A house will stand, a table will bear weight, the sides of a box will hold together, only if the joints are square and the members upright. (The Inheritance of Tools – Best American Essays)

C. So much for endings. Beginnings are always more fun. True connoisseurs, however, are known to favor the stretch in between, since it's the hardest to do anything with. That's about all that can be said for plots, which anyway are just one thing after another, a what and a what and a what. Now try How, and Why.

D. Since humankind is transcendent in intelligence and spirit, so must our species have been released from the iron laws of ecology that bind all other species. No matter how serious the problem, civilized human beings, by ingenuity, force of will and—who knows—divine dispensation, will find a solution

20. In which excerpt is the tone meant to be humorous?
    A. A   B. B   C. C   D. D

21. In excerpt A, the word *deleterious* MOST NEARLY means
    A. harmful   B. distracting   C. sorrowful   D. beneficial

22. In excerpt D, the word *transcendent* MOST NEARLY means
    A. evolved   B. advanced   C. superior   D. enlightened

23. Which excerpt relies MOST heavily on metaphor?
    A. A   B. B   C. C   D. D

24. In which excerpt is the tone intended to be MOST persuasive?
    A. A   B. B   C. C   D. D

25. Pets feel safest when they are at home. They feel least safe in unfamiliar environments, much like humans. These feelings of insecurity influence a pet's ability to communicate and fight. Many pets do fight with other animals, but rarely will they fight to the death. They have a healthy balance of fear and aggression.
    The PRIMARY purpose of the above paragraph is to
    A. tell a story   B. persuade   C. inform   D. offer a solution

KEY (CORRECT ANSWERS)

1. C
2. D
3. C
4. C
5. C

6. C
7. B
8. D
9. B
10. D

11. B
12. B
13. C
14. D
15. C

16. D
17. D
18. A
19. C
20. C

21. A
22. C
23. B
24. D
25. C

EXAMINATION SECTION

TEST 1

DIRECTIONS: Each question or incomplete statement is followed by several suggested answers or completions. Select the one that BEST answers the question or completes the statement. *PRINT THE LETTER OF THE CORRECT ANSWER IN THE SPACE AT THE RIGHT.*

1. *The American people don't want a former pot-smoking draft dodger to be the next President of the United States.*
   The above statement is an example of
   A. faulty use of cause and effect
   B. an ad hominem attack
   C. circular reasoning
   D. a hasty generalization

   1._____

2. *Samuel had received explicit instructions about how to handle the exchange.*
   Which of the following BEST captures the meaning of the word *explicit* as it is used in the above sentence?
   A. Implied
   B. Directly expressed
   C. Terse
   D. Duplicitous

   2._____

3. I soon realized I could not take my studies with Professor Adams any _____.
   Which word BEST completes the above sentence?
   A. further   B. farther   C. more   D. far

   3._____

4. The undercover police officer posed as a person with a chemical dependence when he drove a pre-owned automobile to the economically deprived section of town in order to take out the illegal adult entertainment establishment.
   The above sentence contains too many
   A. analogies   B. metaphors   C. euphemisms   D. aphorisms

   4._____

5. Which of the following represents an appropriate level of diction for the occasion?
   A. I want that job that was in the newspaper.
   B. I would like to apply for the position advertised in the Town Daily.
   C. I want to work as a secretary in that job that was in the paper.
   D. All levels are acceptable.

   5._____

6. Which of the following presents the BEST sequence of the following sentences to make a coherent paragraph?
   I. It was later discovered that nearly all of these people had purchased and eaten hamburgers from the same fast-food franchise.
   II. Two of them, young children, eventually died from their ailments.
   III. The hamburgers had been contaminated by a dangerous strain of the bacteria E. coli and had not been properly cooked.
   IV. In 1993, over 600 people in Washington and Nevada became sick with symptoms that indicated food poisoning.
   The CORRECT answer is:
   A. I, III, II, IV   B. I, III, IV, II   C. IV, III, I, II   D. IV, II, I, III

   6._____

7. *He _____ the pencil down as soon as he was finished with the test.*
   Which word BEST completes the above sentence?
   A. did lay   B. lied   C. laid   D. lay

8. Which of the following presents the BEST sequence of the following sentences to make a coherent paragraph?
   I. Beginning in 1531 with fewer than two hundred men, Pizarro took just two years to subdue the Incas and capture Atahualpa, who attempted to bargain for his life by offering Pizarro a fortune in gold.
   II. His harshness is perhaps best illustrated by his treatment of the Incan emperor, Atahualpa.
   III. Pizarro accepted the gold from Atahualpa, and then killed him anyway.
   IV. Francisco Pizarro was among the most fearsome of the Spanish conquistadors
   The CORRECT answer is:
   A. IV, II, I, III   B. IV, I, II, III   C. II, I, III, IV   D. I, III, IV, II

9. *Neither Sari _____ Joshua could spell the final word in the district spelling bee.*
   Which word BEST completes the above sentence?
   A. nor   B. or   C. either   D. and

10. *They promised when the pageant was over that they would take Sarah out to dinner.*
    The above sentence contains which of the following mistakes?
    A. Faulty parallel construction   B. Faulty coordination
    C. Misplaced modifier   D. Dangling modifier

11. King Lear, Act I, Scene I:
    France: Fairest Cordelia, that art most rich being poor,
    *   Most choice forsaken, and most loved despised, Thee and thy*
    *   virtues here I seize upon.*
    France praises Cordelia because
    A. her sense of morality is more important to him than her material wealth
    B. her dowry has increased, since her father want to get rid of her
    C. of her physical beauty and wealth
    D. she loves him above all others

12. *Michaela's group preceded the lunch break.*
    In the above sentence, the word *preceded* is used to mean which of the following?
    A. Occurred simultaneously   B. Came after
    C. Came before   D. Went forward

Questions 13-17.

DIRECTIONS: Questions 13 through 17 are to be answered on the basis of the following passage.

The Story of An Hour, Kate Chopin:

She could see in the open square before her house the tops of trees that were all aquiver with the new spring life.(1) The delicious breath of rain was in the air.(2) In the street below a peddler was crying his wares.(3) The notes of a distant song which someone was singing reached her faintly, and countless sparrows were twittering in the eaves....(4)
She knew that she would weep again when she saw the kind, tender hands folded in death; the fact that had never looked save with love upon her, fixed and gray and dead.(5) But she saw beyond that bitter moment a long procession of years to come that would belong to her absolutely.(6) And she opened and spread her arms out to them in welcome.(7)

13. Which of the following BEST describes the relationship between the two paragraphs in this passage?
The second paragraph
   A. provides an answer to the questions raised by the first paragraph
   B. contradicts the mood established in the first paragraph
   C. develops and explains the mood established in the first paragraph
   D. illustrates the first paragraph

14. Which of the following MOST accurately characterizes the reason for the woman's mood?
   A. Her husband is dead and she is free.
   B. Although saddened by her husband's death, the weather is so beautiful that she is freed from her sadness for a time.
   C. Her husband is dead and she is overcome with despair.
   D. Although saddened by her husband's death, she looks forward to a life of independence.

15. The descriptive details in the first paragraph establish a
   A. visual image and an emotional tone
   B. tone of sadness and despair
   C. concrete image of the town
   D. concrete image of the room

16. In line 1, the word *aquiver* is used to mean
   A. shivering   B. fluttering   C. shaking   D. blooming

17. This passage is BEST characterized as which of the following? A
   A. descriptive narrative about a self-centered, remorseless woman
   B. dramatization of a woman's overwhelming despair at the loss of her husband
   C. description of the solace one woman finds in nature
   D. descriptive narrative about a woman's dawning sense of independence

18. Which of the following labels in a dictionary indicates that a particular word is used by people who speak a version of a language that is different from the standard version?
    A. Dialect
    B. Derivative
    C. Slang
    D. Archaic

19. *Bob and Sue were a lawyer and a doctor, respectively.*
    In the above sentence, the word *respectively* is used to mean which of the following?
    A. With respect
    B. In the order given
    C. Well respected
    D. Married

20. *She is different than you.*
    The above sentence contains
    A. a split infinitive
    B. a mixed metaphor
    C. a problem with idiom
    D. no errors

21. Spring, Gretel Erlich:
    By mid-March, the lake ice begins to melt where the spring feeds in, and every year the same pair of mallards come ahead of the others and wait. Though there is very little open water, they seem _____. They glide back and forth through a thin estuary, brushing watercress with their elegant folded wings. Which of the following words provides the appropriate connotation to complete the above passage?
    A. content
    B. overjoyed
    C. subdued
    D. excited

22. Which of the following presents the BEST sequence of the following sentences to make a coherent paragraph?
    I. In 1552, a Portuguese historian, Joäo do Barros, wrote that he had heard of a place in Africa where there was a "square fortress of masonry built of stones of marvelous size, and there appears to be no mortar joining them."
    II. The ruins were finally rediscovered by a German geologist, Karl Mauch, in the 1860's.
    III. During the Europeans' first explorations of the African continent, one of the many recurring fables about the mysteries of Africa was a story of some great stone monuments on the southeastern plains.
    IV. Incredibly, tales of this place circulated for more than three hundred years before the first European laid eyes upon their source: the ruins of Great Zimbabwe.
    The CORRECT answer is:
    A. III, IV, II, I
    B. III, I, IV, II
    C. I, III, II, IV
    D. I, IV, II, III

23. *That pumpkin pie was more _____ I could eat.*
    Which word BEST completes the above sentence?
    A. from
    B. of
    C. than
    D. then

24. *Opening the door to let in the heat, the vase was broken.*
 The above sentence contains
 A. faulty parallel construction
 B. faulty coordination
 C. misplaced modifier
 D. dangling modifier

25. _____ late with _____ laundry.
 Which pair of words BEST completes the above sentence?
 A. Their; they're
 B. They're; their
 C. Their; there
 D. There; their

KEY (CORRECT ANSWERS)

1.	B	11.	A
2.	B	12.	C
3.	A	13.	C
4.	C	14.	D
5.	B	15.	A
6.	D	16.	B
7.	C	17.	D
8.	A	18.	A
9.	A	19.	B
10.	C	20.	C

21.	A
22.	B
23.	C
24.	D
25.	B

TEST 2

DIRECTIONS: Each question or incomplete statement is followed by several suggested answers or completions. Select the one that BEST answers the question or completes the statement. *PRINT THE LETTER OF THE CORRECT ANSWER IN THE SPACE AT THE RIGHT.*

1. Which of the following provides the MOST objective point of view on the part of the writer?
   A. Terrified passengers waited in blistering heat as amusement park officials worked to rescue them from the dangerous and life-threatening ride.
   B. Rescuers left terrified passengers stranded for hours while they tried to figure out how to rescue them.
   C. Rescuers spent four hours retrieving passengers from a roller coaster car that inexplicably stopped in mid-ride.
   D. Passengers stranded on a roller coaster cried and moaned so much that rescuers had to waste valuable time trying to calm them down.

1.____

Questions 2-6.

DIRECTIONS: Questions 2 through 6 are to be answered on the basis of the following passage.

Girl, Jamaica Kincaid:

   Wash the white clothes on Monday and put them on the stone heap; wash the color clothes on Tuesday and put them on the clothesline to dry; don't walk bareheaded in the hot sun; cook pumpkin fritters in very hot sweet oil; soak your little cloths right after you take them off; when buying cotton to make yourself a nice blouse, be sure that it doesn't have gum on it, because that way it won't hold up well after a wash; soak salt fish overnight before you cook it; is it true that you sing benna in Sunday school?; always eat your food in such a way that it won't turn someone else's stomach; don't sing benna in Sunday school.

2. What is the point of view of this passage?
   A. First person singular
   B. First person plural
   C. Second person
   D. Third person singular

2.____

3. What can we infer about the speaker of this passage? S/he
   A. holds a position of authority in relation to the person being spoken to
   B. believes the person being spoken to is ignorant
   C. believes the person being spoken to doesn't listen
   D. has absolute authority over the person being spoken to

3.____

4. This passage can BEST be characterized as
   A. descriptive   B. instructional   C. narrative   D. nostalgic

4.____

5. The descriptive details provided in this passage mainly
   A. provide concrete instructions on how to live
   B. provide a concrete image of speaker's faith
   C. provide a concrete image of the speaker's home
   D. establish setting and tone

6. What can we infer about the person being spoken to in this passage? She
   A. is suborn
   B. is disobedient
   C. is a child
   D. resents the speaker

7. *We all wondered how a girl _____ walked with such a limp could play soccer.*
   Which word BEST completes the above sentence?
   A. who   B. whom   C. that   D. which

8. In a dictionary, these serve as an aid to finding the page on which a word appears.
   A. Cross-references
   B. Part of speech labels
   C. Superscript numbers
   D. Guide words

9. On Being Black and Middle Class, Shelby Steele:
   Black though I may be, it is impossible for me to sit in my single-family house with two cars in the driveway and a swing set in the backyard and not see the role class has _____ in my life.
   Which of the following words provides the appropriate connotation to complete the above sentence?
   A. asserted   B. played   C. oppressed   D. dominated

10. Which of the following presents the BEST sequence of the following sentences to make a coherent paragraph?
    I. Before the Incas were conquered by the Spaniards in the 16th century, they had built temples and palaces as large and magnificent as any in the world.
    II. The Incas, a native people whose empire once encompassed much of western South America, have long been admired for their accomplishments in architecture and art.
    III. The Incas' network of roads ran the length of their empire, from the north, in what is now Peru, to Chile in the south.
    IV. But fewer people know that the Incas were also responsible for what was then the world's greatest all-weather road system.
    The CORRECT answer is:
    A. I, II, IV, III   B. I, IV, III, II   C. II, I, IV, III   D. II, IV, III, I

11. Which of the following provides the MOST objective point of view on the part of the writer?
    A. Cisco Systems continued its hostile takeover of small business by purchasing Cerent, a start-up company.
    B. Cisco Systems recently purchased the small start-up company, Cerent, for a record-breaking amount of money.

C. Cisco Systems solidified its role as a great benefactor and helpmate to smaller businesses by buying the start-up company, Cerent.
D. The small start-up company, Cerent, is lucky that Cisco Systems wanted to buy it, considering Cerent's load of debt.

12. _____ driving to the airport? _____ car should we take?
    Which pair of words BEST completes the above sentences?
    A. Whose; who's
    B. Who's; who's
    C. Whose; whose
    D. Who's; whose

13. *Deciding to join the team, the manager shook Susan's hand.*
    The above sentence contains
    A. faulty parallel construction
    B. a dangling modifier
    C. a misplaced modifier
    D. faulty coordination

14. King Lear, Act II, Scene IV:
    Regan: I pray you father being weak, seem so.
    In this excerpt, Regan tells her father, King Lear, that
    A. he looks physically weak and depleted, and should sit down
    B. he is still very powerful
    C. it is unseemly for such a powerful man as him to act so weak
    D. since he no longer has power, he should not act as if he does

15. They Said You Was High Class, Joseph Epstein:
    My fantasy, taken up in early adolescence and not quite dropped to this day, is that I can roam freely from social class, _____ everywhere and everywhere welcome.
    Which of the following words provides the appropriate connotation to complete the above sentence?
    A. comfortable
    B. uncomfortable
    C. joyous
    D. acknowledged

16. Heaven and Nature, Edward Hoagland:
    People with sunny natures do seem to live longer than people who are nervous wrecks; yet mankind didn't evolve out of the animal kingdom by being _____ sunny-minded.
    Which of the following words provides the appropriate connotation to complete the above sentence?
    A. casually
    B. reasonably
    C. unduly
    D. exaggeratedly

17. *Camelia _____ that she knew all about advertising, but her interviewer, _____ that she was inexperienced.*
    Which pair of words BEST completes the above sentences?
    A. implied; inferred
    B. implied; implied
    C. inferred; inferred
    D. inferred; implied

18. The most significant danger of television does not lie in what it produces, but in what it prevents. If you are watching television, chances are that you are not engaging in the talking, game playing, family festivities and arguments that help children to learn about themselves and their world. The television set interferes with the process that helps turn children into thinking adults.
The PRIMARY purpose of the above passage is to
   A. compare   B. classify   C. analyze   D. entertain

19. *The book was written by someone who teaches at Stanford, so it must be good.*
The above statement is an example of
   A. a faulty use of cause and effect   B. an ad hominem attack
   C. circular reasoning   D. a hasty generalization

Questions 20-22.

DIRECTIONS: Questions 20 through 22 are to be answered on the basis of the following passage.

Hills Like White Elephants, Ernest Hemingway:

   The girl stood up and walked to the end of the station. Across, on the other side, were fields of grain and trees along the banks of the Ebro. Far away, beyond the river, were mountains. The shadow of a cloud moved across the field of grain and she saw the river through the trees.

20. This passage is BEST characterized as
   A. instructive   B. persuasive   C. narrative   D. descriptive

21. The descriptive details in this passage MAINLY establish
   A. setting   B. tone   C. point of view   D. time period

22. The point of view of this passage is
   A. first person singular   B. first person plural
   C. third person singular   D. third person plural

23. _____ you go on a trip, _____ to Indiana or India, you should always use traveler's checks instead of cash.
Which pair of words BEST completes the above sentence?
   A. Whether; off   B. Whether; if   C. If; whether   D. If, if

24. Which of the following provides the MOST objective point of view on the part of the writer?
   A. A radical, left-wing professor has violated her students' constitutional rights by refusing to teach male students.
   B. A feminist professor at a major university recently announced that she would no longer teach male students.

C. An embattled feminist professor at a major university works hard to ensure a safe learning environment by only teaching women students.
D. Recently, at a major university, women banded together to throw men out of the classroom of a feminist professor.

25. *Music today is filled with either violence or sex.*
    The above statement is an example of
    A. a false dilemma
    B. a non sequitur
    C. circular reasoning
    D. a hasty generalization

25.____

KEY (CORRECT ANSWERS)

1.	C	11.	B
2.	C	12.	D
3.	A	13.	B
4.	B	14.	D
5.	D	15.	A
6.	C	16.	C
7.	A	17.	A
8.	D	18.	C
9.	B	19.	D
10.	C	20.	D

21.	A
22.	C
23.	C
24.	B
25.	A

TEST 3

DIRECTIONS: Each question or incomplete statement is followed by several suggested answers or completions. Select the one that BEST answers the question or completes the statement. *PRINT THE LETTER OF THE CORRECT ANSWER IN THE SPACE AT THE RIGHT.*

1. *Fresh peaches and cream was a last minute addition to the dinner party.*
   The above sentence contains
   A. a dangling modifier
   B. faulty parallelism
   C. faulty subject-verb agreement
   D. no errors

   1.____

2. *The best mouse trap in the world is, in fact, a snake. The copperhead moves in so quickly on its prey that mice have almost no chance of escape once they have been detected.*
   The PRIMARY purpose of the above passage is to
   A. persuade   B. explain   C. entertain   D. classify

   2.____

3. *Willa Ames still hasn't repaid the money she borrowed yet.*
   The above sentence contains
   A. faulty subject-verb agreement
   B. redundancy
   C. a dangling modifier
   D. no errors

   3.____

4. *The high levels of toxic rain in Canada causes resentment against the U.S. where most of the rain originates.*
   The above sentence contains
   A. a dangling modifier
   B. faulty parallelism
   C. faulty subject-verb agreement
   D. no errors

   4.____

5. *Beth assured her old friend that their troubled past was water over the dam.*
   The above sentence contains
   A. jargon   B. slang   C. an idiom   D. a cliche

   5.____

6. Which of the following presents the BEST sequence of the following sentences to make a coherent paragraph?
   I. Although the Guinness book of world records ignores fossils and honor the American moose's antlers, the size of the Irish Elk's antlers has never even been approached in the history of life.
   II. The Irish Elk, now extinct, was neither exclusively Irish, nor an elk.
   III. It was the largest deer that ever lived, and its enormous antlers were even more impressive.
   IV. Estimates of their total span range up to twelve feet, which seems all the more impressive when we recognize that the antlers were probably shed and regrown every year, as in all other true deer species.
   The CORRECT answer is:
   A. II, I, III, IV   B. II, III, I, IV   C. I, IV, II, III   D. I, III, II, IV

   6.____

7. A library's microfilm collection consists MAINLY of
   A. old newspaper and magazine articles
   B. reference books
   C. the historical records of the town or institution where it is located
   D. the titles and authors of all the books in the library

8. *The relationship between risk and free-enterprise is intimate and powerful.*
   The primary purpose of a passage based on the above sentence would MOST likely be to
   A. explain a process
   B. narrate an event
   C. persuade
   D. compare

9. *When watching a favorite film, commercials are especially annoying.*
   The above sentence contains
   A. a dangling modifier
   B. a misplaced modifier
   C. faulty subject-verb agreement
   D. unnecessary punctuation

10. *The Secretary of State, as well as her Press Secretary, was severely criticized by the media.*
    The above sentence contains
    A. a dangling modifier
    B. faulty parallelism
    C. faulty subject-verb agreement
    D. no errors

11. *Sun-loving plants, such as, sunflowers and geraniums, thrive in hot, open places.*
    The above sentence contains
    A. unnecessary punctuation
    B. faulty parallelism
    C. faulty subject-verb agreement
    D. no errors

12. *Car-jackers should be prosecuted because they broke the law.*
    The above statement is an example of
    A. a faulty use of cause and effect
    B. an ad hominem attack
    C. circular reasoning
    D. a hasty generalization

13. *A man carrying a guitar case runs out of a bank and down the street.*
    Based on the above information, which of the following is a CORRECT logical inference?
    The man
    A. has probably robbed the bank
    B. is in a hurry
    C. plays in a symphony and is late to practice
    D. exercises with his guitar case

Questions 14-20.

DIRECTIONS: Questions 14 through 20 are to be answered on the basis of the following passage.

Discovery of a Father, Sherwood Anderson:

He was a man with big shoulders, a powerful swimmer.(1) In the darkness I could feel the movements of his muscles.(2) We swam to the far edge of the pond and then back to where we had left our clothes.(3) The rain continued and the wind blew.(4) Sometimes my father swam on his back, and when he did he took my hand in his large powerful one and moved it over so that it rested always on his shoulder.(5) Sometimes there would be a flash of lightning and I could see his face quite clearly.(6)

He had become blood of my blood; he the strong swimmer and I the boy clinging to him in the darkness.(7) We swam in silence, and in silence we dressed in our wet clothes and went home.(8)

14. This passage is BEST characterized as a(n)
    A. concrete description of the dangers of swimming during a storm
    B. instructional narrative about swimming
    C. descriptive narrative about a boy's relationship with his father
    D. account of a boy learning how to swim

15. In this passage, the pond and storm are BEST characterized as
    A. elements of nature that encourage reflection
    B. dangerous and unpredictable elements which threaten human connection
    C. mysterious forces that entice people to do dangerous things
    D. elements of nature that encourage a spiritual connection between father and son

16. In line 7, the clause, *He had become blood of my blood*, MOST NEARLY means that
    A. the boy has discovered a deeper emotional connection to his father because of this experience
    B. the boy has just discovered that this man is his biological father
    C. father and son share the same religious beliefs
    D. father and son are alienated from one another

17. Lines 7 and 8 provide a description of the
    A. father's anger
    B. transformation of the son's relationship to his father
    C. son's anger
    D. alienation which separates the son from the father

18. The narrator in this passage relies MOST heavily on which of the following?
    A. Metaphor
    B. Analogy
    C. Imagery
    D. Emotional appeal

4 (#3)

19. In describing the relationship between the two paragraphs in this passage, the second paragraph 19.____
    A. provides an answer to the questions raised by the first paragraph
    B. contradicts the mood established in the first paragraph
    C. illustrates the first paragraph
    D. develops and explains the mood established in the first paragraph

20. The MAIN implication of this passage is that the narrator 20.____
    A. has discovered that he is afraid of his father
    B. has discovered a powerful and mysterious connection to his father
    C. has discovered that he doesn't understand his relationship to his father
    D. and his father do not know how to communicate with one another

21. Which of the following presents the BEST sequence of the following sentences to make a coherent paragraph? 21.____
    I. Begun around 1200, the ceremony has evolved over time through various stages.
    II. After about a hundred years of this phase, tea-drinking became associated with luxury and was practiced by members of high society who often held "tea tournaments," which were much like present-day wine-tastings.
    III. One of the most important Japanese cultural practices is the tea ceremony.
    IV. At first, tea was drunk for medical reasons, by people who made outrageous claims about tea's ability to cure almost any known illness.
    The CORRECT answer is:
    A. III, I, IV, II   B. I, IV, II, III   C. IV, II, III, I   D. III, IV, II, I

22. King Lear, Act V, Scene III: 22.____
    Lear: Come, let's away to prison:
           We two alone will sing like birds I' th' cage:
           When thou dost ask me blessing, I'll kneel down
           and ask of thee forgiveness: so we'll live,
           and pray, and sing, and tell old tales, and laugh
           at gilded butterflies, and hear poor rogues
           talk of court news; and we'll talk with them too,
           who loses and who wins, who's in, who's out;
           and take upon us the mystery of things,
           as if we were God's spies: and we'll wear out,
           in a walled prison, packs and sects of great oones
           that ebb and flow by the moon.
    In the above scene, King Lear tells Cordelia that, while in prison, the two of them will
    A. act as spies so that they can discover the important news of the royal court and use it for their own benefit
    B. tell false tales about members of the royal court, thereby destroying them from within their prison cells

C. entertain themselves with tales and stories, granting no importance to issues of fashion and royal favor, and so will outlive all the schemers outside of prison
D. ignore everything worldly, only concentrating on prayer and meditation, thereby saving their eternal souls

23. Speech on the Signing of the Treaty of Port Elliott, 1855, Chief Seattle:
Yonder sky that has wept tears of compassion upon my people for centuries untold, and which to us appears changeless and eternal, may change. Today is fair. Tomorrow may be overcast with clouds. My words are like the stars that never change.
The diction in the above passage is BEST characterized as
A. formal
B. colloquial
C. slang
D. formal with slang references

24. Which of the following presents the BEST sequence of the following sentences to make a coherent paragraph?
I. These natives had not yet invented the wheel, and the land around them had none of the animals—horses, donkeys, or camels—that had been domesticated to serve as pack animals in other parts of the world.
II. During the earliest years of their civilizations, the native people of South America, especially the inhabitants of the mountainous Andes region, had no means for transporting heavy loads.
III. Llamas lived on the high plateau of the Andes and, as early as 4,000 years ago, were being used by South American natives as a transport animal.
IV. However, the mountain highlands of South America were populated by another animal that had adapted well to this harsh environment—the gentle llama.
The CORRECT answer is:
A. II, III, I, IV   B. II, I, IV, III   C. III, I, IV, II   D. III, II, IV, I

25. *Saritha's suitcase felt light as a feather without her books.*
The above sentence contains
A. slang   B. jargon   C. a cliche   D. an idiom

KEY (CORRECT ANSWERS)

1.	D	11.	A
2.	B	12.	C
3.	B	13.	B
4.	C	14.	C
5.	D	15.	D
6.	B	16.	A
7.	A	17.	B
8.	D	18.	C
9.	A	19.	D
10.	D	20.	B

21. A
22. C
23. A
24. B
25. C

TEST 4

DIRECTIONS: Each question or incomplete statement is followed by several suggested answers or completions. Select the one that BEST answers the question or completes the statement. *PRINT THE LETTER OF THE CORRECT ANSWER IN THE SPACE AT THE RIGHT.*

1. When you restate the relevant information from a passage in your own words, you have _____ the passage.
   A. paraphrased   B. summarized   C. plagiarized   D. quoted

1._____

Questions 2-7.

DIRECTIONS: Questions 2 through 7 ae to be answered on the basis of the following passage.

The Inheritance of Tools, Scott Russell Sanders:

I had botched a great many pieces of wood before I mastered the right angle with a saw, botched even more before I learned to miter a joint.(1) The knowledge of these things resides in my hands and eyes and the webwork of muscles, not in the tools.(2) There are machines for sale—powered miter boxes and radial arms, saws, for instance—that will enable any casual soul to cut proper angles in boards. (3) The skill is invested in the gadget instead of the person who uses it, and this is what distinguishes a machine from a tool.(4)

2. What is the point of view of this passage?
   A. First person singular
   B. Second person
   C. Third person singular
   D. Third person

2._____

3. This passage is BEST characterized as a(n)
   A. instructive narrative about the proper use of tools
   B. persuasive narrative about the merits of manual tools
   C. reminiscence about the author's childhood experience with tools
   D. descriptive narrative about the author's relationship to manual tools

3._____

4. The narrator relies MOST heavily on which of the following in this excerpt?
   A. Metaphor   B. Analogy   C. Contrast   D. Persuasion

4._____

5. In line 2, the word *resides* MOST NEARLY means
   A. informs   B. exists   C. controls   D. moves

5._____

6. In this passage, power tools are BEST characterized as
   A. tools which require les training to operate than manual tools
   B. emblems of a dangerous trend away from hard work
   C. tools used only by ignorant people
   D. tools used by amateurs, not expert craftsmen who depend on tools to make their living

6._____

7. The MAIN implication of this passage is that
   A. it takes a lot of time to learn how to use manual tools
   B. manual tools are better to use than modern tools
   C. modern tools are better to use than older tools
   D. modern tools rely more on technology than the skill of the craftsman

8. Which of the following presents the BEST sequence of the following sentences to make a coherent paragraph?
   I. The purpose of this monument would be to honor the memory of the Americans who had served and died in the Vietnam War.
   II. When the name of the winner was revealed, artists and architects all over the world were stunned.
   III. The winner was not a nationally famous artist, but a twenty-one-year-old student at Yale University named Maya Lin, unknown to virtually everyone in the fields of art and architecture.
   IV. In 1980, the Vietnam Veterans Memorial Fund announced a competition, open to all Americans, for the design of a monument that would stand on the Mall in Washington, D.C.
   The CORRECT answer is:
   A. I, II, III, IV   B. I, IV, III, II   C. IV, II, III, I   D. IV, I, II, III

9. A woman in a grocery store has her cart loaded with baby food.
   Based on the above information, which of the following is a CORRECT logical inference? She
   A. feeds baby food to her animals   B. is a store employee
   C. probably has a baby   D. likes to eat baby food

10. *Sheryl had to go off of the medicine.*
    The above sentence contains problems with
    A. split infinitives   B. idiom
    C. mixed metaphors   D. jargon

11. *People who hate their jobs are unhappy because they hate what they're doing.*
    The above statement is an example of
    A. a faulty use of cause and effect   B. an ad hominem attack
    C. circular reasoning   D. a hasty generalization

12. *The quarter horse skipped, pranced, galloping onto the track.*
    The above sentence contains problems with
    A. parallel construction   B. elliptical phrasing
    C. a dangling modifier   D. coordination

13. *Camping in Yosemite was more thrilling for us than, staying in the loveliest most exclusive hotels.*
    The above sentence contains
    A. a dangling modifier   B. unnecessary punctuation
    C. faulty subject-verb agreement D. no errors

14. *I learned the skills of a master carpenter: however, I never learned the necessary patience.*
    The above sentence contains
    A. faulty use of a colon
    B. faulty use of a semicolon
    C. faulty subject-verb agreement
    D. no errors

15. *Some of the students looked dazed and confused _____ others looked as if they hadn't yet awakened.*
    Which of the following would BEST complete the above sentence?
    A. Parentheses   B. A dash   C. A semicolon   D. A colon

16. Anarchy in the Tenth Grade, Greg Graffin:
    People asked me, "Dude! Do you party?" It took me about six months to realize it was a synonym for getting high. I did not know what a bong was, or why someone would call it bitchin'.
    The diction in the above passage is BEST characterized as
    A. slang
    B. colloquial, containing slang references
    C. slang, containing colloquial references
    D. informal, containing colloquial references

Questions 17-21.

DIRECTIONS: Questions 17 through 21 are to be answered on the basis of the following passage.

Heart of Darkness, Joseph Conrad:

The sea-reach of the Thames stretched before us like the beginning of an interminable waterway.(1) In of the offing the sea and the sky were welded together without a joint, and in the luminous space the tanned sails of the barges drifting up with the tide seemed to stand still in the red clusters of canvas sharply peaked, with gleams of varnished spirits.(2) A haze rested on the low shores that ran out to sea in vanishing flatness.(3) The air was dark above Gravesend , and farther back still seemed condensed into a mournful gloom, brooding motionless over the biggest, and the greatest, town on Earth.(4)

17. In line 1, the word *interminable* MOST NEARLY means
    A. wide   B. ongoing   C. endless   D. vast

18. This passage is BEST characterized as a(n)
    A. objective description of the modern-day Thames
    B. persuasive narrative about the Thames
    C. descriptive narrative about the Thames from a child's point of view
    D. descriptive narrative about the Thames

19. The narrator relies MOST heavily on which of the following in this excerpt?
    A. Imagery   B. Metaphor   C. Analogy   D. Contrast

20. The tone of this excerpt is BEST characterized as
    A. despairing
    B. foreboding
    C. humorous
    D. emotionally objective

21. This excerpt is written in which point of view?
    A. First person
    B. Second person
    C. Third Person
    D. Third person plural

22. Which of the following presents the BEST sequence of the following sentences to make a coherent paragraph?
    I. Almost immediately, he noticed a change in the behavior of his co-workers—in the past they had constantly argued with each other, but now they had become unusually friendly.
    II. Almost thirty years ago, a scientist named David Berliner, who was studying human skin tissues, left some samples in open vials around his laboratory.
    III. When Berliner later removed the vials, the group returned to its grouchy ways.
    IV. Berliner's search to solve this mystery has led him to the discovery of human *pheromones*—behavior-influencing chemical compounds that are transmitted from one member of a species to another—in samples of human skin.
    The CORRECT answer is:
    A. II, I, III, IV
    B. II, III, I, IV
    C. IV, II, I, III
    D. IV, III, I, II

23. *This is a personal day, a terrible day, the day to which his entire sojourn has been tending. It is the day he realizes that there are no untroubled countries in this fearfully troubled world.*
    The diction in the above passage is BEST characterized as
    A. colloquial, with slang references
    B. slang
    C. colloquial
    D. formal

24. *The sheepdog herded the animals quickly, chasing and guarding them, but he didn't bite them.*
    The above sentence contains problems with
    A. subordination
    B. coordination
    C. elliptical phrasing
    D. parallel construction

25. *No pain, no gain.*
    The above sentence contains
    A. nouns in apposition to one another
    B. balanced elliptical phrases
    C. a dangling modifier
    D. euphemism

KEY (CORRECT ANSWERS)

1.	A	11.	C
2.	A	12.	A
3.	D	13.	B
4.	C	14.	A
5.	B	15.	C
6.	A	16.	B
7.	D	17.	C
8.	D	18.	D
9.	C	19.	A
10.	B	20.	B

21. A
22. A
23. D
24. D
25. B

EXAMINATION SECTION
TEST 1

DIRECTIONS: Each question or incomplete statement is followed by several suggested answers or completions. Select the one that BEST answers the question or completes the statement. *PRINT THE LETTER OF THE CORRECT ANSWER IN THE SPACE AT THE RIGHT.*

Questions 1-6.

DIRECTIONS: Questions 1 through 6 are to be answered on the basis of the following passage.

Death in the Woods, Sherwood Anderson

    She was an old woman and lived on a farm near the town in which I lived.(1) All country and small-town people have seen such old women, but no one knows must about them.(2) Such an old woman comes into town driving an old worn-out horse or she comes afoot carrying a basket.(3) She may own a few hens and have eggs to sell.(4) She brings them in a basket and takes them to a grocer.(5) There she trades them in.(6) She gets some salt pork and some beans.(7) Then she gets a pound or two of sugar and some flour.(8)
    Afterwards she goes to the butcher's and asks for some dog-meat.(9) She may spend ten or fifteen cents, but when she does she asks for something.(10) Formerly the butchers gave liver to any one who wanted to carry it away.(11) In our family we were always having it.(12) Once one of my brothers got a whole cow's liver at the slaughterhouse near the fairgrounds in our town.(13) We had it until we were sick of it.(14) It never cost a cent.(15) I have hated the thought of it ever since.(16)

1. This passage is BEST characterized as a(n)
   A. exact description of the old woman's day
   B. narrative explaining why the narrator hates liver so much
   C. descriptive narrative about the conditions of the old woman's life
   D. descriptive narrative about the conditions of the narrator's life

2. What is the point of view of this passage?
   A. First person
   B. Second person
   C. Third person singular
   D. Third person plural

3. How does the narrator know so much about the old woman's life?
   A. The townspeople spent a great deal of time gossiping about the old woman's strange habits.
   B. Because the town in which the narrator grew up was so small, people knew everything about one another.
   C. The narrator was very close to the old woman as a child.
   D. She is like many old women the narrator has observed in small towns such as the one he grew up in.

4. The tone of this excerpt is BEST characterized as
   A. despairing
   B. solemn
   C. scolding
   D. emotionally objective

5. The details in line 3 mainly establish
   A. point of view
   B. tone
   C. time period
   D. place

6. How do the townspeople regard the old woman?
   They
   A. hardly notice her
   B. love her dearly
   C. treat he with pity
   D. treat her with scorn

7. Which of the following essay titles employs a formal tone?
   A. Of Crumpled Wings and Little Girls
   B. Speech on the Signing of the Treaty of Port Elliott, 1855
   C. Of Cruelty and Clemency, and Whether It is Better to be Loved or Feared
   D. All employ a formal tone

8. *Ms. Davies is such a good judge that it is hard to believe she has such terrible taste in clothes.*
   The above statement is an example of
   A. a faulty use of cause and effect
   B. a non sequitur
   C. circular reasoning
   D. a hasty generalization

9. Which of the following presents the BEST sequence of the following sentences to make a coherent paragraph?
   I. In 1773, Phillis Wheatley, a young slave girl who was owned by a Boston tailor named John Wheatley, published a book of poetry.
   II. At an early age, Phillis began to write about God and her neighboring townspeople, and her first poem was printed when she was only fourteen.
   III. African-American literary history began long before African slaves were granted American citizenship—in fact, it began when the original thirteen states were still British colonies.
   IV. Unlike most slaveowners who punished slaves for learning to read and write, the Wheatley family encouraged Phillis's religious and scholarly education.
   The CORRECT answer is:
   A. III, II, I, IV
   B. III, I, IV, II
   C. I, IV, II, III
   D. I, II, IV, III

10. If the River Was Whiskey, T.C. Boyle:
    His shoulders quaked. He huddled and stamped his feet, but he never took his eyes off the tip of the rod. Twitching it suggestively, he reeled with the jerky, hesitant motion that would drive lunker fish to a frenz. Or so he'd read, anyway.
    The diction in the above passage is BEST characterized as
    A. colloquial
    B. formal
    C. informal
    D. slang

11. *The children ran down the hill, skipped across the lawn and into the pool.* 11.____
    The above sentence contains problems with
    A. subordination
    B. coordination
    C. parallel construction
    D. elliptical phrasing

Questions 12-17.

DIRECTIONS: Questions 12 through 17 are to be answered on the basis of the following passage.

An Occurrence at Owl Creek Bridge, Ambose Bierce:

A man stood upon a railroad bridge in Northern Alabama, looking down into the swift waters twenty feet below.(1) The man's hands were behind his back, the wrists bound with a cord.(2) A rope loosely encircled his neck.(3) It was attached to a stout cross-timber above his head, and the slack feel to the level of his knees.(4) Some loose boards laid upon the sleepers supporting the metals of the railway supplied a footing for him and his executioners two private soldiers of the Federal army, directed by a sergeant, who in civil life may have been a deputy sheriff.(5) At a short remote upon the same temporary platform was an officer in the uniform of his rank, armed.(6) He was a captain.(7)

12. This passage is BEST characterized as a 12.____
    A. concrete description of the preparations for a hanging
    B. descriptive narrative about a man who is about to die
    C. vivid argument against the use of capital punishment
    D. descriptive narrative about a man preparing for a dramatic escape

13. What is the point of view of this passage? 13.____
    A. First person
    B. Second person
    C. Third person singular
    D. Third person plural

14. The tone of this excerpt is BEST characterized as 14.____
    A. solemn
    B. humorous
    C. fantastic
    D. emotionally objective

15. The descriptive details in sentence 5 MAINLY establish 15.____
    A. point of view   B. tone   C. setting   D. situation

16. The narrator relies MOST heavily on which of the following in this excerpt? 16.____
    A. Imagery   B. Metaphor   C. Analogy   D. Contrast

17. In sentence 5, the word *civil* MOST NEARLY means 17.____
    A. military   B. civilian   C. polite society   D. peacetime

18. Falling Into Life, Leonard Kriegel: 18.____
    My legs were lifeless, useless, but their loss had created a dancing image in whose shadowy _____ I recognized a strange but potentially interesting new self. I world survive.

Which of the following words provides the appropriate connotation to complete the above sentence?
A. Gyrations B. Shaking C. Twitching D. Silence

19. A parenthetical citation typically lists
    A. an author's last name
    B. an author's last name and the page number where the referenced material can be found
    C. an author's last name and the title of the referenced work
    D. the title of the referenced work, and the date of its first publication

20. Miss U.S.A., Studs Terkel:
    You used to sit around the TV and watch Miss America and it was exciting, we thought glamorous. Fun, we thought. But by the time I was eight or nine, I didn't feel comfortable. Soon I'm hitting my adolescence like fourteen, but I'm not doing any dating and I'm feeling awkward and ugly.
    The diction in the above passage is BEST characterized as
    A. slang, with some colloquial references
    B. formal
    C. colloquial
    D. slang

21. Which of the following presents the BEST sequence of the following sentences to make a coherent paragraph?
    I. Marion Walter Jacobs was born in Louisiana in 1930 and grew up in the Delta, where he acquired the deep blues tradition of the region.
    II. Like many Delta blues musicians, Walter moved north to pursue a career among the larger blues audiences of Chicago.
    III. Walter discovered that a small hand-held microphone could amplify the harmonica's sound to take on an entirely different tone—a sound more like a saxophone's.
    IV. It was in Chicago that he took on the stage name of Little Walter, and made the simple breakthrough that would irreversibly change the sound of blues music.
    The CORRECT answer is:
    A. II, I, IV, III B. I, IV, II, III C. I, II, III, IV D. I, II, IV, III

22. *The duties of the position include babysitting, house-cleaning, and preparation of meals.*
    The above sentence contains problems with
    A. subordination   B. coordination
    C. elliptical phrasing   D. parallel construction

23. *I never have and never will accept a bribe.*
    The above sentence contains problems with
    A. subordination   B. coordination
    C. elliptical phrasing   D. parallel construction

24. *We will abide by the new rules.*
    In the above sentence, the phrase *abide by* is an example of a(n)
    A. idiom
    B. cliche
    C. slang expression
    D. simile

25. Which of the following presents the BEST sequence of the following sentences to make a coherent paragraph?
    I. The ancient Egyptians later discovered a better writing material—the thin bark of the papyrus reed, a plant that grew near the mouth of the Nile River.
    II. Although the tablets were cheap and easy to produce, they had two major disadvantages: they were difficult to store, and once the clay had dried and hardened a person could not write on them.
    III. People wrote on these tablets by pressing a sharpened stick into the wet clay.
    IV. The earliest known writing materials were thin clay tablets, used in Mesopotamia more than 5,000 years ago.
    The CORRECT answer is:
    A. IV, III II, I
    B. I, III, II, IV
    C. IV, I, III, II
    D. II, IV, III, I

KEY (CORRECT ANSWERS)

1.	C	11.	C
2.	A	12.	A
3.	D	13.	C
4.	B	14.	D
5.	C	15.	C
6.	A	16.	A
7.	D	17.	B
8.	B	18.	A
9.	B	19.	B
10.	A	20.	D

21.	D
22.	D
23.	C
24.	A
25.	A

TEST 2

DIRECTIONS: Each question or incomplete statement is followed by several suggested answers or completions. Select the one that BEST answers the question or completes the statement. *PRINT THE LETTER OF THE CORRECT ANSWER IN THE SPACE AT THE RIGHT.*

Questions 1-6.

DIRECTIONS: Questions 1 through 6 are to be answered on the basis of the following passage.

A Distant Episode, Paul Bowles:

The September sunsets were at their reddest the week the Professor decided to visit Ain Tadourit, which is in the warm country.(1) He came down out of the high, flat region in the evening by bus, with two small overnight bags full of maps, sun lotions, and medicines.(2) Ten years ago he had been in the village for three days; long enough, however to establish a fairly firm friendship with a café keeper, who had written him several times during the first year after his visit, if never since.(3) "Hassan Ramani," the Professor said over and over, as the bus bumped downward through ever warmer layers of air.(4) Now facing the flaming sky in the west, and now facing the sharp mountains, the car followed the dusty trail down the canyons into the air which began to smell of other things besides the endless ozone of the heights: orange blossoms, pepper, sun-baked excrement, burning olive oil, rotten fruit.(5) He closed his eyes happily and lived for an instant in a purely olfactory world.(6)

1. This passage is BEST characterized as a
   A. description of a sunset at Ain Tadourit
   B. descriptive narrative about a harrowing bus ride
   C. descriptive narrative about the Professor's trip to visit an old friend
   D. descriptive narrative about a trip the Professor took to visit his friend ten years before

1.____

2. The information in sentence 3 mainly establishes
   A. setting   B. point of view   C. tone   D. situation

2.____

3. In sentence 4, *Hassan Ramani* MOST likely refer to the
   A. Professor's friend
   B. town to which the Professor is traveling
   C. town which the Professor has just left
   D name of the country in which the Professor is traveling

3.____

4. Sentences 5 and 6 provide a
   A. description of Ain Tadourit
   B. vivid contrast between the world the Professor has just left, and the one he is about to enter
   C. physical connection between past and present
   D. description of the Professor's alienation from the town around him

4.____

5. In sentence 6, the word *olfactory* MOST NEARLY means 5._____
   A. sensual B. smell C. imaginary D. past

6. The author relies MOST heavily on which of the following in this excerpt? 6._____
   A. Imagery B. Metaphor C. Analogy D. Contrast

7. A recent study concluded that almost 90 percent of children from upper- and middle class families entered college, whereas fewer than 20 percent of children from lower-working-class families did. 7._____
   Based on the above information, which of the following is a CORRECT logical inference?
   A. The children of lower-working-class children are not as smart as children from upper- and middle-class families.
   B. The families of lower-working-class children don't emphasize school.
   C. There is a relationship between college attendance and social class.
   D. Children from upper- and middle-class families enjoy school more than other students.

8. Wounded Chevy at Wounded Knee, Diana Hume George: 8._____
   I was fifteen when I started my romance with Indians, and I only knew that I was in love with life outside the constricting white mainstream and with all the energy that _____ on the outer reaches of cultural stability.
   Which of the following words provides the appropriate connotation to complete the above sentence?
   A. exists B. lies dormant C. vibrates D. explodes

Questions 9-14.

DIRECTIONS: Questions 9 through 14 are to be answered on the basis of the following passage.

The Distance of the Moon, Italo Calvino:

How well I know!—old Qfwfq cried,—the rest of you can't remember, but I can.(1) We had her on top of us all the time, that enormous Moon: when she was full—nights as bright as day, but with a butter-colored light—it looked as if she were going to crush us; when she was new, she rolled around the sky like a black umbrella blown by the wind; and when she was waxing, she came forward with her horns so low she seemed about to stick into the peak of a promontory and get caught there.(2) But the whole business of the Moon's phases worked in a different way then: because the distances from the Sun were different, and the orbits, and the angle of something or other, I forget what; as for eclipses, with Earth and Moon stuck together the way they were, why, we had eclipses every minute: naturally, those two big monsters managed to put each other in the shade constantly, first one, then the other(3).

9. This passage is BEST characterized as a(n)
   A. historical description of the moon's orbit
   B. descriptive narrative about the narrator's childhood
   C. fantastic description of the moon's orbit
   D. descriptive narrative about the narrator's love of astronomy

10. What is the point of view of this passage?
    A. First person   B. Second person
    C. Third person singular D. Third person plural

11. The author relies MOST heavily on which of the following in this excerpt?
    A. Fact   B. Metaphor   C. Analogy   D. Imagery

12. In sentence 2, the word *promontory* MOST NEARLY means
    A. stage   B. mountain   C. building   D. range

13. The tone of this passage is BEST described as
    A. humorous   B. sarcastic   C. fantastic   D. ironic

14. Which writing technique does the author rely on MOST heavily?
    A. Subordination   B. Parallel structure
    C. Repetition   D. Fragmentation

15. *Just 3 weeks after raising the speed limit on that stretch of highway, three young people were killed in car accidents.*
    The above statement is an example of
    A. a faulty use of cause and effect   B. an ad hominem attack
    C. circular reasoning   D. a hasty generalization

16. Most young people go into the Army with the same mindset. They are young, scared, and advised that joining the Army will free them from probation if they have committed any minor crimes. Young men are told they will come out as men. This, combined with the free rent, free food and adventure, convinces them to join. Then they learn about the real Army.
    Based on the above information, which of the following is a CORRECT logical inference?
    A. Parents shouldn't encourage their children to join the Army.
    B. The Army lies in its advertisements and recruiting efforts.
    C. The experience of being in the Army is different from what most people expect.
    D. One way to become a "man" is to join the Army.

17. Kubota, Garret Hongo:
    He gave his testimony to me and I held it at first _____ in my conscience like it was an heirloom too delicate to expose to strangers and anyone outside of the world Kubota made with his words.

Which of the following words provides the appropriate connotation to complete the above sentence?
A. happily   B. absently   C. gingerly   D. cautiously

18. Which of the following provides the CLEAREST description of a scene?
    A. With a small gathering of people toward a shelter at the edge of a field in northern Indiana, I walked silently in the dusk of a late summer evening.
    B. In the dusk of a late summer evening, I walked silently with a small gathering of people toward a shelter at the edge of a field in northern Indiana.
    C. At the edge of a field in northern Indiana, I walked silently in the dusk of a late summer evening with a small gathering of people toward a shelter.
    D. Toward a shelter at the edge of a field in northern Indiana I walked in the dusk of a late summer evening silently with a small gathering of people.

19. *She finished the project according with schedule.*
    The above sentence contains problems with
    A. split infinitives   B. subject-verb agreement
    C. parallel construction   D. idiom

20. Which of the following provides the MOST objective point of view on the part of the writer?
    A. Central City School Board Members recently voted to eliminate several district positions in order to cut costs.
    B. Central City School Board Members finally voted to eliminate some wasteful jobs from the bloated budget.
    C. Many workers will soon find themselves unemployed thanks to the recent decision by the Central City School Board to fire them.
    D. Lazy workers will soon have to look elsewhere for work thanks to the Central City School Board.

21. Which of the following presents the BEST sequence of the following sentences to make a coherent paragraph?
    A. The Apollo space program, conducted by the National Aeronautics and Space Administration (NASA), had reached its goal, set eight years earlier, of landing a man on the moon.
    B. In the United States, public support for the cost of NASA missions began to fade even before the Apollo 11 landing—the Apollo program ended up costing a total of $25 billion—and as a result the final two Apollo flights were scrapped.
    C. On July 20, 1969, astronauts Neil Armstrong and Edwin "Buzz" Aldrin stepped onto the surface of the moon and accomplished what is still considered to be one of the greatest achievements of human history.
    D. The Apollo 11 landing is so widely celebrated that few people care to know about the controversy created by this and other government-funded space programs.

22. Counters and Cable Cars, Stephen Jay Gould:
    We also respect an authenticity of place. Genuine objects out of context and milieu may foster intrigue, but rarely _____. London Bridge dismantled and reassembled in America becomes a mere curiosity.
    Which of the following words provides the appropriate connotation to complete the above sentence?
    A. happiness   B. inspiration   C. joy   D. reflection

23. *One day our culinary class assignment was to cook a five course dinner. You were graded on well your part of the meal turned out.*
    The above passage contains
    A. a shifting point of view
    B. faulty parallel construction
    C. a split infinitive
    D. faulty apposition

24. *Sarah is late for dinner, but at least she brought good wine.*
    The above sentence contains
    A. a shifting point of view
    B. an inconsistent verb tense
    C. a dangling modifier
    D. faulty parallel construction

25. *Patients should try if possible to avoid getting in and out of bed.*
    The above sentence contains
    A. a shifting point of view
    B. faulty parallel construction
    C. a split infinitive
    D. a misplaced modifier

KEY (CORRECT ANSWERS)

1.	C		11.	D
2.	D		12.	B
3.	A		13.	C
4.	B		14.	A
5.	B		15.	A
6.	A		16.	C
7.	C		17.	D
8.	C		18.	B
9.	C		19.	D
10.	A		20.	A

21. D
22. B
23. A
24. B
25. C

TEST 3

DIRECTIONS: Each question or incomplete statement is followed by several suggested answers or completions. Select the one that BEST answers the question or completes the statement. *PRINT THE LETTER OF THE CORRECT ANSWER IN THE SPACE AT THE RIGHT.*

1. *Though only 12 years old, Harvard accepted Stuart as a student.*
   The above sentence contains
   A. faulty parallel construction
   B. problems with subject-verb agreement
   C. a misplaced modifier
   D. a dangling modifier

2. *Some of them are friends whom we see at the store or who live in our town.*
   The above sentence contains
   A. elliptical phrasing
   B. parallel construction
   C. appositive nouns
   D. misplaced modifiers

3. *These are the kitchen rules: Coffee to be made only by staff. Coffee service to stop at 3:00 P.M. Doughnuts in cabinet.*
   The above announcement contains
   A. problems with elliptical phrasing
   B. faulty parallel construction
   C. faulty subordination
   D. faulty coordination

4. *Doctors are criticized for doing too much when they're not needed, and too little when you are.*
   The above sentence contains
   A. a split infinitive
   B. a dangling modifier
   C. a shifting point of view
   D. faulty parallel construction

5. Which of the following provides the MOST objective point of view on the part of the writer?
   A. Pilots confirmed our worst fears today, admitting that they often nap during flights.
   B. Terrified passengers discover that their pilots are often napping on the job.
   C. Pilots for a major airline admitted to acting recklessly and endangering the lives of passengers by taking naps during flights.
   D. Pilots for a major airline recently acknowledged that many of them take naps during flights.

Questions 6-11.

DIRECTIONS: Questions 6 through 11 are to be answered on the basis of the following passage.

The Hollow Nut, Colette:

    Next year, Bel-Gazou will be past nine years old.(1) She will have ceased to proclaim those inspired truths that confound her pedagogues.(2) Each day carries her farther from that first stage of her life, so full, so wise, so perpetually mistrustful, so loftily disdainful of experience, of good advice, and humdrum wisdom.(3) Next year, she will come back to the sands that glid her, to the salt butter and the foaming cider.(4) She will find again her dilapidated hut, and her citified feet will once more acquire their natural horny soles, slowly roughened on the flints and ridges of the rough ground.(5) But she may well fail to find again her childish subtlety and the keenness of her senses that can taste a scene, feel a color, and see—"thin as a hair, thin as a blade of grass" —the cadence of an imaginary song.(6)

6. This passage is BEST characterized as a
   A. descriptive narrative about the loss of childhood
   B. descriptive narrative about the author's childhood
   C. concrete description of Bel-Gazou's love for her summer home
   D. descriptive narrative about the author's love for Bel-Gazou

7. In sentence 2, the word *pedagogues* MOST NEARLY means
   A. admirers   B. friends   C. teachers   D. critics

8. In sentence 3, which of the following stylistic techniques does the author mainly rely on?
   A. Repetition
   B. Coordination
   C. Subordination
   D. Parallel structure

9. The details in sentence 3 mainly serve to
   A. detail the negative aspects of childhood which Bel-Gazou will soon outgrow
   B. detail the positive aspects of childhood which will be lost as Bel-Gazou grows up
   C. describe and chastise Bel-Gazou's bad behavior
   D. provide a psychological portrait of childhood

10. In sentence 6, *cadence* MOST NEARLY means
    A. melody   B. rhythm   C. words   D. imagery

11. The MAIN implication of this passage is that
    A. although Bel-Gazou must leave her beloved summer cottage, it will still be waiting when she returns next year
    B. it is time for Bel-Gazou to leave her childish world behind
    C. childhood is a time of carefree joy and curiosity
    D. the sensibilities which characterize childhood are fleeting

12. **The Stone Horse, Barry Lopez:**
    I waited until I held his eye. I assured him I would not tell anyone else how to get there. He looked at me with _____ despair, like a man who had been robbed twice, whose belief in human beings was offered without conviction.
    Which of the following words provides the appropriate connotation to complete the above passage?
    A. suffering   B. stoical   C. sad   D. intense

13. Which of the following presents the BEST sequence of the following sentences to make a coherent paragraph?
    I. The guide apparently didn't understand the question because he answered by saying "Kangaroo," which is an Aboriginal term meaning, "I don't know."
    II. Perhaps the worst mistake ever made in translation by an explorer is the word "kangaroo."
    III. Upon seeing one of the creatures, Cook turned to one of the native Australians he had brought along as a guide and asked what it was.
    IV. It entered the language in 1770 through the famous English sea captain, James Cook, while he was exploring the coast of Australia.
    The CORRECT answer is:
    A. IV, II, III, I   B. III, I, IV, II   C. II, IV, III, I   D. II, III, I, IV

14. *When I was in the fourth grade, I was called upon to participate in a school-wide spelling bee in an auditorium filled with restless students. Waiting nervously in my seat, I chewed my fingernails and tugged my socks.*
    The PRIMARY purpose of the above passage is to
    A. tell a story   B. offer a solution
    C. describe something   D. define something

15. *The young woman was _____ and fashionable.*
    Which of the following words provides the appropriate connotation to complete the above sentence?
    A. skeletal   B. chubby   C. skinny   D. slender

16. *Upon seeing the washed-out bridge, our bikes screeched to a halt.*
    The above sentence contains
    A. faulty parallel construction   B. faulty coordination
    C. a misplaced modifier   D. a dangling modifier

17. *Harold intended on doing things differently.*
    The above sentence contains problems with
    A. mixed metaphors   B. jargon
    C. idiom   D. split infinitives

18. *Joe is a man who means what he says, and says what he means.*
    The above sentence contains
    A. parallel construction   B. elliptical phrasing
    C. a dangling modifier   D. a false analogy

19. *History became popular, and historians became alarmed.*   19.____
    The above sentence contains
    A. parallel construction   B. elliptical phrasing
    C. a dangling modifier   D. a false analogy

20. *The candidate will make a good President because he speaks so well in*   20.____
    front of the cameras.
    The above statement is an example of
    A. a faulty use of cause and effect   B. a non sequitur
    C. circular reasoning   D. a hasty generalization

Questions 21-25.

DIRECTIONS: Questions 21 through 25 are to be answered on the basis of the following passage.

Walls, Kenneth McClane:

The prisons—at least the prisons I have encountered—are infinitely more hellish than our Hollywood dream makers relate.(1) Inmates in these places are not planning breakouts or prison riots; they are not planning anything.(2) To dream of escape is to believe that one has something worthy of salvaging; to believe, that is, in the proposition of a self-orchestrated future.(3) The prisons I have visited are spirit killers: the inmates—no matter how smart, capable, or engaging—have little sense of their own inextinguishable worth, their own human possibility.(4) And this is not by accident.(5)

21. This passage is BEST characterized as a   21.____
    A. persuasive narrative advocating the use of harsh punishment for prison inmates
    B. persuasive narrative against poor treatment of inmates in prisons
    C. descriptive narrative about the psychological effects of prisons on inmates
    D. descriptive narrative about the author's experience as an inmate

22. In sentence 3, the word *proposition* MOST NEARLY means   22.____
    A. impossibility   B. offer   C. bargain   D. idea

23. The MAIN purpose of sentence 5 is to   23.____
    A. create a transition into the next paragraph
    B. conclude the paragraph
    C. blame prisoners' problems on the prison staff and wardens
    D. answer the question raised in the first sentence of the paragraph

24. The MAIN implication of this passage is that   24.____
    A. most prisoners fail to take advantage of the amount of free-time they have in prison to plan for their futures
    B. prisons deliberately work to undermine the prisoners' sense of self and worth

C. most prisoners bide their time in prison by planning for their future outside the prison walls
D. prisons rightfully work to undermine the prisoners' sense of self and worth

25. What can we infer about the author of this passage? 25.____
    He
    A. has no opinion on the facts he presents in this paragraph
    B. believes these prisoners have been punished enough and should be freed
    C. is in favor of the kind of punishment he describes in this paragraph
    D. is against the kind of punishment he describes in this paragraph

---

KEY (CORRECT ANSWERS)

1.	D	11.	D
2.	A	12.	B
3.	B	13.	C
4.	C	14.	A
5.	D	15.	D
6.	A	16.	D
7.	C	17.	C
8.	D	18.	B
9.	B	19.	A
10.	B	20.	B

21. C
22. D
23. A
24. B
25. D

TEST 4

DIRECTIONS: Each question or incomplete statement is followed by several suggested answers or completions. Select the one that BEST answers the question or completes the statement. *PRINT THE LETTER OF THE CORRECT ANSWER IN THE SPACE AT THE RIGHT.*

1. *Katrice's new neighbor seemed nutty as a fruitcake.* 1.____
   The above sentence contains a(n)
   A. cliche   B. euphemism   C. metaphor   D. idiom

2. Which of the following is an example of a reference book? 2.____
   A. African-American Biographies
   B. Webster's New American Dictionary
   C. Collier's Encyclopedia
   D. All of the above

3. Which of the following provides the CLEAREST description of a scene? 3.____
   A. When I was a child, my great-grandfather used to read to me; I remember him pointing to a tree, a cloud a dog, and naming them in the Miami language, giving them back to me in the language of his own childhood.
   B. Reading to me as a child, my great-grandfather used to give them back to me in the language of his own Miami childhood, pointing to a tree, a cloud, a dog.
   C. Pointing to a tree, a cloud, a dog, and naming them in the Miami language, giving them back to me in the language of his own childhood, my great-grandfather used to read to me as a child.
   D. Giving them back to me in the Miami language of his own childhood, my great-grandfather used to pointing to a tree, a cloud, a dog, reading to me as a child.

4. *A Homemade Education, Malcolm X:* 4.____
   It was because of my letters that I happened to stumble upon starting to acquire some kind of a homemade education.
   The diction in the above passage is BEST characterized as
   A. colloquial   B. formal
   C. slang   D. colloquial, with slang references

5. *She worked the fields all morning, bending for the strawberries, and the* 5.____
   _____ she worked up evaporated in the dry air, cooling her hot skin.
   Which of the following words provides the appropriate connotation to complete the above sentence?
   A. saltwater   B. perspiration   C. stink   D. sweat

6. Which of the following presents the BEST sequence of the following sentences to make a coherent paragraph?
   I. An amateur should practice this toe-raising technique by sitting well back in a chair with the legs together and straightened, the feet flexed or bent at the ankles.
   II. While keeping your knees straight, your feet should then be arched, slowly, working through the arches to the balls of the feet, and finally onto the points of the toes, which should be squeezed together to increase their ability to support your weight.
   III. Ballet dancers follow a strict code of artistic expectations that usually prohibits them from moving their bodies into positions that do not follow straight, well-balanced lines.
   IV. The dancers' code is so strict that when raising themselves onto their toes, the toes are expected to follow the straight line suggested by the rest of the leg, rather than flexing or "knuckling under."
   The CORRECT answer is:
   A. IV, III, I, II   B. IV, I, II, III   C. III, IV, I, II   D. III, II, I, IV

7. *Patrick enjoyed playing with fire by missing his deadlines.*
   The above sentence contains a(n)
   A. split infinitives
   B. subject-verb agreement
   C. parallel construction
   D. idiom

8. *She is capable to finish the job.*
   The above sentence contains problems with
   A. split infinitives
   B. subject-verb agreement
   C. parallel construction
   D. idiom

9. *That we die may be the meaning of life. That we communicate may be the measure of life.*
   The above sentence contains
   A. parallel construction
   B. elliptical phrasing
   C. a dangling modifier
   D. a false analogy

10. *The shooter celebrated, racing past me. It was obvious that the elephant would never _____ again.*
    Which of the following words provides the appropriate connotation to complete the above sentence?
    A. stand   B. rise   C. walk   D. get up

Questions 11-16.

DIRECTIONS: Questions 11 through 16 are to be answered on the basis of the following passage.

The Stunt Pilot, Annie Dillard:

In 1975, with a newcomer's willingness to try anything once, I attended the Bellingham Air Show.(1) The Bellingham airport was a wide clearing in a forest of tall Douglas firs; its runways suited small planes.(2) It was June.(3) People wearing blue or tan zipped jackets stood loosely on the concrete walkways and runways outside the coffee shop.(4) At that latitude in June, you stayed outside because you could, even most of the night, if you could think up something to do.(5) The sky did not darken until ten o'clock or so, and it never got very dark.(6) Your life parted and opened in the sunlight.(7) You tossed your dark winter routines, thought up mad projects, and improvised everything from hour to hour.(8) Being a stunt pilot seemed the most reasonable thing in the world; you could wave your arms in the air all day and night, and sleep next winter.(9)

11. This passage is BEST characterized as a descriptive narrative about the author's
    A. first experience at an air show
    B. experiences in her new home of Bellingham
    C. new acquaintances
    D. favorite season

12. In sentence 5, the narrative shifts point of view from
    A. first person singular to first person plural
    B. first person to second person
    C. second person to third person
    D. first person to third person

13. The shift in point of view mainly serves to
    A. create a sense of communal experience in which the reader is included
    B. create a sense of communal experience from which the reader is excluded
    C. underscore the author's position within the community
    D. underscore the author's position outside the community

14. The MAIN purpose of sentence 7 is to
    A. describe the author's growing sense of self
    B. describe the quality of light
    C. introduce the author's state of mind
    D. introduce the emotional effects of the season

15. In sentence 8, which of the following stylistic techniques does the author mainly rely on?
    A. Repetition
    B. Coordination
    C. Subordination
    D. Parallel structure

16. The tone of this passage is BEST described as
    A. humorous   B. sarcastic   C. exuberant   D. fantastic

17. *She kept herself busy as a bee all summer long.*
    The above sentence contains a(n)
    A. cliche   B. idiom   C. metaphor   D. euphemism

18. *Actors are often more interesting on the screen than in the flesh.*
    The above sentence contains
    A. parallel construction
    B. elliptical phrasing
    C. a dangling modifier
    D. a false analogy

19. Which of the following provides the MOST objective point of view on the part of the writer?
    A. In Othello, Desdemona is another sexist stereotype created by a man.
    B. In Othello, Desdemona acts out of a sense of love, even though that love results in her death.
    C. Desdemona is a boring character who never learns to take control of her own life.
    D. Othello kills his wife, Desdemona, because she is too spineless to stand up for herself.

20. *As I dance, whirling and _____, I feel happier than I have ever felt in my life.*
    Which of the following words provides the appropriate connotation to complete the above sentence?
    A. pleased   B. happy   C. joyous   D. content

21. Which of the following is the CLEAREST explanation?
    A. Developing a code for the U.S. military which would become one of the most successful codes in military history during World War II, a group of Navajo Indians used their unique language.
    B. A group of Navajo Indians during World War II developed a code for the U.S. military which would become one of the most successful codes in military history using their unique language.
    C. One of the most successful codes in military history was developed during World War II from the unique language used by Navajo Indians.
    D. During World War II, a group of Navajo Indians used their unique language to develop a code for the U.S. military which would become one of the most successful codes in military history.

22. *Work with a friend who is in your class or who is good at math.*
    The above sentence contains
    A. elliptical phrases
    B. parallel construction
    C. euphemisms
    D. a dangling modifier

23. *I know that the crime rate has increased because the drinking age was lowered.*
    The above statement is an example of
    A. a faulty use of cause and effect
    B. an ad hominem attack
    C. circular reasoning
    D. a hasty generalization

24. *To please the children, some presents were opened Christmas Eve.* 24.____
    The above sentence contains
    A. faulty parallel construction   B. faulty subject-verb agreement
    C. a misplaced modifier   D. a dangling modifier

25. *It was crystal clear to Maria that Anthony was lying.* 25.____
    The sentence above contains a(n)
    A. metaphor   B. idiom   C. cliché   D. euphemism

KEY (CORRECT ANSWERS)

1.	A		11.	A
2.	D		12.	B
3.	A		13.	A
4.	B		14.	D
5.	D		15.	D
6.	C		16.	C
7.	D		17.	A
8.	B		18.	A
9.	A		19.	B
10.	B		20.	C

21. D
22. B
23. A
24. D
25. C

EXAMINATION SECTION
TEST 1

DIRECTIONS: Each question or incomplete statement is followed by several suggested answers or completions. Select the one that BEST answers the question or completes the statement. *PRINT THE LETTER OF THE CORRECT ANSWER IN THE SPACE AT THE RIGHT.*

Questions 1-11.

DIRECTIONS: The following sentences in Questions 1 through 11 contain problems in grammar, usage, diction (choice of words), idiom, and punctuation. Some sentences are correct. No sentence contains more than one error. You will find that the error, if there is one, is underlined and lettered. Assume that all other elements of the sentence are correct and cannot be changed. If there is an error, select the one underlined part that must be changed in order to make the sentence correct. If there is no error, select answer D.

1. Halfway through his <u>speech,</u> Val forgot what he'd planned to say and began to 1.____
                          A
   ramble, saying whatever came to <u>mind,</u> it was obvious to everyone listening that
                                            B
   he <u>hadn't prepared</u> his speech carefully. <u>No error</u>
         C   D

2. Although Gwendolyn Brooks <u>had received</u> much praise from fellow poets 2.____
                              A
   throughout her illustrious career, the people who <u>have had</u> the most direct
                                         B
   influence upon her work are <u>parents</u>. <u>No error</u>
                         C   D

3. Tom did not feel well the morning after the big <u>party,</u> and <u>decides</u> that in the 3.____
                                 A   B
   future he <u>would drink</u> alcohol only in moderation. <u>No error</u>
           C   D

4. After several months of <u>steadily</u> dropping sales, the <u>executives</u> <u>were forced</u> to 4.____
                    A   B   C
   acknowledge the failure of their advertising campaign. <u>No error</u>
                                             D

5. The factory strike lasted <u>so long a time</u> that the management and <u>workers</u> 5.____
                    A   B
   agreed to hire an impartial judge to decide <u>upon</u> a fair solution to their
                                          C
   dispute. <u>No error</u>
           D

6. People who watch the display of fireflies on a clear summer evening are actually
   witnessing a complex chemical reaction called bioluminescence, turn certain
      A   B
   organisms into living light bulbs. No error
      C   D

7. Since the beginning of this century many members of the Caughnawaga
                                           A
   Mohawk tribe make their living high above New York City. No error
            B   C   D

8. Maria Tallchief, the daughter of a full-blood Osage Indian, will perhaps
   mostly be remembered as America's first internationally celebrated
      A   B
   prima ballerina. No error
      C   D

9. Angela's parents were stern and old-fashioned they considered it improper for
      A   B   C
   her to call boys on the telephone. No error
                                        D

10. Although former congresswoman Barbara Jordan led a life marked by
                     A
    groundbreaking accomplishments, her insistence that she was no different
                   B
    from anyone else may be her greatest lesson. No error
                     C   D

11. The old man was a hermit who lived by himself at a cabin in the woods;
                              A   B
    nobody in town had ever spoken with him. No error
                   C   D

12. Quotation marks should be used for which of the following?
    A. Paraphrasing quotations
    B. Summarizing another person's ideas
    C. Direct quotations
    D. To emphasize an idea

13. Which of the following is CORRECTLY punctuated?
    A. Her story was titled, "Apples in Autumn".
    B. Her story was titled, "Apples in Autumn."
    C. Her story was titled "Apples in Autumn".
    D. Her story was titled; "Apples in Autumn."

14. (qtd. in Smith 27)
    What does the above parenthetical reference indicate about the source?
    A. Information regarding the quotation can be found in footnote 27.
    B. Smith is the author of the quotation.
    C. The source is direct.
    D. The source is indirect.

15. The Modern Language Association (MLA) format for documenting sources uses which of the following?
    A. References page
    B. Works Cited page
    C. Bibliography page
    D. All are acceptable

16. A direct quote is MOST beneficial in an essay when you
    A. want to emphasize a person's opinions
    B. need to include a long passage in order to selectively record a person's main ideas
    C. want to outline a person's general argument
    D. want to provide lengthy background information on a person's expertise

17. If you are writing a research essay on a new development in medical technology and you need the most current information available, where should you look?
    A. Library Reference Section
    B. Library Periodical Index
    C. Library Book Index
    D. Internet

18. www.ncu.edu
    What does the above internet address indicate?
    The site is
    A. in northern California
    B. affiliated with an educational institution
    C. affiliated with a government institution
    D. affiliated with a publishing institution

Questions 19-22.

DIRECTIONS: Questions 19 through 22 are to be answered on the basis of the following passage.

So This Was Adolescence by Annie Dillard

For as long as I could remember, I had been transparent to myself, unselfconscious, learning, doing, most of every day.(1) Now I was in my own way; I myself was a dark object I could not ignore.(2) I couldn't remember how to forget myself.(3) I didn't want to think about myself, to reckon myself in, to deal with myself every livelong minute on top of everything else – but swerve as I might, I couldn't avoid it.(4) I was a boulder blocking my own path.(5) I was a dog barking between my own ears, a barking dog who wouldn't hush.(6)

19. This excerpt can BEST be classified as which of the following? 19._____
    A. Narrative   B. Descriptive
    C. Argumentative   D. Explanatory

20. The imagery in this excerpt depends MOST heavily on which of the following? 20._____
    A. Exaggeration   B. Comparison   C. Metaphor   D. Simile

21. What has changed for the author in this paragraph? 21._____
    She
    A. doesn't know
    B. has recalled a painful memory
    C. has experienced a nervous breakdown
    D. has grown self-conscious

22. The phrase *reckon myself in* in sentence 5 is BEST characterized as which of 22._____
    the following?
    A. Formal   B. Colloquial   C. Poetic   D. Abstract

Questions 23-25.

DIRECTIONS: Questions 23 through 25 are to be answered on the basis of the following passage.

People Have Multiple Intelligences by Howard Gardner

Intelligence is not an absolute such as height that can be measured simply, largely because people have multiple intelligences rather than one single intelligence.(1) In all, I have identified seven forms of intelligence.(2) The two that are valued most highly in this society are linguistic and logical-mathematical intelligences.(3) When people think of someone as smart, they are usually referring to those two, because individuals who possess linguistic and logical-mathematical abilities do well on tests that supposedly measure intelligence.(4)

23. The effect of this excerpt depends MOST heavily on the use of which of the 23._____
    following?
    A. Multiple examples   B. Definition
    C. Narration   D. Imagery

24. The main verb of the first sentence is 24._____
    A. is   B. can be   C. is and have   D. have

25. The phrase *linguistic intelligence* in sentence 3 refers to which of the following? 25._____
    A. Spatial and language abilities   B. Knowledge of multiple languages
    C. Language abilities   D. Public speaking abilities

KEY (CORRECT ANSWERS)

1.	B		11.	B
2.	A		12.	C
3.	B		13.	B
4.	D		14.	D
5.	A		15.	B
6.	B		16.	A
7.	C		17.	D
8.	A		18.	B
9.	C		19.	A
10.	D		20.	C

21. D
22. B
23. B
24. A
25. C

TEST 2

DIRECTIONS: Each question or incomplete statement is followed by several suggested answers or completions. Select the one that BEST answers the question or completes the statement. *PRINT THE LETTER OF THE CORRECT ANSWER IN THE SPACE AT THE RIGHT.*

Questions 1-6.

DIRECTIONS: Questions 1 through 6 are to be answered on the basis of the following passage.

Declaration of Sentiments and Resolutions by Elizabeth Cady Stanton

   When, in the course of human events, it becomes necessary for one portion of the family of man to assume among the people of the earth a position different from that which they have hitherto occupied, but one to which the laws of nature and nature's God entitle them, a decent respect to the opinions of mankind requires that they should declare the causes that impel them to such a course.(1)
   We hold these truths to be self-evident: that all men and women are created equal; that they are endowed by their creator with certain inalienable rights; that among these are life, liberty and the pursuit of happiness; that to secure these rights governments are instituted, deriving their just powers from the consent of the governed.(2)

1. This passage is BEST characterized as
   A. interpretive   B. narrative   C. an allegory   D. persuasive

2. *...from that which they have hitherto occupied, but one to which the laws of nature and of nature's God entitle them, a decent respect to the opinions of mankind requires that they should declare the causes that impel them to such a course...*
   The above excerpt from the first sentence relies MOST heavily on which of the following?
   A. Parallel construction   B. Example
   C. Imagery   D. Coordination

3. In sentence 1, the word *hitherto* is BEST replaced by
   A. will one day   B. again   C. previously   D. never

4. What point of view is this excerpt written in?
   A. First person singular   B. First person plural
   C. Third person singular   D. Third person plural

5. Which of the following BEST expresses the main purpose of this excerpt?
   A. To explain the illegal actions this political group is planning to take
   B. To explain the need for women's legal rights
   C. To argue for the legal rights of women
   D. To argue for the legal rights of men and women

6. This excerpt, from sentence 2, is an example of a(n)   6.____
   A. noun phrase   B. dangling modifier
   C. dependent clause   D. independent clause

Question 7.

DIRECTIONS: Question 7 contains problems in grammar, usage, diction (choice of words), idiom, and punctuation, or it can be correct. The sentence does not contain more than one error. You will find that the error, if there is one, is underlined and lettered. Assume that all other elements of the sentence are correct and cannot be changed. If there is an error, select the one underlined part that must be changed in order to make the sentence correct. If there is no error, select answer D.

7. <u>Although</u> scientists have succeeded in creating robots able to process huge   7.____
       A
   amounts of information, the <u>are</u> still struggling to create one <u>who's</u> reasoning
                                 B   C
   ability matches that of a human baby. <u>No error</u>
                                              D

8. One Sunday, Katy Smith noticed that her new neighbor did not leave home to   8.____
   go to church. As a result, Katy concluded that her neighbors were atheists.
   Katy's flaw in logic is an example of
   A. ad hominem attack   B. faulty deduction
   C. faulty induction   D. a logical fallacy

Questions 9-14.

DIRECTIONS: In each of the following sentences, you are given two or more sentences to combine into one. After each set of sentences, there is a question that will help you decide how the sentences are to be combined. In combining some of the sentences, you will change the order of the original a great deal; in combining others, you will change the order only a little. Be sure that the new sentence you create is a complete sentence, that it contains all of the essential facts given in the original set of sentences, that it maintains the proper relationship of ideas, and that is clearly and effectively written.

9. My grandfather has dramatic mood swings. He was diagnosed as manic-   9.____
   depressive.
   Your new sentence will contain which of the following?
   A. swings, he
   B. manic-depressive grandfather
   C. grandfather, who
   D. with dramatic mood swings, my grandfather

10. A politician thinks of the next election. A statesman thinks of the next generation.
    Which of the following is the BEST word to join the two sentences?
    A. whereas   B. furthermore   C. hitherto   D. although

11. Ulysses was written by James Joyce. It is an important book. It examines the human psyche.
    Your new sentence will begin with which of the following?
    A. The human psyche, an important
    B. James Joyce, an important
    C. Ulysses, an important
    D. Ulysses and James Joyce

12. I visited my friend Anna. She owns a wolf. It ate my steak one night.
    Your new sentence will begin with which of the following?
    A. After
    B. When
    C. I visited
    D. My friend Anna, who

13. I had a job in high school. I worked for a family. I babysat their children. I was responsible for house-cleaning.
    Your new sentence will contain which of the following?
    A. babysitting and housecleaning
    B. babysat their children and was responsible for
    C. responsible for housecleaning and to babysit
    D. to babysit and for housecleaning

Questions 14-17.

DIRECTIONS: Question 14 through 17 are to be answered on the basis of the following passage.

Asking How Much is Enough by Alan Durning

Consumption has become a central pillar of life in industrial lands and is even embedded in social values.(1) Opinion surveys in the world's two largest economies—Japan and the United States show consumerist definitions of success becoming ever more prevalent.(2)
In Taiwan, a billboard demands "Why Aren't You a Millionaire Yet?"(3) The Japanese speak of the "new three sacred treasures": color television, air conditioning and the automobile.(4)
The affluent life-style born in the United States is emulated by those who can afford it around the world.(5) And many can: the average person today is 4.5 times richer than were his or her great-grandparents at the turn of the century.(6)

14. The effect of this passage depends MOST heavily on the use of which of the following?
    A. Definition of terms
    B. Narrative scene
    C. Extended example
    D. Multiple examples

15. In sentence 2, the phrase *consumerist definitions of success* MOST NEARLY means which of the following?
Success
   A. determined by consumer surveys
   B. that is measured by material wealth
   C. that includes spiritual and psychological considerations
   D. measured by greed

15.____

16. In sentence 5, the word *affluent* is BEST replaced by which of the following?
   A. Frugal   B. Wasteful   C. Wealthy   D. Luxurious

16.____

17. This passage can BEST be characterized as which of the following?
   A. Narrative   B. Expository   C. Persuasive   D. Symbolic

17.____

Questions 18-23.

DIRECTIONS: Questions 18 through 23 are to be answered on the basis of the following passage.

Nonmoral Nature by Stephen Jay Gould

When the Right Honorable and Reverend Francis Henry, earl of Bridgewater, died in February, 1829, he left $8,000 to support a series of books "on the power, wisdom and goodness of God, as manifested in the creation."(1) William Buckland, England's first official academic geologist and later dean of Westminster, was invited to compose one of the nine Bridgewater Treatises.(2) In it he discussed the most pressing problem of natural theology: If God is benevolent and the Creation displays his "power, wisdom and goodness," then why are we surrounded with pain, suffering, and apparently senseless cruelty in the animal world?(3)

18. What is the main verb in the first sentence?
   A. to support   B. left and died   C. died   D. left

18.____

19. In sentence 3, the word *benevolent* is BEST replaced by
   A. good   b. mild   C. just   D. stern

19.____

20. This passage is BEST described as
   A. persuasive   B. narrative   C. expository   D. comparative

20.____

21. The phrase *pain, suffering, and apparently senseless cruelty* from sentence 3 is an example of
   A. a subordinate clause   B. parallel construction
   C. an independent clause   D. a phrase

21.____

151

22. Which of the following BEST expresses the main idea of the excerpt? 22._____
   A. Historians who believed that nature reflected God's goodness were often disappointed.
   B. Historians believed that nature reflected God's goodness, but they were wrong
   C. God is good, and nature reflects this goodness.
   D. If God is good, then why doesn't nature reflect this goodness?

23. ...England's first official academic geologist and later dean of Westminster... 23._____
   The above excerpt, from sentence 2, is an example of which of the following?
   A. A dependent clause   B. An independent clause
   C. A phrase   D. Parallel construction

Question 24.

DIRECTIONS: See directions for Question 7.

24. <u>After</u> the basketball team lost by forty points, the angry A coach gathered <u>it</u> 24._____
      A   B
    into the locker room and told <u>them their</u> performance had been a disgrace.
                                              C

    <u>No error</u>
    D

Question 25.

DIRECTIONS: See directions for Questions 9-14.

25. I saw him far down the road. He rode an old dusty horse. An old song played 25._____
    on the radio. I sat on the upper rail of our small corral.
    Your new sentence will begin with which of the following?
    A. Riding an old dusty horse   B. I was on the upper rail
    C. The song playing on the radio   D. Seeing him far down the road

KEY (CORRECT ANSWERS)

1.	D	11.	C
2.	A	12.	B
3.	C	13.	A
4.	B	14.	D
5.	C	15.	B
6.	D	16.	C
7.	C	17.	B
8.	C	18.	D
9.	C	19.	A
10.	A	20.	C

21.	B
22.	D
23.	C
24.	B
25.	B

TEST 3

DIRECTIONS: Each question or incomplete statement is followed by several suggested answers or completions. Select the one that BEST answers the question or completes the statement. *PRINT THE LETTER OF THE CORRECT ANSWER IN THE SPACE AT THE RIGHT.*

Questions 1-9.

DIRECTIONS: In each of the following sentences, you are given two or more sentences to combine into one. After each set of sentences, there is a question that will help you decide how the sentences are to be combined. In combining some of the sentences, you will change the order of the original a great deal; in combining others, you will change the order only a little. Be sure that the new sentence you create is a complete sentence, that is contains all of the essential facts given in the original set of sentences, that is maintains the proper relationship of ideas, and that is clearly and effectively written.

1. Bhavesh runs in front of the trains. Bhavesh is crazy.
   Your new sentence will contain which of the following?
   A. whose   B. that   C. who   D. whom

2. Frank is frustrated by how slow his bicycle is. Frank bought a new Toyota.
   Your new sentence will begin with which of the following?
   A. Buying a new Toyota
   B. His bicycle being frustrating
   C. The new Toyota
   D. Frank, frustrated

3. The police officer met his informer. They met at a diner in another city. No one from the neighborhood went there.
   Your new sentence will contain which of the following?
   A. away from the neighborhood
   B. meeting at a neighborhood diner
   C. informer at an out-of-the-way
   D. informing in the neighborhood

4. That window was fine yesterday. Today it is broken.
   Your new sentence will contain which of the following?
   A. which   B. that   C. it   D. its

5. There was a fight. Three students were suspended. No one was hurt.
   Your new sentence will begin with which of the following?
   A. Fighting with each other
   B. Three students were
   C. Suspended for fighting
   D. Unhurt from fighting

6. The town of Happy is four square miles. It is bounded on the North by Holler Creek, and on the South by an Interstate. Seven hundred people live there.
   Your new sentence will begin with which of the following?
   A. Four square miles and called Happy
   B. Bounded by Holler Creek
   C. Seven hundred people
   D. Bounded on the South by an Interstate

7. The horse was a nice, friendly horse. It never caused any trouble. It let me slip the bridle off. It stood quietly as I combed the burrs from its hide.
   Your new sentence will contain which of the following?
   A. standing quietly as I combed
   B. horse, it never caused
   C. letting me slip the bridle off
   D. which was nice and friendly and had never caused any trouble

8. There was an emergency with the patient. Two doctors were called in to operate. The patient lived.
   Your new sentence will begin with which of the following?
   A. Called in to operate
   B. Two doctors were
   C. The patient's emergency
   D. Living through the surgery

9. The losing team was made up of superstars. These superstars acted as isolated individuals on the court.
   Your new sentence will contain which of the following?
   A. superstars, these
   B. losing team superstars these
   C. superstars who
   D. acting isolated on the superstar court

10. Ernest was surprised to discover that Angela was a smoker. She didn't have yellow teeth or a terrible cough.
    Ernest's flaw in logic is an example of
    A. ad hominem attack
    B. faulty deduction
    C. faulty induction
    D. a logical fallacy

Questions 11-15.

DIRECTIONS: Questions 11 through 15 are to be answered on the basis of the following passage.

On the Ball, by Roger Angell

    It weighs just over five ounces and measures between 2.86 and 2.94 inches in diameter.(1) It is made of a composition-cork nucleus encased in two thin layers of rubber, one black and one red, surrounded by 121 yards of tightly wrapped blue-gray wool yarn, 45 yards of white wool yarn 53 more yards of blue-gray wool yarn, 150 yards of fine cotton yarn, a coat of rubber cement, and a cowhide (formerly horsehide) exterior which is held together with 216 slightly raised red cotton stitches.(2)

11. The effect of this passage relies MOST heavily on which of the following?
    A. Argument
    B. Extended example
    C. Description
    D. Narration

12. ...*by 121 yards of tightly wrapped blue-gray wool, 45 yards of white wool yarn, 53 more yards of blue-gray wool yarn...*
    The above excerpt, taken from sentence 2, is an example of
    A. parallel construction
    B. non-parallel construction
    C. an independent clause
    D. a dependent clause

    12._____

13. The main verb of sentence 2 is
    A. surrounded   B. is made   C. wrapped   D. is held

    13._____

14. This passage is BEST characterized as
    A. narrative
    B. ironic
    C. argumentative
    D. informative

    14._____

15. Which of the following techniques is MOST frequently used by the writer?
    A. Vivid detail
    B. Extended examples
    C. Imagery
    D. Simile

    15._____

16. In competition against a rival bookstore, the owner of the smaller store began running ads about his competitor's gambling history.
    This is an example of a(n)
    A. false analogy
    B. hasty generalization
    C. faulty use of authority
    D. ad hominem attack

    16._____

17. An unpopular monarch was criticized for being too authoritarian with his subjects. He replied by saying, "Would you prefer anarchy instead?"
    His reasoning is an example of a
    A. false analogy
    B. slippery slope argument
    C. faulty dilemma
    D. doubtful cause

    17._____

Questions 18-22.

DIRECTIONS: The following sentences in Questions 18 through 22 contain problems in grammar, usage, diction (choice of words), idiom, and punctuation. Some sentences are correct. No sentence contains more than one error. You will find that the error, if there is one, is underlined and lettered. Assume that all other elements of the sentence are correct and cannot be changed. If there is an error, select the one underlined part that must be changed in order to make the sentence correct. If there is no error, select answer D.

18. In the past few <u>decades,</u> while much of the <u>worlds</u> imagination has focused on
                        A   B
    the possibilities of outer space some scientists <u>have been</u> exploring a different
                                                        C
    frontier —the ocean floor. <u>No error</u>
                                    D

    18._____

19. Many treasure hunters and archaeologists believe the sea floor around the   19.____

    <u>Azores,</u> a group of <u>islands west of</u> Portugal, still <u>harbor</u> some of the richest
       A   B   C
    sunken treasure in the world. <u>No error</u>
                                      D

20. Throughout the <u>Age of Exploration,</u> explorers <u>like</u> Columbus and Vespucci   20.____
                         A   B
    relied on the <u>Trade Winds</u> of the North Atlantic to fuel and sustain their long
                       C
    journeys. <u>No error</u>
                  D

21. The undersea canyon that <u>began</u> just west of the <u>Monterey peninsula</u> in   21.____
                                A   B
    California has provided marine biologists a rare opportunity <u>to study</u> the
                                                                    C
    life of the deep ocean up close. <u>No error</u>
                                         D

22. Though they may not realize it, many modern restaurants <u>have adopted</u> <u>menus</u>   22.____
                                                                A   B
    reminiscent of an old Swedish tradition called the <u>smorgasbord</u>. <u>No error</u>
                                                            C   D

23. Sylvia was sad when she heard that Mr. Roe had had a heart attack. She   23.____
    wasn't surprised, however, since Mr. Roe did not like to see his doctor anymore
    than necessary.
    Sylvia's flaw in logic is an example of
        A. a logical fallacy   B. faulty deduction
        C. faulty induction   D. ad hominem attack

24. Cynthia couldn't believe that, at 6'9" tall, Thomas didn't play basketball.   24.____
    Cynthia's flaw in logic is an example of
        A. ad hominem attack   B. faulty deduction
        C. faulty induction   D. a logical fallacy

Question 25.

DIRECTIONS: See directions for Questions 1-9.

25. Every student should have access to a computer. Access to the internet should   25.____
    be free.
    Which of the following is the BEST word to join the two sentences?
        A. and   B. however   C. therefore   D. furthermore

KEY (CORRECT ANSWERS)

1.	C	11.	C
2.	D	12.	A
3.	C	13.	B
4.	A	14.	D
5.	B	15.	A
6.	C	16.	D
7.	D	17.	C
8.	B	18.	B
9.	C	19.	C
10.	B	20.	D

21.	A
22.	D
23.	B
24.	B
25.	D

TEST 4

DIRECTIONS: Each question or incomplete statement is followed by several suggested answers or completions. Select the one that BEST answers the question or completes the statement. *PRINT THE LETTER OF THE CORRECT ANSWER IN THE SPACE AT THE RIGHT.*

Questions 1-6.

DIRECTIONS: Questions 1 through 6 are to be answered on the basis of the following passage.

Finding a Voice, by Eudora Welty

Through learning at my later date things I hadn't known, or had escaped or possibly feared realizing, about my parents—and myself—I glimpse our whole family life as if it were freed of that clock time which spaces us apart so inhibitingly, divides young and old, keeps our living through the same experiences at separate distances.(1)
It is our inward journey that leads us through time—forward or back,, seldom in a straight line, most often spiraling.(2) Each of us is moving, changing, with respect to others.(3) As we discover, we remember; remembering, we discover; and most intensely do we experience this when our separate journeys converge.(4)

1. The main verb in the first sentence is
   A. spaces
   B. hadn't known and had escaped
   C. learning
   D. glimpse

2. *Through learning at my later date things I hadn't known.*
   The above excerpt, taken from sentence 1, is an example of which of the following?
   A. Parallel construction
   B. An independent clause
   C. A dependent clause
   D. A phrase

3. *As we discover, we remember; remembering, we discover.*
   The above excerpt, taken from sentence 4, is an example of which of the following?
   A. Parallel construction
   B. An independent clause
   C. A dependent clause
   D. A phrase

4. *…forward or back, seldom in a straight line, most often spiraling…*
   The above excerpt, taken from sentence 2, is an example of which of the following?
   A. Parallel construction
   B. An independent clause
   C. A dependent clause
   D. A phrase

5. In sentence 4, the word *converge* is BEST replaced with
   A. separate
   B. come together
   C. subordinate
   D. end

6. The author's main point is BEST summarized by which of the following statements? 6._____
    A. Time is the dominant force in our lives.
    B. Time is irrelevant in our lives.
    C. Our lives are better measured by emotional time than chronological time.
    D. Our lives are better measured by chronological time than emotional time.

Questions 7-13.

DIRECTIONS: In each of the following sentences, you are given two or more sentences to combine into one. After each set of sentences, there is a question that will help you decide how the sentences are to be combined. In combining some of the sentences, you will change the order of the original a great deal; in combining others, you will change the order only a little. Be sure that the new sentence you create is a complete sentence, that is contains all of the essential facts given in the original set of sentences, that is maintains the proper relationship of ideas, and that is clearly and effectively written.

7. The rodeo arena was crowded. The crowd made no impression on me. 7._____
   Your sentence will begin with which of the following?
   A. And   B. However   C. Although   D. Furthermore

8. People turn on the television. Three hours later, people find themselves still in front of the television. They've eaten many bags of snacks. 8._____
   Your new sentence will contain which of the following?
   A. are eating   B. people find themselves
   C. they've eaten   D. hours, and many bags

9. Watching television is a popular way to spend leisure time. It makes people apathetic. 9._____
   Which of the following is the BEST word to join the two sentences?
   A. and   B. but   C. because   D. furthermore

10. I don't like seafood. My mother doesn't like seafood either. 10._____
    Your new sentence will contain which of the following?
    A. Either…or   B. Either…nor   C. Neither…nor   D. Neither…or

11. Thurmount means "gateway to the mountains." It is minutes from the Blue Ridge mountains. It is also minutes from the historic town of Surley. 11._____
    Your new sentence will begin with which of the following?
    A. Thurmount, which means
    B. Minutes from Surely, the historic town
    C. Gateway to the mountains, Thurmount
    D. Surley and the Blue Ridge mountains close by

12. Her job was to sell to vendors. She also helped with marketing. There were some advertising opportunities, too.
    Your new sentence will contain which of the following?
    A. to sell to vendors, market and sometimes advertising
    B. selling to vendors, to market and some advertising
    C. selling to vendors, marketing and some advertising
    D. to sell, marketing and advertising

    12.____

13. I want not only to survive. I want to live.
    Your new sentence will contain which of the following?
    A. want to live
    B. survive and live
    C. and
    D. but also

    13.____

Questions 14-20.

DIRECTIONS: The following sentences in Questions 14 through 20 contain problems in grammar, usage, diction (choice of words), idiom, and punctuation. Some sentences are correct. No sentence contains more than one error. You will find that the error, if there is one, is underlined and lettered. Assume that all other elements of the sentence are correct and cannot be changed. If there is an error, select the one underlined part that must be changed in order to make the sentence correct. If there is no error, select answer D.

14. Among the Tlingit people of Western Canada, the tradition of the potlatch <u>was used</u> to redistribute wealth within the <u>tribe,</u> and <u>marked</u> all ceremonial
                  A   B   C
    occasions. <u>No error</u>
                   D

    14.____

15. One of the <u>great,</u> and least publicized, <u>legacies</u> of Native American culture
                   A   B
    <u>has been</u> the worldwide cultivation of food staples such as tomatoes, potatoes,
      C
    and corn through careful farming methods. <u>No error</u>
                                                                   D

    15.____

16. Although the <u>Japanese art of Bonsai</u> began <u>more then</u> 1,000 years ago, it has
                         A   B
    become a modern antidote to the cramped <u>gardens</u> of densely populated urban
                                                           C
    areas. <u>No error</u>
           D

    16.____

17. Feng Shui, the ancient Chinese science of studying the natural environment's 17.____
                                                                           A
    affect on a person's well-being, has gained new popularity in the design and
      B   C
    decoration of buildings. No error
                              D

18. Karala had to write her article more quick than the other reporters, because 18.____
                                            A   B   C
    her flight was scheduled to leave an hour after the deadline. No error
                                                                   D

19. After careful consideration, the committee have decided to extend our 19.____
                    A   B   C
    contract for another four years. No error
                                      D

20. Of the eight attorneys at the law firm, Martha is the most qualified to handle 20.____
                 A   B   C
    this case. No error
                D

Questions 21-25.

DIRECTIONS: Questions 21 through 25 are to be answered on the basis of the following passage.

Letter From Birmingham Jail, Martin Luther King, Jr.

   I have earnestly worked and preached against violent tension, but there is a type of constructive nonviolent tension that is necessary for growth.(1) Just as Socrates felt that it was necessary to create a tension in the mind so that individuals could rise from the bondage of myths and half-truths to the unfettered realm of creative analysis and objective appraisal, we must see the need for having nonviolent gadflies to create the kind of tension in society that will help men rise from the dark depths of prejudice and racism to the majestic heights of understanding and brotherhood.(2)

21. ...mind so that individuals could rise from the bondage of myths and half-truths 21.____
    to the unfettered realm of creative analysis and objective appraisal...
    The above excerpt from sentence 2 contains examples of which of the
    following?
        A. Coordination   B. Prepositional phrasing
        C. Dangling modifiers   D. Parallel construction

22. In sentence 2, the word *gadflies* is BEST replaced by 22.____
        A. soldier   B. protester
        C. underachievers   D. indigent men

23. This passage is BEST characterized as which of the following? 23.____
    A. Moral argument B. Narrative episode
    C. Poetic statement D. A tribute

24. The writer depends MOST heavily on which of the following devices? 24.____
    A. Hyperbole B. Understatement
    C. Metaphor and simile D. Personification

25. Based on the tone and style of the excerpt, what can you infer about the 25.____
    writer's feelings for his intended audience?
    He
    A. believes they are ignorant B. hates them
    C. agrees with their views D. disagrees with their view

KEY (CORRECT ANSWERS)

1.	D		11.	A
2.	C		12.	C
3.	A		13.	D
4.	D		14.	C
5.	B		15.	A
6.	C		16.	B
7.	C		17.	B
8.	D		18.	A
9.	B		19.	B
10.	C		20.	D

21. D
22. B
23. A
24. C
25. D

EXAMINATION SECTION
TEST 1

DIRECTIONS: Each question or incomplete statement is followed by several suggested answers or completions. Select the one that BEST answers the question or completes the statement. *PRINT THE LETTER OF THE CORRECT ANSWER IN THE SPACE AT THE RIGHT.*

Questions 1-3.

DIRECTIONS: In each of the following sentences, you are given two or more sentences to combine into one. After each set of sentences, there is a question that will help you decide how the sentences are to be combined. In combining some of the sentences, you will change the order of the original a great deal; in combining others, you will change the order only a little. Be sure that the new sentence you create is a complete sentence, that is contains all of the essential facts given in the original set of sentences, that is maintains the proper relationship of ideas, and that is clearly and effectively written.

1. Finding a job is hard. The job market is competitive. You must be sharp in the job market. It can eat up your confidence.
   Your new sentence will contain which of the following?
   A. sharp and confident
   B. sharp market with confidence
   C. competitive, sharp, confident market
   D. hard market

1._____

2. I like to ski. I like to snowboard. I like making Adirondack chairs.
   Your new sentence will contain which of the following?
   A. skiing, snowboarding and to make
   B. skiing, snowboarding, and making
   C. to snowboard, ski and making
   D. make, ski and snowboarding

2._____

3. Our waitress was costumed in a kimono. She had painted her face white. She had arranged her hair in an upswept lacquered beehive.
   Your new sentence will begin with which of the following?
   A. Wearing her hair
   B. In a kimono, with painted face and lacquered beehive
   C. Our waitress, who
   D. Painting her face

3._____

Questions 4-20.

DIRECTIONS: The following sentences in Questions 4 through 20 contain problems in grammar, usage, diction (choice of words), idiom, and punctuation. Some sentences are correct. No sentence contains more than one error. You will find that the error, if there is one, is underlined and lettered. Assume that all other elements of the sentence are correct and cannot be changed. If there is an error, select the one underlined part that must be changed in order to make the sentence correct. If there is no error, select answer D.

4. The <u>Sioux Indians</u> wasted no part of a bison kill, and even used <u>it's</u> bones to
     A   B
make knives, cooking <u>tools,</u> and sewing needles. <u>No error</u>
                          C   D

4. _____

5. Due to <u>Lily's</u> years of care and grooming, her <u>sleek</u> healthy Holstein won the
         A   B
dairy cattle competition at the <u>state fair</u>. <u>No error</u>
                                     C   D

5. _____

6. Due to the changing nature of the cattle <u>industry,</u> <u>there</u> <u>are not</u> real cowboys
                                                 A   B   C
left in America. <u>No error</u>
                    D

6. _____

7. This <u>weekend,</u> the gas <u>company's</u> bowling team, made up of both managers
        A   B
and workers, won <u>their</u> fifth straight championship. <u>No error</u>
                  C   D

7. _____

8. The <u>grizzly bears</u> of Yellowstone National Park have begun to relearn their
      A
old hunting and foraging techniques, <u>however</u> there <u>has been</u> an increase
                                            B   C
in the bear population. <u>No error</u>
                            D

8. _____

9. You must exercise, <u>eating sensibly</u> and <u>think positively</u> if you want to <u>lose</u>
                          A   B   C
weight. <u>No error</u>
        D

9. _____

10. If Carlton <u>Was</u> to put any more weight on that <u>hayrack</u>, it <u>would</u> surely be
         A   B   C
too heavy for the tractor to pull. <u>No error</u>

10. _____

11. Diving from her chair into the pool's deep end, the lifeguard had saved the
                                    A   B   C
    children. No error
              D

12. Hank made Sheila and I promise to meet him at the fairgrounds when the
                         A   B
    state fair came to town. No error
                C   D

13. Luther put his children to bed, read them a story, and kissed them good
                                A   B   C
    night. No error
           D

14. Our kitchen table, along with the Adirondack chairs in the yard, were made
                 A   B
    by my grandfather, who is a skilled carpenter. No error
          C   D

15. The tenants of the apartment complex wanted to show their appreciation for
        A
    the work of Arthur, the building superintendent at his retirement party they
                                     B
    gave him a gold watch, a plaque and a certificate. No error
    C   D

16. My Aunt Audrey used to have a gold tooth that shined brightly whenever she
                       A   B   C
    laughed. No error
             D

17. The only person in the county who's relatives are all natives, Abel makes
                                   A   B
    sure everyone knows it. No error
                         C D

18. After Luc scored the goal that won the hockey game, his teammates treated
                              A   B
    him as if he was a king. No error
                C   D

19. Mr. Lopez was angry when he discovered the latch on the corral gate
                                A
    had been broken by one of his ranch hands. No error
    B   C   D

20. Stewart burned the gravy and ruined the <u>dinner,</u> but we told him not to worry   20._____
                                              A

    <u>because</u> none of us are <u>are perfect cooks</u>. <u>No error</u>
      B   C   D

21. Susanne refused to allow her son to buy a red car because she knew it would   21._____
    result in more speeding tickets for him. Susanne's flaw in logic is an example
    of
    A. ad hominem attack   B. faulty deduction
    C. faulty induction   D. hasty generalization

Questions 22-25.

DIRECTIONS: Use the following information to answer Questions 22 through 25.

    003.42   Schuster, Mary B
    CAM   Student's Guide to Home Sewing Projects/Mary Schuster—
              Bedford, Mass.: Addison-Wesley Pub. Co.
              c. 1998.
              ix, 254 p.: ill., 36 cm.
              ISBN 0-000-00836-2 (pbk)
              1. Crafts – Sewing
              2. Home – Craft Projects
              3. Mary Schuster

22. What do the numbers 003.42 (along the lefthand margin) represent?   22._____
    A. Library of Congress number
    B. Size of the book (in height and depth)
    C. The number of pages in the book
    D. Library call numbers

23. ix, 254 p.: ill., 36 cm.   23._____
    What does the above line indicate?
    A. Volume number, Library of Congress number, and height of book
    B. Number of pages, use of illustrations, and height of book
    C. Volume number, number of pages, and height of book
    D. Number of pages, location of book, and height of book

24. Bedford, Mass.: Addison-Wesley Pub. Co.© 1998   24._____
    What does the above information indicate?
    A. Publisher and year that book was accepted for publication
    B. Location of publisher, publisher, and year that book was accepted for
       publication
    C. Location of publisher, publisher, and year of publication
    D. Publisher and year publishing house was established

25.
1. Crafts – Sewing
2. Home – Craft Projects
3. Mary Schuster

What does the above information indicate?
A. Other Library of Congress listings for the same book
B. Subjects related to the book's subject
C. Other books by the same author
D. Other library catalog listings for the same book

25.____

KEY (CORRECT ANSWERS)

1.	A		11.	C
2.	B		12.	A
3.	C		13.	D
4.	B		14.	B
5.	D		15.	B
6.	C		16.	B
7.	C		17.	A
8.	B		18.	C
9.	A		19.	D
10.	A		20.	C

21. B
22. D
23. B
24. C
25. D

TEST 2

DIRECTIONS: Each question or incomplete statement is followed by several suggested answers or completions. Select the one that BEST answers the question or completes the statement. *PRINT THE LETTER OF THE CORRECT ANSWER IN THE SPACE AT THE RIGHT.*

Questions 1-5.

DIRECTIONS: Questions 1 through 5 are to be answered on the basis of the following passage.

No Name Woman, Maxine Hong Kingston

    The round mooncakes and round doorways, the round tables of graduated size that fit one roundness inside another, round windows and rice bowls—these talismans had lost their power to warn this family of the law: a family must be whole, faithfully keeping the descent line by having sons to feed the old and the dead, who in turn look after the family.(1) The villagers came to show my aunt and her lover-in-hiding a broken house.(2) The villagers were speeding up the circling of events because she was too shortsighted to see that her infidelity had already harmed the village, that waves of consequences would return unpredictably, sometimes in disguise, as now, to hurt her.(3)

1. This passage is BEST characterized as which of the following? 1.____
   - A. Persuasive
   - B. Narrative
   - C. Classification
   - D. Definition

2. The author relies MOST heavily on which of the following? 2.____
   - A. Definition
   - B. Hyperbole
   - C. Personification
   - D. Imagery

3. In sentence 1, the word *talismans* is BEST replaced by which of the following? 3.____
   - A. Objects   B. Images   C. Symbols   D. Superstitions

4. ...that her infidelity had already harmed the village, that waves of consequences would return unpredictably... 4.____
   The above excerpt, from sentence 3, contains examples of which of the following?
   - A. Fragments
   - B. Dangling modifiers
   - C. Parallel construction
   - D. Coordination

5. What is the MAIN verb of the first sentence? 5.____
   - A. had lost   B. fit   C. to warn   D. graduated

170

Questions 6-9.

DIRECTIONS: Questions 6 through 9 are to be answered on the basis of the following passage.

Winged: The Creatures on My Mind, Ursula K. LeGuin

    Gulls on Klatsand Beach, on any North Pacific shore, are all alike in their two kinds: white adults with black wingtips and yellow bills; and yearlings, adult-sized but with delicately figured brown features.(1) They soar and cry, swoop, glide, dive, squabble, and grab; they stand in their multitudes at evening in the sunset shallows of the creek mouth before they rise in silence to fly out to sea, where they will sleep the night afloat on waves far out beyond the breakers, like a fleet of small white ships with sails furled and no riding lights.(2)

6. This passage is BEST characterized as
 A. narrative   B. ironic   C. persuasive   D. descriptive

7. Which of the following is used MOST frequently by the writer?
 A. Irony
 B. Imagery
 C. Subordination
 D. Simile

8. The final image of the gulls, in sentence 2, suggests which of the following?
 A. Isolation
 B. Foreboding
 C. Communal identity
 D. Individual identity

9. In sentence 1, the word *yearlings* is BEST replaced by
 A. adolescents   B. children   C. aged adults   D. young males

Questions 10-13.

DIRECTIONS: Questions 10 through 13 are to be answered on the basis of the following passage.

Leisure Will Kill You, Art Buchwald

    This country is producing so much leisure equipment for the home that nobody has any leisure time anymore to enjoy it.(1) A few months ago I bought a television tape recorder to make copies of programs when I was out of the house.(2)
    Last week I recorded the Nebraska-Oklahoma football game.(3) When I came home in the evening, I decided to play it back.(4) But my son wanted to play "Baseball" on the TV screen with his Atari Computer.(5) We finished four innings when my wife came in the room and asked me if I would like to listen to the Vienna Opera on our hi-fi stereo set.(6)

10. The tone of this passage is BEST described as
 A. sarcastic
 B. argumentative
 C. ironic
 D. sentimental

11. The effect of the passage relies MOST heavily on which of the following? 11._____
    A. Definition   B. Metaphor   C. Argument   D. Example

12. The MAIN verb in sentence 6 is 12._____
    A. finished   B. came   C. asked   D. would like

13. Which of the following BEST describes the author's writing style? 13._____
    A. Academic   B. Direct   C. Abstract   D. Poetic

Questions 14-17.

DIRECTIONS: Questions 14 through 17 are to be answered on the basis of the following passage.

The Women, Harriet Jacobs

I would ten thousand times rather that my children should be the half-starved paupers of Ireland than to be the most pampered among the slaves of America.(1) I would rather drudge out my life on a cotton plantation, till the grave opened to give me rest, than to live with an unprincipled master and a jealous mistress.(2) The felon's home in a penitentiary is preferable.(3) He may repent, and turn from the error of his ways, and so find peace, but it is not so with a favorite slave.(4) She is not allowed to have any pride or character.(5) It is deemed a crime in her to wish to be virtuous.(6)

14. The effect of this passage relies MOST heavily on which of the following? 14._____
    A. Argument   B. Imagery
    C. Extended example   D. Comparison

15. The word *pampered*, in sentence 1, is BEST replaced with 15._____
    A. coddled   B. rich   C. abused   D. large

16. The underlined excerpt from sentence 2 is an example of 16._____
    A. an independent clause   B. a dependent clause
    C. a phrase   D. parallel construction

17. This passage can BEST be characterized as 17._____
    A. persuasive   B. ironic   C. sarcastic   D. poetic

Questions 18-25.

DIRECTIONS: The following sentences in Questions 18 through 25 contain problems in grammar, usage, diction (choice of words), idiom, and punctuation. Some sentences are correct. No sentence contains more than one error. You will find that the error, if there is one, is underlined and lettered. Assume that all other elements of the sentence are correct and cannot be changed. If there is an error, select the one underlined part that must be changed in order to make the sentence correct. If there is no error, select answer D.

4 (#2)

18. Saku, the anchor of the <u>women's</u> crew <u>team,</u> has the strongest forearms I 18.____
          A   B
<u>ever saw</u>. <u>No error</u>
    C   D

19. <u>Carlos,</u> who visited the museum to see the collection of Olmec <u>figurines,</u> was 19.____
    A   B
amazed <u>by</u> the mystical expressions on their faces. <u>No error</u>
        C   D

20. I want all <u>employees</u> to attend the company picnic this <u>afternoon,</u> so post the 20.____
              A   A
notice <u>however</u> it can be seen by everyone. <u>No error</u>
        C   D

21. Whenever Rakesh and <u>me</u> go to the community <u>center,</u> we <u>like</u> to sit near 21.____
                         A   B   C
the baby pool and watch the children play. <u>No error</u>

22. Everyone <u>knew</u> Irina was an experienced <u>pilot</u> and they wondered why she 22.____
              A   B
hadn't filed a flight plan before leaving for <u>Bermuda</u>. <u>No error</u>
                                                C   D

23. <u>Its</u> not a good idea to disturb my <u>father when</u> he <u>is napping</u>. <u>No error</u> 23.____
    A   B   C   D

24. The committee <u>are</u> opposed to the new dress <u>code which</u> <u>requires</u> men 24.____
                  A   B   C
to wear suits and women to wear skirts. <u>No error</u>
                                          D

25. After mowing Mr. <u>Tanner's lawn</u>, <u>I went</u> to the pool <u>to meet</u> my friends. 25.____
                      A   B   C
<u>No error</u>
    D

KEY (CORRECT ANSWERS)

1. B
2. D
3. C
4. C
5. A

6. D
7. B
8. C
9. A
10. C

11. D
12. A
13. B
14. D
15. A

16. C
17. A
18. C
19. D
20. C

21. A
22. D
23. A
24. A
25. D

TEST 3

DIRECTIONS: Each question or incomplete statement is followed by several suggested answers or completions. Select the one that BEST answers the question or completes the statement. *PRINT THE LETTER OF THE CORRECT ANSWER IN THE SPACE AT THE RIGHT.*

1. *The Irish Elk, now extinct, was neither exclusively Irish, nor an elk.(1) Although the Guiness book of world records honors the American moose's antlers, the size of the Irish Elk's antlers has never even been approached in the history of life.(2)*
   Which of the following would be the MOST suitable sentence to insert immediately after sentence 1 in the above paragraph?
   A. Before attracting the attention of scientists, they had been used as gateposts.
   B. By some accounts, their antlers were over eight wide.
   C. It was the largest deer that ever lived, and its enormous antlers were even more impressive.
   D. We now know that the giant deer ranged as far east as Siberia and China and as far south as Northern Africa.

   1.____

2. *Cornbread is a food that originated during the settlement of the American Midwest, and is still popular in both urban and rural sections of the country's interior. Unlike most American foods, which were variations of dishes that pioneers brought from their home countries, cornbread originated on this continent, in the Kansas territory, as a direct descendant of the "ashcake" of the Kansas Indians.*
   Which of the following would be the MOST suitable sentence to conclude this paragraph?
   A. For many years this method of baking cornbread remained unchanged by people who settled the frontier.
   B. Ashcake was mixed from cornmeal and water, made into thick cakes, and baked directly on the cinders and ashes of prairie camp fires.
   C. Today corn-dodger days are remembered in Illinois by occasional corn-dodger dinners.
   D. Illinois pioneers created a variation of cornbread, a small loaf called the corn-dodger.

   2.____

Questions 3-15.

DIRECTIONS: In each of the following sentences, you are given two or more sentences to combine into one. After each set of sentences, there is a question that will help you decide how the sentences are to be combined. In combining some of the sentences, you will change the order of the original a great deal; in combining others, you will change the order only a little. Be sure that the new sentence you create is a complete sentence, that is contains all of the essential facts given in the original set of sentences, that is maintains the proper relationship of ideas, and that is clearly and effectively written.

3. The particles are known as *stealth liposomes*. They can hide in the body a long time without detection.
   Your new sentence will begin with which of the following?
   A. Stealthy liposomes
   B. Hiding in the body
   C. Known as
   D. Particles hiding in the body without detection

   3._____

4. Cory felt like a soldier. He felt like a soldier who had been comfortably wounded. A soldier who knows the war, for him, is over. Cory felt a heavy, sighing peace.
   Your new sentence will begin with which of the following?
   A. Cory felt a heavy, sighing peace
   B. Feeling a heavy, sighing peace, the soldier
   C. Comfortably wounded and knowing
   D. Knowing that war was over for him

   4._____

5. Six boys ran over the hill. The six boys breathed hard. They worked their arms as they ran.
   Your new sentence will begin with which of the following?
   A. Arms at work   B. The six boys breathed
   C. Running over the hill D. With their hearts pounding

   5._____

6. Stress is hard on body and soul. Some people suffer from being unable to sleep. Some people have low self-esteem. Some people have nervous breakdowns.
   Your new sentence will contain which of the following?
   A. sleeplessness, low self-esteem and even nervous breakdowns
   B. unable to sleep, low self-esteem and nervous breakdowns
   C. no sleeping, low self-esteem and to have a nervous breakdown
   D. to have nervous breakdowns and sleeplessness and low self-esteem

   6._____

7. Susan went from the new part of the library through to the old part. Susan walked around awhile. She went to the periodicals section.
   Your new sentence will contain which of the following?
   A. however   B. afterwards   C. therefore   D. during

   7._____

8. I had made a decision. It was time to prove myself. I was scared.
   Your new sentence will begin with which of the following?
   A. However,   Therefore   C. And   D. Even though

   8._____

9. Mrs. Stevenson was a heavyset woman. Mrs. Stevenson lived in a yellow house behind the elementary school
   Your new sentence will contain which of the following?
   A. she   B. that   C. whom   D. who

   9._____

10. People come home from work feeling tired. People turn on the television. People watch the evening news.
    Your new sentence will contain which of the following?
    A. people turn and watch
    B. tired people turn
    C. tired and they
    D. working tired

10.____

11. I walked to the ticket window at the train station. I laid my money on the counter. I could not decide where to go.
    Your new sentence will begin with which of the following?
    A. Not deciding
    B. Unable to decide
    C. Laying my money on the counter
    D. My money on the counter

11.____

12. Some people attend college for the wrong reasons. Some only want to have fun. Some want to find a mate. Some would rather not get a job.
    Your new sentence will contain which of the following?
    A. not get jobs, have fun or find a mate
    B. having fun, find a mate or put off getting a job
    C. have fun, find a mate or put off getting a job
    D. having fun, finding mates and getting jobs

12.____

13. I will always remember my elementary school uniforms. The girls wearing blue skirts. The boys had to wear blue pants.
    Your new sentence will contain which of the following?
    A. wearing skirts and pants, boys and girls, of blue
    B. the wearing of blue skirts for girls, and boys wore
    C. wearing blue skirts and the boys wore
    D. wearing blue skirts, the boys wearing

13.____

14. Eva went to class. She picked up Yolanda at the marina.
    Which of the following is the BEST word to join the two sentences?
    A. then   B. than   C. so than   D. because

14.____

15. Bay Street is located in the heart of downtown Nassau. It houses the straw market.
    Your new sentence will begin with which of the following?
    A. Downtown Nassau
    B. Housing the straw market on Bay Street
    C. Bay Street, located
    D. Locating at Bay Street

15.____

16. During his campaign for City Council, Adam decided to focus on the fact that his opponent had been married and divorced three times.
    Adam's decision is an example of
    A. ad hominem attack
    B. faulty deduction
    C. hasty generalization
    D. a logical fallacy

16.____

Questions 17-23.

DIRECTIONS: Questions 17 through 23 are to be answered on the basis of the following passage.

Of Cruelty and Clemency, Niccolo Machiavelli

From this arises the question whether it is better to be loved more than feared, or feared more than loved.(1) The reply is, that one ought to be both feared and loved, but as it is difficult for the two to go together, it is much safer to be feared than loved, if one of the two has to be wanting.(2) For it may be said of men in general that they are ungrateful, voluble dissemblers, anxious to avoid danger, and covetous of gain; as long as you benefit them, they are entirely yours; they offer you their blood, their goods, their life, and their children, as I have before said, when the necessity is remote; but when it approaches, they revolt.(3)

17. This paragraph is BEST characterized as
    A. interpretive   B. symbolic   C. explanatory   D. persuasive

18. The MAIN verb of the first sentence is
    A. arises   B. loved   C. feared   D. to be

19. In sentence 1, the phrase *loved more than feared, and feared more than loved* is an example of
    A. a noun phrase   B. parallel construction
    C. simile   D. metaphor

20. In sentence 2, the word *wanting* is BEST replaced with
    A. required   B. present   C. needed   D. absent

21. In sentence 3, the phrase *ungrateful, voluble dissemblers* contains which of the following?
    A. Coordinate nouns   B. Coordinate adjectives
    C. Subordinate adverbs   D. Subordination

22. Sentence 3 of this passage relies MOST heavily on which of the following?
    A. Subordination   B. Coordination
    C. Imagery   D. Metaphor

23. The main point of this passage is BEST expressed by which of the following statements?
    A. Men are best controlled through love, whereas women are best controlled through fear.
    B. Men are best controlled through fear, whereas women are best controlled through love.
    C. Because men are basically untrustworthy, it is easier to control them through fear than through love.
    D. Because men are basically trustworthy, it is better to control them through love than through fear.

24. Little Susan Richter hates to take her evening bath. One night, Susie's mother scolded Susie for standing too close to the oven. She explained that she didn't want Susie to get hurt. Susie countered by asking why her mother didn't let her escape her evening bath rituals, since she could fall in the tub and hurt herself. Susie's reasoning is an example of
    A. a false analogy
    B. hasty generalization
    C. a faulty use of authority
    D. a doubtful cause

24.____

25. *During World War II, important military communications often took place in code, so that messages could not be intercepted and translated by enemy forces.(1) This problem was solved by a man named Philip Johnston, who grew up on a Navajo Indian Reservation in the American Southwest.(2)*
    Which of the following would be MOST suitable to insert after sentence 1 in the above paragraph?
    A. Johnston's idea was used by the military, and the Navajo codetalkers devised a code so effective that it was not declassified by the military until more than twenty years later.
    B. The American military faced a significant problem: the similarities between the English and German languages would make English codes easy for a German to translate, and many Japanese soldiers who had graduated from American universities were used as codebreakers.
    C. Johnston's idea was to use Navajo soldiers as code-talkers; the Navajo language was tonal, meaning that its vowels rise and fall, changing meaning with different pitches that cannot be communicated in writing.
    D. Devising an effective code was a problem the American military had to solve.

25.____

KEY (CORRECT ANSWERS)

1.	C		11.	B
2.	B		12.	C
3.	C		13.	D
4.	A		14.	A
5.	D		15.	C
6.	A		16.	A
7.	B		17.	D
8.	D		18.	A
9.	D		19.	B
10.	C		20.	D

21. B
22. A
23. C
24. A
25. B

TEST 4

DIRECTIONS: Each question or incomplete statement is followed by several suggested answers or completions. Select the one that BEST answers the question or completes the statement. *PRINT THE LETTER OF THE CORRECT ANSWER IN THE SPACE AT THE RIGHT.*

Questions 1-5.

DIRECTIONS: Questions 1 through 5 are to be answered on the basis of the following passage.

Think About It, Frank Conroy

Indeed, in our intellectual lives, our creative lives, it is perhaps those problems that will never resolve that rightly claim the lion's share of our energies.(1) The physical body exists in a constant state of tension as it maintains homeostasis, and so too does the active mind embrace the tension of never being certain, never being absolutely sure, never being done, as it engages the world.(2) That is our special fate, our inexpressibly valuable condition.(3)

1. The MAIN verb in sentence 1 is
   A. is and claim   B. claim   C. is   D. resolve

2. The passage is BEST described as which of the following?
   A. Persuasive   B. Expository   C. Ironic   D. Poetic

3. ...*never being certain, never being absolutely sure, never being done*...
   The above excerpt, taken from sentence 2, is an example of which of the following?
   A. Coordinate independent clauses   B. An independent clause
   C. A dependent clause   D. Parallel construction

4. In sentence 2, the word *homeostasis* is BEST replaced by
   A. balance   B. dominance
   C. subordination   D. confusion

5. Which of the following BEST summarizes the writer's main point?
   A. The state of being uncertain requires a great deal of energy.
   B. We should avoid uncertainty at all costs.
   C. Uncertainty is the basis of our most important creativity.
   D. Uncertainty is the basis of our most debilitating insecurities.

6. Although Althea had heard that the new park was beautiful, she refused to take her son there since it was in the city and Althea had heard that city parks were dangerous.
   Althea's flaw in logic is an example of
   A. ad hominem attack   B. faulty deduction
   C. faulty induction   D. a logical fallacy

Questions 7-11.

DIRECTIONS: Questions 7 through 11 are to be answered on the basis of the following passage.

The Collective Unconscious, Karl Jung

The collective unconscious is a part of the psyche which can be negatively distinguished from a personal unconscious by the fact that it does not, like the latter, owe its existence to personal experience and consequently is not a personal acquisition.(1) While the personal unconscious is made up essentially of contents which have at one time been conscious but which have disappeared from consciousness, and therefore have never been individually acquired, but owe their existence exclusively to heredity.(2) Whereas the personal unconscious consists for the most part of complexes, the content of the collective unconscious is made up essentially of archetypes.(3)

7. The effect of this passage relies MAINLY on the use of
   A. definition   B. narration   C. analogy   D. metaphor

8. This passage is BEST characterized as
   A. psychological   B. narrative   C. persuasive   D. analytical

9. In sentence 1, the word *acquisition* is BEST replaced by
   A. accomplishment   B. attainment
   C. possession   D. means

10. *While the personal unconscious is made up essentially of contents which have at one time been conscious.*
    The above excerpt from sentence 2 is an example of which of the following?
    A. Noun phrase   B. Parallel construction
    C. Subordinate clause   D. Independent clause

11. Which of the following BEST describes the primary difference between the personal and the collective unconscious?
    A. The personal unconscious is based on individual experience while the collective unconscious is not.
    B. The collective unconscious is based on individual experience while the personal unconscious is not.
    C. The collective unconscious is beyond human understanding, whereas the personal unconscious is within the bounds of human understanding.
    D. The personal unconscious is unreliable, whereas the collective unconscious is reliable.

12. *Following its discovery in 1492, the New World's exploration includes in its history many stories of ambitious, sometimes greedy explorers who exploited the new land and its people in order to achieve wealth and fame.(1) Pizarro's harshness is perhaps best illustrated by his treatment of Atahualpa, emperor of*

the Incan empire.(2) The Incas were a native civilization that ranged over most of western South America, and were known for their sophisticated technology, roads, and architecture.(3)

Which of the following would be the MOST suitable sentence to insert immediately after sentence 2 in the above paragraph?
- A. Beginning in 1531 with fewer than two hundred men, Pizarro took less than two years to conquer the Incas and capture Atahualpa at his palace in the city of Cuzco.
- B. As it turned out, the Incan empire contained enough gold to fill many rooms.
- C. Pizarro made many enemies during the years of his brutal career.
- D. Of all these men, one of the most ruthless and coldblooded was Francisco Pizarro, the Spanish conquistador.

13. *The name "Piltdown Man" refers to a skull, unearthed from the English countryside, that was brought before the London Geological Society in 1912.(1) This unusual size and shape led many scientists to proclaim the skull was hard evidence of the common ancestry of apes and humans, and the skull was placed in the British Museum.(2)*

    Which of the following would be the MOST suitable sentence to insert immediately after <u>sentence 1</u> in the above paragraph?
    - A. In an effort to fool the world's scientists, somebody had buried a human skull with an ape's jawbone, and pulled off a practical joke that lasted more than forty years.
    - B. The skull had a large cranium, which suggested a brain like a human's, but its jawbone was unusually long and heavy, with pronounced canine teeth.
    - C. It wasn't until many years after the skull's discovery that a few skeptics were able to prove what they had long suspected Piltdown Man was a fake.
    - D. The presenter was Sir Edmund Georges, a prominent English geologist.

14. *It seems appropriate, then, that ketchup, a sauce made from tomatoes, has become a sort of All-American addition to foods such as hot dogs and hamburgers. In spite of the tomato's origin, however, ketchup isn't even close to being All-American.*

    Which of the following would be the MOST suitable to insert at the <u>beginning</u> of the above paragraph?
    - A. Tomatoes originated in North America, and were cultivated for centuries by natives before becoming popular in other parts of the world.
    - B. Ketchup is believed to have come from a Malaysian pickled fish sauce called "kechap" and a similar Chinese sauce called "ke-tsiap."
    - C. Tomatoes have a diverse history and origin.
    - D. Nobody knows for sure, but it is assumed that these sauces made the immigration from the Far East to America and were eventually changed into what we now call ketchup.

15. *Because the temperature during atmospheric re-entry is so incredibly hot, it took NASA's engineers some time to find a substance capable of protecting the shuttles. Eventually, the engineers were led to a material that is as old as our most ancient civilizations—glass.*
Which of the following would be the MOST suitable to insert at the beginning of the above paragraph?
   A. One of the most easily manipulated substances on earth, glass can be made into ceramic tiles that are composed of over 90% air.
   B. These ceramic tiles are such effective insulators that when a tile emerges from the oven in which it was fired, it can be held safely in a person's hand.
   C. NASA's space shuttles are the first spacecraft ever designed to leave and re-enter the Earth's atmosphere while remaining intact.
   D. NASA astronauts require protection from the heat generated by re-entering the Earth's atmosphere.

Questions 16-20.

DIRECTIONS: Questions 16 through 20 are to be answered on the basis of the following passage.

A Bend in the Road, Colin Fletcher

When we contemplate such rents in the fabric as Los Angeles and the Love Canal, Beirut, and Chernobyl, Ethiopia and the East Bronx, most of us tend to bleat about politicians or multi-nationals or drug cartels or other handy breeds of "them."(1) Indictments of this kind are easy and exculpating and slightly titillating; but perhaps we should be looking closer to home.(3)

16. In sentence 1, the word *rents* is BEST replaced by
    A. upheavals   B. mistakes   C. rips   D. surprises

17. *…as Los Angeles and the Love Canal, Beirut and Chernobyl, Ethiopia and the East Bronx…*
The above excerpt, from sentence 2, is an example of which of the following?
    A. Parallel construction   B. An independent clause
    C. A dependent clause   D. Coordinate clauses

18. In the context of this passage, the word *bleat*, in sentence 1, is BEST characterized as
    A. academic   B. technical   C. poetic   D. colloqial

19. This passage is BEST characterized as which of the following?
    A. Poetic   B. Expository   C. Narrative   D. Persuasive

20. In sentence 1, the MAIN verb is
    A. rents   B. contemplate   C. tend   D. bleat

21. *Archimedes, the ancient Greek scientist, once used the exclamation "Eureka (I have found it)!" in such dramatic fashion that it is still part of the English language today.(1) Archimedes' benefactor, Hiero, wanted to know if his crown was made of pure gold or had been diluted with an amount of silver, and he assigned Archimedes the problem.(2)*
    Which of the following would be MOST suitable to insert after sentence 2 in the above paragraph?
    - A. He knew that gold and silver had different densities, and that pieces of gold and silver that weighed the same would displace different amounts of water.
    - B. Archimedes was thinking about the problem when he stepped into his bathtub, and some of the water overflowed, giving him inspiration he needed to find a solution.
    - C. When he realized he could use this principle to answer Hiero's question, he ran into the streets shouting, "Eureka!" without remembering to put on his clothes.
    - D. Archimedes was a very successful scientist in his time.

21.____

22. *Many white Americans, who then dictated the tastes of society, were wary of music that was played almost exclusively in black clubs in the poorer sections of cities and towns. However, jazz didn't take long to develop from early ragtime melodies into more complex, sophisticated forms, such as Charlie Parker's "bebop" style of jazz.*
    Which of the following would be MOST suitable to insert at the beginning of the above paragraph?
    - A. After charismatic band leaders such as Duke Ellington and Count Basie brought jazz to a larger audience, white audiences began to accept and even to enjoy the new American art form.
    - B. Soon, by the 1940's, jazz was the most popular type of music among American intellectuals and college students.
    - C. Jazz soon developed into very complicated and sophisticated forms.
    - D. In the early days of jazz, it was considered "lowdown" music, or music that was played only in rough, disreputable bars and taverns.

22.____

23. *The computer technology known as virtual reality, now in its very first stages of development, is already revolutionizing some aspects of contemporary life.(1) No more than a computer program that is designed to build and display graphic images, the virtual reality program takes graphic programs a step further by sensing a person's head and body movements.(2)*
    Which of the above would be MOST suitable to insert after sentence 2 in the above paragraph?
    - A. A virtual reality program responds to these movements by adjusting the images that a person sees on a screen or through goggles, creating an "interactive" world.
    - B. Plastic surgeons have already begun to use virtual reality to map out the complex nerve and tissue structures of a particular patient's face, in order to prepare for delicate surgery.

23.____

C. This ability to sense real movement is truly revolutionary.
D. Virtual reality computers are also being used by the space program, most recently to simulate conditions for the astronauts who were launched on a repair mission to the Hubble telescope.

24. *The macaws of South America are not only among the largest and most beautifully colored of the world's flying birds, but they are also one of the smartest.(1) For example, all macaws flock to riverbanks at certain times of the year to eat the clay that is found in river mud.(2)*
Which of the following would be MOST suitable to insert <u>after sentence 1</u> in the above paragraph?
    A. Though uncertain of the definite reasons for this behavior, scientists believe the birds digest the clay in order to counteract toxins contained in the seeds of certain fruits that are eaten by macaws.
    B. The macaw's intelligence has led to intense study by scientists, who have discovered some macaw behaviors that have not yet been explained.
    C. It is believed that macaws are forced to resort to these toxic fruits during the dry season, when foods are more scarce.
    D. Scientists have studied their intelligence for many years.

24.____

25. *Because they were some of the first explorers to venture into the western frontier of North America, the French were responsible for the naming of several native tribes. Perhaps the most poorly-conceived French name for an Indian tribe is Eskimo, the name for the natives of the far North which translates roughly as "eaters of raw flesh."*
Which of the following would be MOST suitable for concluding the above paragraph?
    A. Some of these names were actually just nicknames that stuck; the Gros Ventre ("Big Bellies") and Nez Perce ("Pierced Noses") were two of the large tribes that were named in this way.
    B. A smaller tribe, the Sans Arcs ("No Bows") were so named because the French believed the tribe had not yet discovered the bow and arrow.
    C. The French explorers enjoyed granting French names to people and places they had discovered.
    D. The name is incorrect; these people have always cooked their fish and game, and they now call themselves the Inuit, a native term that means "the people."

25.____

KEY (CORRECT ANSWERS)

1.	C		11.	A
2.	B		12.	D
3.	D		13.	B
4.	A		14.	A
5.	C		15.	C
6.	B		16.	C
7.	A		17.	A
8.	D		18.	D
9.	B		19.	B
10.	C		20.	C

21. B
22. D
23. A
24. B
25. D

EXAMINATION SECTION
TEST 1

DIRECTIONS: Each question or incomplete statement is followed by several suggested answers or completions. Select the one that BEST answers the question or completes the statement. *PRINT THE LETTER OF THE CORRECT ANSWER IN THE SPACE AT THE RIGHT.*

Questions 1-14.

DIRECTIONS: Questions 1 through 14 are to be answered on the basis of the following passage. Read the passage carefully before you choose your answers.

    The Sunday morning service began when Brother Elisha sat down at the piano and raised a song. This moment and this music had been with John, so it seemed, since he had first drawn breath. It seemed that there had never been a time when he had not known this moment of waiting while the packed church paused—the sisters in white,
(5) heads raised, the brothers in blue, heads back; the white caps of the women seeming to glow in the charged air like crowns, the kinky, gleaming heads of the men seeming to be lifted up—and the rustling and the whispering ceased and the children were quiet; perhaps someone coughed, or the sound of a car horn, or a curse from the streets came in; then Elisha hit the keys, beginning at once to sing, and everybody joined him, clapping their
(10) hands, and rising, and beating the tambourines.
    The song might be: *Down at the cross where my Saviour died!*
    Or: *Jesus, I'll never forget how you set me free!*
    Or: *Lord, hold my hand while I run this race!*
    They sang with all the strength that was in them, and clapped their hands for joy.
(15)   There had never been a time when John had not sat watching the saints rejoice with terror in his heart, and wonder. Their singing caused him to believe in the presence of the Lord; indeed it was no longer a question of belief, because they made that presence real. He did not feel it himself, the joy they felt, yet he could not doubt that it was, for them, the very bread of life—could not doubt it, that is, until it was too late to doubt. Something
(20) happened to their faces and their voices, the rhythm of their bodies, and to the air they breathed; it was as though wherever they might be became the upper room, and the Holy Ghost were riding on the air. His father's face, always awful, became more awful now; his father's daily anger was transformed into prophetic wrath. His mother, her eyes raised to heaven, hands arced before her, moving, made real for John that patience, that
(25) endurance, that long suffering, which he had read of in the Bible and found so hard to imagine.
    On Sunday mornings the women all seemed patient, all the men seemed mighty. While John watched, the Power struck someone, a man or woman; they cried out, a long, wordless crying, and, arms outstretched like wings, they began the Shout. Someone
(30) moved a chair a little to give them room, the rhythm paused, the singing stopped, only the pounding feet and the clapping hands were heard; then another cry, another dancer; then the tambourines began again, and the voices rose again, and the music swept on again, like fire, or flood, or judgment. Then the church seemed to swell with the Power it held,

2 (#1)

and, like a planet rocking in space, the temple rocked with the Power of God. John
(35) watched, watched the faces, and the weightless bodies, and listened to the timeless cries.
One day, so everyone said, this Power would possess him; he would sing and cry as they
did now, and dance before his King.

1. The passage is PRIMARILY concerned with   1.____
    A. John's attitude toward the Sunday service
    B. John's theories about the power of the Lord
    C. the impact of music on John's church
    D. John's relationship with his parents
    E. the role of John's church in his future

2. In lines 7-8, the effect of the words *perhaps someone coughed, or the sound of*   2.____
   a car horn, or a curse from the streets came in is to
    A. retard the tempo of the speaker's prose
    B. satirize the faith of the churchgoers
    C. highlight the distractions that spoil the audience's concentration
    D. change, for a moment, the point of view of the speaker
    E. emphasize, by contrast, the hushed silence in the church

3. The effect produced by the repetition of the phrase *there had never been a time*   3.____
   when in lines 3 and 15 is that it
    A. signals to the reader that attending church is an unpleasant event for
       John
    B. emphasizes how vague John's memory of his youth is
    C. establishes the contrast between John's past and future
    D. emphasizes the persuasiveness of the Sunday service in John's memory
    E. alerts the reader to John's naïveté

4. It can be inferred from the phrase *with terror in his heart, and wonder* (lines 15-16)   4.____
   that John
    A. dreaded attending church services on Sundays
    B. responded strongly but ambivalently to the church service
    C. found the music in the church mystifying and unpleasant
    D. was indifferent to the emotional force that lay behind the singing
    E. was disturbed by the insincerity of those singing

5. In line 18, the pronoun *it* in the phrase *it was, for them* refers to   5.____
    A. *wonder* (line 16)   B. *singing* (line 16)
    C. *question* (line 17)   D. *joy they felt* (line 18)
    E. *bread of life* (line 19)

6. In the narrative progress of the passage, the specific function of the depiction   6.____
   of John's father's *prophetic wrath* and his mother's *long suffering* (lines 23-25)
   is that it
    A. diverts the reader's attention from John's point of view
    B. retards the pace of the narration prior to the climax

C. provides a specific example of a preceding general description
D. counters earlier references to the demeanor of the congregation
E. offers a parallel to the transformation John undergoes in the passage

7. In context, *the saints* (line 15), *bread of life* (line 19), and *arms outstretched like wings* (line 29) serve to
   A. evoke an otherworldly atmosphere resonant of the Bible
   B. situate the passage within a socially conservative framework
   C. highlight the bitter, sardonic humor of the passage
   D. mask the passage's truly secular emphasis
   E. endorse a particular approach to spiritual matters

8. The qualifiers *for them* (line 18) and *so everyone said* (line 36) suggest that
   A. John is confident that he will replace his doubt with joy and ecstasy
   B. John shares the experience of those around him sympathetically
   C. John feels himself to be isolated from the rest of the congregation
   D. the speaker views the congregation as the ultimate authority over John
   E. the speaker is more interested in the experience of the congregation than in that of John

9. The image of a *planet rocking in space* (line 34) suggests all of the following EXCEPT the
   A. energy generated by the worshippers
   B. power of God in the heavens
   C. swaying of the congregation to the music
   D. cohesiveness and unity of the congregation
   E. despair of those who are bound to earth

10. The attention the speaker pays to the details of sound serves PRIMARILY to
    A. distract the reader from the disconcerting issues raised in the passage
    B. offer the reader a physical sense of the church service
    C. construct a metaphor for John's position in the congregation
    D. entertain the reader prior to the presentation of more challenging material
    E. complement the attention paid to the visual and the tactile

11. The style of the passage as a whole is characterized by
    A. simple declarative sentences containing a minimum of descriptive language
    B. complex sentences interspersed with short, exclamatory sentences
    C. sentences that contain several modifying phrases and subordinate clauses
    D. sentences that grow progressively more argumentative as the passage continues
    E. expository sentences at the beginning that give way to interpretive sentences at the end

12. The irony in the passage as a whole rests CHIEFLY on the conflict between
    A. the solemnity of the occasion and the joy of the worshippers
    B. John's father's prophetic wrath and his mother's long suffering
    C. the air of expectancy prior to the morning service and the sounds from the street
    D. John's acute observation of religious ecstasy and his inability to participate in it
    E. the change that takes place in the churchgoers on Sunday and their daily appearance and demeanor

13. The point of view in the passage is that of a
    A. participating observer who is partial to John
    B. third-person narrative who is aware of John's thoughts
    C. nonparticipating spectator who is unfamiliar with John's thoughts
    D. first-person narrator who chooses to speak of himself in the third person
    E. third-person narrator who provides insight into the thoughts of several characters

14. The effect of the repetition of the words *seeming* and *seemed* throughout the passage is that it
    A. serves to emphasize John's particular, individual perspective on the events described
    B. functions as a reminder to the reader that the speaker is only telling a story
    C. suggests that John's memory of the events described is vague and indistinct
    D. provides support for the extended allegory developed in the passage
    E. highlights the speaker's capacities as an omniscient narrator

Questions 15-28.

DIRECTIONS: Questions 15 through 28 are to be answered on the basis of the following poem. Read the poem carefully before you choose your answers

My Picture

Here, take my likeness with you, whilst 'tis so;
    For when from hence you go,
    The next sun's rising will behold
    Me pale, and lean, and old.
(5)   The man who did this picture draw
Will swear next day my face he never saw.

I really believe, within a while,
    If you upon this shadow smile,
    Your presence will such vigour give,

(10)   (Your presence which makes all things live)
        And absence so much alter me,
    This will the substance, I the shadow be.

    When from your well-wrought cabinet you take it,
        And your bright looks awake it;
(15)   Ah, be not frighted, if you see,
        The new-soul'd picture gaze on thee,
        And hear it breathe a sigh or two;
    For those are the first things that it will do.

    My rival-image will be then thought blest,
(20)   And laugh at me as dispossessed;
        But thou, who (if I know thee right)
        I'th' substance does not much delight,
        Wilt rather send again for me,
    Who then shall but my picture's picture be.

15. The poem dramatizes the moment when the speaker
    A. perceives the sun rising on his beloved
    B. has to depart from his beloved
    C. receives a commissioned portrait of himself
    D. meditates on his beloved's present activities
    E. faces the imminent departure of his beloved

16. The poem contains a(n)
    I. extended metaphor
    II. lover's self-incrimination
    III. compliment to the poet's beloved
    The CORRECT answer is:
    A. I only   B. I, II   C. I, III   D. II, III   E. I, II, III

17. In the context of the poem, the phrase *whilst 'tis so* (line 1) is BEST paraphrased as while
    A. things are so between us   B. it is necessary that we be apart
    C. art abides unchanged   D. I am still like the picture
    E. you spend your time thus

18. Which of the following pairs of words refers to different entities?
    A. *likeness* (line 1) and *picture* (line 5)
    B. *shadow* (line 8) and *shadow* (line 12)
    C. *presence* (line 9) and *presence* (line 10)
    D. *picture* (line 15) and *it* (line 18)
    E. *me* (line 23) and *picture* (line 24)

19. When the speaker says the artist will deny ever having seen him (lines 5-6), he means that
    A. no one would wish to be associated with someone so broken by age
    B. not even the artist's precise knowledge of him could detect any likeness
    C. the picture was drawn with no knowledge of the speaker
    D. no one was available to receive the picture when it was finished
    E. the portrait was a likeness in every respect but facial features

20. A PRINCIPAL purpose of the use of shadow (line 12) is to
    A. foreshadow the departure of the speaker
    B. emphasize the disintegration of the picture
    C. serve as a balance for the use of *presence* (lines 9-10)
    D. compensate for the negative connotation of *absence* (line 11)
    E. contrast with the meaning of *substance* (line 12)

21. In the context of the poem, the expression *bright looks* (line 14) is BEST interpreted to mean
    A. curious scrutiny and haughty appearance
    B. flirtatious glances and downcast eyes
    C. affectionate interest and personal beauty
    D. tearful observation and wise aspect
    E. intelligent inquiry and longing face

22. Lines 14-17 describe an example of
    A. animation   B. convalescence   C. maternal pride
    D. stolen pleasures   E. spiritual devotion

23. In line 21, *I know thee right* is BEST paraphrased as
    A. you are as loyal as you should be
    B. my understanding of your feelings is correct
    C. I recognize your importance in my life
    D. your sense of propriety is the same as mine
    E. I tell you honestly of my love

24. By the expression *but my picture's picture be* (line 24), the speaker means that he will have
    A. proved that the picture does indeed represent him
    B. moved toward the perfection of the picture
    C. made himself a perfect replica of the picture
    D. improved his looks substantially over those of the picture
    E. declined in vitality so that he is more lifeless than a picture

25. Which of the following pairs of phrases MOST probably refers to the same moment in the sequence of events in the poem?
    A. *whilst* (line 1); *next sun's rising* (line 3)
    B. *when* (line 2); *next day* (line 6)
    C. *within a while* (line 7); *When* (line 13)
    D. *first* (line 18); *again* (line 23)
    E. *then* (line 19); *then* (line 24)

25.____

26. In the final stanza, the speaker anticipates
    A. the triumph of his rival
    B. new freedom from the necessity to care for his appearance
    C. his beloved's preference for the insubstantial
    D. his willingness to laugh with his beloved at the change in himself
    E. the repossession of youthful good looks as an effect of his beloved's presence

26.____

27. Which of the following is LEAST important to the theme of the poem?
    A. *pale* (line 4)
    B. *smile* (line 8)
    C. *vigour* (line 9)
    D. *well-wrought* (line 13)
    E. *delight* (line 22)

27.____

28. The tone throughout the poem is BEST described as one of
    A. playful seriousness
    B. ironic grimness
    C. cheerful glee
    D. somber melancholy
    E. irreversible despair

28.____

Questions 29-40.

DIRECTIONS: Questions 29 through 40 are to be answered on the basis of the following passage. Read the passage carefully before you choose your answers.

    If mere parsimony would have made a man rich, Sir Pitt Crawley might have become very wealthy—if he had been an attorney in a country town, with no capital but his brains, it is very possible that he would have turned them to good account, and might have achieved for himself a very considerable influence and competency. But he was unluckily
(5) endowed with a good name and a large though encumbered estate, both of which went rather to injure than to advance him. He had a taste for law, which cost him any thousands yearly; and being a great deal too clever to be robbed, as he said, by any single agent, allowed his affairs to be mismanaged by a dozen, whom he all equally mistrusted. He was such a sharp landlord, that he could hardly find any but bankrupt tenants; and
(10) such a close farmer, as to grudge almost the seed to the ground, whereupon revengeful Nature grudged him the crops which she granted to more liberal husbandmen. He speculated in every possible way; he worked mines; bought canal-shares; horsed coaches; took government contracts, and was the busiest man and magistrate of his county. As he would not pay honest agents at his granite-quarry, he had the satisfaction
(15) of finding that four overseers ran away, and took fortunes with them to America. For want of proper precautions, his coal-mines filled with water: the government flung his contract of damaged beef upon his hands: and for his coach-horses, every mail proprietor in the

kingdom knew that he lost more horses than any man in the country, from under-feeding and buying cheap. In disposition he was sociable, and far from being proud; nay, he
(20) rather preferred the society of a farmer or a horse-dealer to that of a gentleman, like my Lord, his son: he was fond of drink, of swearing, of joking with the farmers' daughters: he was never known to give away a shilling or to do a good action, but was of a pleasant, sly, laughing mood, and would cut his joke, and drink his glass with a tenant and sell him up the next day; or have his laugh with the poacher he was transporting with equal good
(25) humour. His politeness for the fair sex has already been hinted at by Miss Rebecca Sharp—in a word, the whole baron-etage, peerage, commonage of England, did not contain a more cunning, mean, selfish, foolish, disreputable old man. That blood-red hand of Sir Pitt would be in anybody's pocket except his own; and it is with grief and pain that as admirers of the British aristocracy, we find ourselves obliged to admit the existence of so
(30) many ill qualities in a person whose name is in Debrett.
   One great cause why Mr. Crawleye had such a hold over the affections of his father, resulted from money arrangements. The Baronet owed his son a sum of money out of the jointure of his mother, which he did not find it convenient to pay; indeed he had an almost invincible repugnance to paying anybody, and could only be brought by force to discharge
(35) his debts. Miss Sharp calculated (for she became, as we shall hear speedily, inducted into most of the secrets of the family) that the mere payment of his creditors cost the honourable Baronet several hundreds yearly; but this was a delight he could not forego; he had a savage pleasure in making the poor wretches wait, and in shifting from court to court and from term to term the period of satisfaction. What's the good of being in Parliament,
(40) he said, if you must pay your debts? Hence, indeed, his position as a senator was not a little useful to him.

29. Which of the following descriptions is an example of the narrator's irony?
    A. *he was unluckily endowed with a good name* (lines 4-5)
    B. *grudge almost the seed to the ground* (line 10)
    C. *He speculated in every possible way* (lines 11-12)
    D. *his coal-mines filled with water* (line 16)
    E. *the government flung his contract of damaged beef upon his hands* (lines 16-17)

30. Which of the following phrases MOST pointedly refers to Sir Pitt's parsimonious character?
    A. *a very considerable influence and competency* (line 4)
    B. *a great deal too clever to be robbed* (line 7)
    C. *allowed his affairs to be mismanaged by a dozen* (line 8)
    D. *far from being proud* (line 19)
    E. *invincible repugnance to paying anybody* (line 34)

31. In context, the adjective *close* (line 10) is BEST interpreted as meaning
    A. strict and rigorous
    B. secretive and reclusive
    C. overly cautious in spending
    D. restricted to a privileged class
    E. accurate and precise

32. The use of the word *satisfaction* in line 14 is an example of a(n)
    A. exaggerated description of a trivial event in Sir Pitt's life
    B. ironic reference to the price Sir Pitt had to pay for his business mismanagement
    C. euphemism for Sir Pit's words of anger
    D. allusion to Sir Pitt's ambivalent reaction to financial failures
    E. suggestion that Sir Pitt perversely tool delight in discovering the defection of his overseers

33. In the context of the sentence, the phrases *pleasant, sly, laughing mood* (lines 22-23) and *good humour* (lines 24-25) are used to show Sir Pitt's
    A. haughty condescension to members of a lower social class
    B. uninhibited passions and misguided optimism
    C. desire to instill a democratic sensibility in his son
    D. awkwardness in the execution of his responsibilities as a landlord
    E. duplicity and capacity for treachery

34. Which of the following terms is(are) meant to be taken ironically?
    I. *honourable* (line 37)   II. *delight* (line 37)
    III. *pleasure* (line 38)
    The CORRECT answer is:
    A. I only   B. II only   C. III only   D. I, II   E. I, II, III

35. The passage suggests that, as a member of Parliament, Sir Pitt was
    A. competent and respected by his colleagues
    B. devoted to the interests of country gentlemen like himself
    C. a servant of the cause of the British aristocracy
    D. inadequately compensated
    E. using his position for selfish ends

36. In his relationship with his son, Sir Pitt
    A. is devoted to his son only out of a sense of moral obligation to his son's mother
    B. makes a display of loving his son because of the debt he owes his son
    C. pretends to cherish his son because he has designs on his son's inheritance
    D. is unwilling to accept and provide for his son because of the personal grudge he holds against his son's mother
    E. treats his son with disdain because he is jealous of the estate his son has inherited

37. The effect of the last paragraph is that it
    A. illustrates how Sir Pitt's political and family affairs reflect his character
    B. counters speculations about Sir Pitt's character
    C. shows how Sir Pitt's shortcomings are beneficial to his political career
    D. introduces Miss Sharp's role as an observer of Sir Pitt's actions
    E. suggests the causes of Sir Pitt's moral transformation

38. The narrator attributes Sir Pitt's attitude and behavior to which of the following factors?   38.____
   A. Lack of formal education
   B. Absence of religious beliefs
   C. Traits of his ancestors
   D. Social rank and flawed character
   E. Unsuccessful marriage and unprofitable projects

39. The style of the passage as a whole can be BEST characterized as   39.____
   A. humorless and pedantic
   B. effusive and subjective
   C. descriptive and metaphorical
   D. terse and epigrammatic
   E. witty and analytical

40. The narrator's attitude toward Sir Pitt can be BEST described as one of   40.____
   A. pity
   B. objectivity
   C. sardonic condemnation
   D. emotional judgment
   E. jaded disgust

Questions 44-55.

DIRECTIONS: Questions 44 through 55 are to be answered on the basis of the following poem. Read the poem carefully before you choose your answers.

A Whippoorwill in the Woods

Night after night, it was very nearly enough.
they said, to drive you crazy: a whippoorwill
in the wood repeating itself like a stuck groove
of an LP with a defect, and no way possible
(5) of turning the thing off.

And night after night, they said, in the insomniac
small hours the whipsawing voice of obsession
would have come in closer, the way a sick
thing does when it's done for—or maybe the reason
(10) was nothing more melodramatic

than a night-flying congregation of moths, lured in
in their turn by house-glow, the strange heat
of it—imagine the nebular dangerousness, if one
were a moth, the dark pockmarked with beaks, the great
(15) dim shapes, the bright extinction—

if moths are indeed, after all, what a whippoorwill
favors. Who knows? Anyhow, from one point of view
insects are to be seen as an ailment, moths above all:
the filmed-over, innumerable nodes of spun-out tissue
(20) untidying the trees, the larval

spew of such hairy hordes, one wonders what use
they can be other than as a guarantee no bird
goes hungry. We're like that. The webbiness,
the gregariousness of the many are what we can't abide.
(25) We single out for notice

above all what's disjunct, the way birds are,
with their unhooked-up, cheekily anarchic
dartings and flashings, their uncalled-for color—
the indelible look of the rose-breasted grosbeak
(30) an aunt of mine, a notice

of such things before the noticing had or needed
a name, drew my five-year-old attention up to, in
the green deeps of a maple. She never married,
believed her cat had learned to leave birds alone,
(35) and for years, node after node,

by lingering degrees she made way within for
what wasn't so much a thing as it was a system,
a webwork of error that throve until it killed her.
What is health? We must all die sometime.
(40) Whatever it is out there

in the woods, that begins to seem like
a species of madness, we survive as we can:
the hooked-up, the humdrum, the brief, tragic
wonder of being at all. The whippoorwill out in
(45) the woods, for me, brought back

as by a relay, from a place at such a distance
no recollection now in place could reach so far,
the memory of a memory she told me of once:
of how her father, my grandfather, by whatever
(50) now unfathomable happenstance,

carried her (she might have been five) into the breathing night.
"Listen!" she said he'd said. "Did you hear it?
That was a whippoorwill." And she (and I) never forgot.

41. In the first stanza, the whippoorwill is presented CHIEFLY as a(n)   41.____
    A. kind of poet   B. symbol of death   C. emblem of freedom
    D. annoyance   E. messenger

12 (#1)

42. The whippoorwill is MOST probably called a *voice of obsession* (line 7) because it
    A. has a shrill cry
    B. repeats itself
    C. is invisible
    D. constantly tries to come nearer
    E. is probably sick

43. How many reasons does the speaker give to try to explain why the whippoorwill *would have come in closer* (line 8)?
    A. One   B. Two   C. Three   D. Four   E. Five

44. The speaker hypothesizes that moths might be
    A. bent on self-destruction
    B. dangerous to whippoorwills
    C. more like human beings than whippoorwills are
    D. heroic actors in a tragic drama
    E. food for whippoorwills

45. The diction used to describe moths in lines 19-21 suggests that
    A. science is slowly beginning to understand certain mysteries
    B. the speaker finds some aspects of nature alien to her
    C. nature is able to provide a truly tragic spectacle
    D. nature is governed by a higher power
    E. the beauty of nature is a source of comfort to the speaker

46. In line 26, *what's disjunct* refers to something that
    A. cannot be seen by most observers
    B. stands outside the purely natural world
    C. is broken and fragmented
    D. faces a constant threat of extinction
    E. is not incorporated in a larger entity

47. The object of *to* in line 32 is
    A. *look* (line 29)   B. *aunt* (line 30)   C. *things* (line 31)
    D. *name* (line 32)   E. *deeps* (line 33)

48. For the speaker, the rose-breasted grosbeak and the whippoorwill are similar in that they both
    A. have the ability to disturb people's sleep
    B. feed principally on moths
    C. stand out as individuals amid their surroundings
    D. symbolize the individuality of the speaker
    E. are natural creatures that seem to violate the laws of nature

49. In line 34, the speaker implies that the aunt
    A. had lived most of her life fearing natural disaster
    B. was curious about scientific information that dealt with nature

13 (#1)

C. understood nature better than the speaker
D. preferred not to face certain realities about nature
E. was largely indifferent to her natural surroundings

50. In line 39, the cause of the aunt's death is described in language MOST similar to that used by the speaker to describe
    A. cats   B. birds   C. moths
    D. the whippoorwill   E. the grandfather

51. In the poem as a whole, the speaker views nature as being essentially
    A. inspiring   B. comforting   C. unfathomable
    D. vicious   E. benign

52. The speaker makes a categorical assertion at all of the following places in the poem EXCEPT lines
    A. 1-2   B. 17-8   C. 23-24   D. 25-26   E. 40-43

53. Of the following, line _____ contains an example of personification.
    A. 33   B. 39   C. 43   D. 48   E. 51

54. Lines 44-53 have all of the following functions EXCEPT to
    A. return to the initial subject of the poem
    B. illustrate the influence of childhood experience
    C. link the present to the past
    D. emphasize the chaotic quality of natural events
    E. evoke a family relationship

55. The grandfather's words (lines 52-53) convey a sense of
    A. regret   B. awe   C. tragedy   D. hope   E. danger

KEY (CORRECT ANSWERS)

1.	A	11.	C	21.	C	31.	C	41.	D	51.	C
2.	E	12.	D	22.	A	32.	B	42.	B	52.	A
3.	D	13.	B	23.	B	33.	E	43.	B	53.	E
4.	B	14.	A	24.	E	34.	D	44.	E	54.	D
5.	D	15.	E	25.	C	35.	E	45.	B	55.	B
6.	C	16.	C	26.	C	36.	B	46.	E		
7.	A	17.	D	27.	D	37.	A	47.	A		
8.	C	18.	B	28.	A	38.	D	48.	C		
9.	E	19.	B	29.	A	39.	E	49.	D		
10.	B	20.	E	30.	E	40.	C	50.	C		

ESSAY WRITING

THE WRITING PROCESS

Under ideal conditions, writing involves a series of steps:

1. Pre-writing activities which facilitate understanding the purpose and the audience for a particular piece of writing and which might include generating ideas through brainstorming, notes, reflection, research, or discussion;

2. Focusing the material generated in step one by framing a thesis (controlling idea) and a direction (organization);

3. Getting the first draft on paper, using standard grammar, correct mechanics, and accurate spelling;

4. Assessing the success of the first draft by yourself or in consultation with a reliable reader;

5. Revising the draft by clarifying the thesis, topic sentences, supporting detail, and word choice; and

6. Proofreading for mistakes in grammar and spelling.

Ideal conditions do not always exist in the real world. Often you have to write under pressure and produce a clear statement. This is the case in a test situation. You must streamline the writing process to compose an acceptable essay in approximately one hour. This section will help you to practice necessary strategies by describing how you might do the following:

1. Turn the directions into a purpose statement.
2. Brainstorm for material to put in the essay.
3. Group and focus your ideas.
4. Compose your essay with clear signals for the reader.
5. Proofread for word choice, grammar, and mechanics.

TURN DIRECTIONS INTO PURPOSE STATEMENTS

For each of the following sets of essays, the directions specify a topic, an audience, and some possible ways to develop the essay. You have some choice about how to develop the essay, but you must stick to the topic given and a style appropriate to the audience. The directions consist of four sentences which give

1. an indication of audience,
2. a description of audience,
3. suggestions for development, and
4. a restatement of the topic.

You can distinguish the sentences that suggest development because they contain words which give options rather than commands; for example, the sentences that give you commands about the topic will look like this:

In writing, tell the panel why you are considering teaching as a career.

On the other hand, sentences that suggest development will look like this:
The reasons may include...
You might want to consider...
The experiences could be...

Your first step, then, is to sort out the essential commands in the directions and convert them into a clear purpose statement such as *I will explain my reasons for choosing teaching as a career.* The purpose statement must cover all the essential parts of the assignment.

EXERCISE B

For each of the following sets of directions, underline the sentences that give you commands about the topic and write a purpose statement, using your own words if possible.

Prompt 1
A committee of teachers and administrators is reviewing your qualifications for a scholarship. In writing, tell the committee about a special activity you engage in, either in school or outside of school. It could be a job, an organization you belong to, a hobby or sport you participate in, or something you do with your family. Tell the committee what your special activity is and explain why this activity is important to you.

Prompt 2
A superintendent of schools has reviewed your application for a teaching position. Before holding a formal interview with you, the superintendent wants you to provide a writing sample that tells what motivated you to choose teaching as a profession. You might want to discuss a special learning experience you had or your interest in a chosen field or subject. Tell the superintendent what your motivation is and explain why your learning experience or your interest in a special field or subject is important to you.

Prompt 3
Your college advisor has just notified you that the college has instituted an open curriculum. As a result, you may choose any three courses or activities you wish to take next semester. You will be given equal course credit for academic subjects and activities such as sports, cultural

activities (music, theater, art), school newspaper or literary magazine activities, fraternities, sororities, community projects, or any other activity whose importance you can justify. In writing, indicate what three courses you would select and how each one would make you a better person.

Prompt 4
You have just been given the opportunity to write a letter of application to the Director of Admissions at the college of your choice. Imagine that cost is not a concern to you; you may choose a college that offers a traditional liberal arts curriculum or one that allows you to study only those courses that relate to your field of interest. In your essay, tell the Director of Admissions the type of college you are choosing and identify the reasons for your choice.

Prompt 5
A committee of teachers is reviewing your application for admission into the teacher education program of your choice. The committee has asked you to write an essay that describes a book that made the most lasting impression on you or from which you believe you learned some valuable lesson. The book may be on any subject, fiction or nonfiction, that is meaningful to you. The book need not be something you read for a course. Explain to the committee what your impression or lesson is and why it is important to you.

BRAINSTORM FOR MATERIAL TO PUT IN THE ESSAY

The directions on the subtest often contains suggestions for areas to explore. The sample directions which ask for an essay on your reasons for choosing a teaching career suggest that you consider *examples set by other people, benefits you expect from a teaching career, or the challenges you think teaching offers.* Remember that these suggestions are only suggestions. Before you respond to them, you should think about how you would accomplish the writing task if the suggestions had not been made. To be convincing, the material in your essay must come from your own experiences and knowledge. Brainstorming can help you accomplish this.

There are different ways to brainstorm. Some people prefer to write freely for 5-10 minutes. Others like to make lists or sketches. Others mull over ideas and ask themselves questions before jotting down a few key words. If you have a method that works for you, stick with it. If you don't, try one of the three approaches just mentioned.

EXERCISE C

1. Think about your reasons for wanting to teach and jot down a list of those reasons.

2. Compare your list with the suggestions given for considering teaching as a career: (examples, benefits, and challenges).

3. Which reasons fit the category of the rewards of teaching?

4. Which reasons could be labeled challenges of teaching?

5. Which reasons are related to examples set by other people?

6. What labels or categories do your other reasons fall under?

7. Are some of your reasons related to experiences that you have had as a learner or teacher (e.g., sports, scouting, 4-H, religious classes)?

8. Are some of your reasons related to your interest in a particular subject such as mathematics or art?

9. Are some of your reasons related to particular qualities you possess such as patience, enthusiasm, or tolerance?

LISTEN TO YOUR INNER VOICE

The purpose of brainstorming is to come up with enough detail or elaboration to satisfy the evaluation requirements. You should aim to produce enough material for an introduction and at least three additional paragraphs. Once you list a few initial ideas, the best way to generate more detail is to imagine a voice saying, *Tell me more about that.* Let's suppose that your initial list of reasons for wanting to teach looked like this.

- I like kids.
- Summers off.
- Make a contribution to society.
- Encouragement from teachers.

Responding to that imaginary voice saying, *Tell me more*, might help you elaborate the first reason as follows:

I like kids…
    because they all have some undeveloped potential.
    because their responses aren't always predictable.
    because they get so excited when they learn something new.

Another way to elaborate on the first reason is through examples:

- The two boys I used to babysit.
- The girl I helped to get over her fear of water.
- The special education student who was my *little brother*.

Imagine the voice asking for more information until you believe you have enough for a satisfactory essay. Not every statement will give you as much room for development as others, but you can expand upon all of the statements. Each time you elaborate, your writing becomes more specific. Including specific detail makes your ideas concrete and your writing more convincing. Specific detail is one of the criteria for evaluating your essay.

EXERCISE D

1. Go back to the list of purpose statements that you developed in Exercise C, and brainstorm for material you might include in an essay.

2. Go back to your list of reasons for wanting to teach and elaborate as much as you can on each one.

GROUP AND FOCUS YOUR IDEAS

A good essay is unified by a controlling idea or thesis which dictates a pattern of organization. The thesis should be stated in one or two sentences. The words you choose to write the thesis statement should repeat or echo the directions for the essay. This strategy will ensure that you state the topic clearly. One way to write a thesis is to do one of the following:

1. Look at your purpose statement.
   Example 1: I must explain my reasons for choosing teaching as a career.
   Example 2: I must explain how a learning experience motivated me to go into teaching.

2. Look at the list of ideas you generated by brainstorming and try to sum up the ideas in a sentence or two:
   Sample Thesis 1: I have chosen teaching as a career because I enjoy young children, particularly those who have a learning disability. Teaching is a career that will enable me to make a contribution to society.
   Sample Thesis 2: The experience that I had as a *big brother* to a special education student helped me to realize that everyone has the potential to learn. This experience strengthened my interest in teaching as a career.

The thesis prepares the reader for what is to follow. It is a promise that you will discuss certain ideas and not others.

You will not always use all the material you generated during the brainstorming step. In the sample that we have been discussing, you might have decided not to use material related to summers off or the encouragement of teachers. However, if you decide that there is some material you want to include in the body of your essay material which is not indicated by the thesis, you need to revise the thesis. Suppose you decide to include the information about summers off and the encouragement of teachers, how could you revise the thesis? Here is one possibility:

Revised Thesis: There are many reasons why I have chosen teaching as a career. The pleasure of working with children, the opportunity to make a contribution to society, the encouragement of teachers, and time during the summer to continue my own education and interests are a few of them.

6

You should understand that it is not necessary or advisable to give every reason why you would like to teach. Be selective. Choose reasons on which you can elaborate and ones you feel strongly about. This will make a more convincing essay.

OUTLINING

There are different ways of grouping brainstorming ideas. The traditional format is the outline. Here is one example, based on the thesis we have been discussing.

Thesis: There are many reasons why I have chosen teaching as a career; some of them are the pleasure of working with children, the opportunity to make a contribution to society, the encouragement of teachers, and time during the summer to continue my own education and interests.

   I. I enjoy working with children.
       A. All children have potential.
       B. Their responses are unpredictable.
       C. They are excited when they learn something.

   II. I will make a contribution to society.
       A. Many jobs have questionable social value even if they have high salaries.
       B. Teachers can help children develop a good self-image and give them necessary skills.

   III. Teachers have encouraged me.
        A. They say I can express myself clearly.
        B. They see that I am enthusiastic about learning.

   IV. Summers will be time to continue my education and interests.
       A. Teachers must be lifelong learners.
       B. Intensity of teaching requires time for pursuing other interests.

CLUSTERING

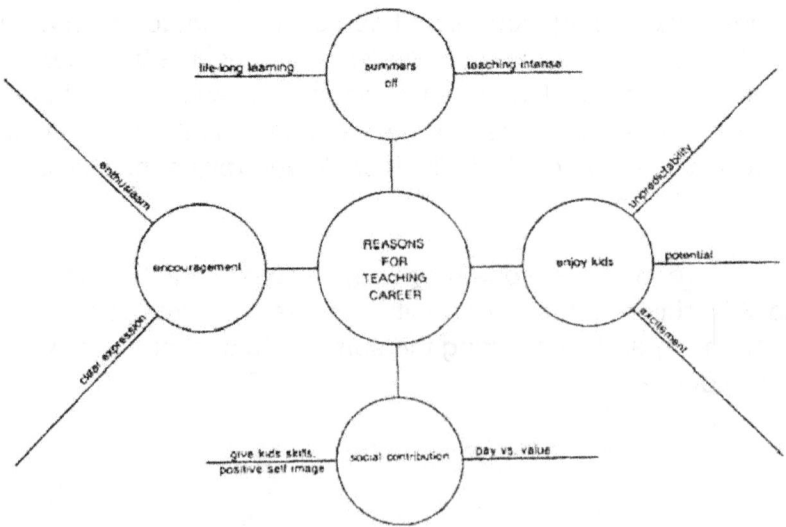

208

FLOW CHARTS

Still another way to map ideas is with the help of a flow chart. The main idea is placed in a box at the top, and other categories branch off below.

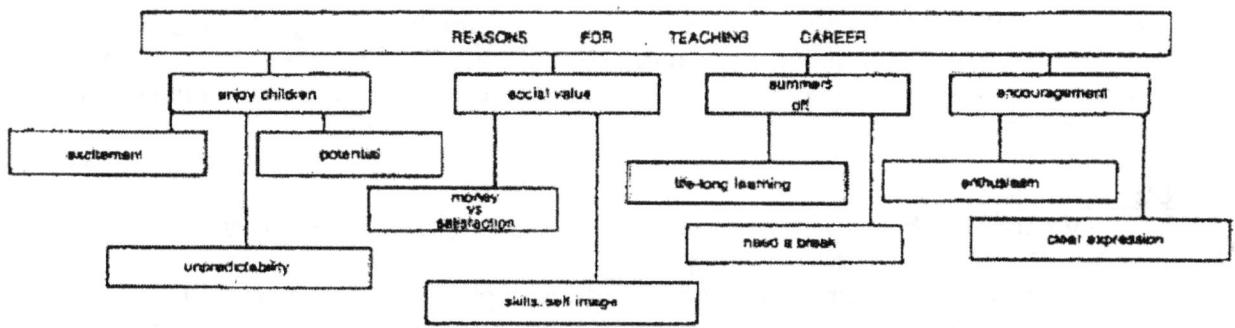

INFORMAL LISTS

An informal list is an easy way to group ideas.

My Reasons:

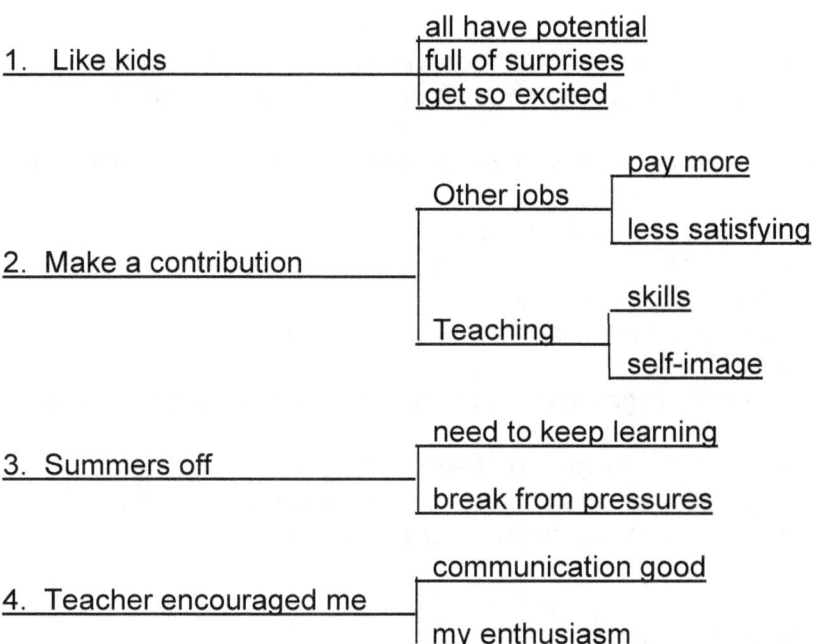

Regardless of which method you use to group your ideas, the goal is to pull together related bits of information and sketch the paragraph structure for your essay before you actually start writing your essay in the test booklet.

EXERCISE E

1. Go back to the material that you produced through brainstorming in Exercise D.2 and group the ideas by using one of the formulas illustrated.

2. Using one of the strategies mentioned previously, group the ideas given below in each set. For each set, read through the ideas in the set and identify or create a thesis statement; group related sentences; and find or create a sentence or phrase that will hold each group of sentences together.

   SET A.
   1. TV cartoons show characters recovering quickly from serious injury.
   2. Mr. Rogers never loses his temper.
   3. Ads associate happiness and good times with possession of a product.
   4. The ads show cereal boxes opening by themselves and dancing on the table.
   5. TV gives children a distorted sense of reality.
   6. Mr. Rogers always takes off his shoes when he comes inside.
   7. A character falls off a mountain top, shakes his head, and gets up.
   8. Positive role models, like Mr. Rogers, are unlike any real-life adult.
   9. Mr. Rogers never raises his voice.
   10. The ads are deceptive and manipulative.
   11. Characters who smash into walls are never badly hurt.

   SET B.
   1. I felt welcome when I went to see my math teacher during his office hours.
   2. The activity fair during orientation week had something to offer everyone.
   3. The counselors were helpful.
   4. Many teachers ask if students need help rather than wait for the students to get in trouble.
   5. The counselors helped with course selection.
   6. Resident advisors counsel students about adjustment problems.
   7. The counselors provided placement testing.
   8. Teachers talk to students after class rather than just rushing off.
   9. Students on campus are friendly.
   10. My experience at Winona College has been good, and I would recommend it to others.
   11. Teachers go over sample tests before you take the first test.
   12. The dorm council plans activities and projects to bring students together.
   13. The counselors offer minicourses on taking notes and tests.

   SET C.
   1. I don't belong to any organizations.
   2. I'm not involved in any special activities.
   3. I go to classes, work at the store, and see my friends on weekends.
   4. My job isn't special.
   5. I work at a supermarket.
   6. I need the job for spending money and college expenses.

7. I have learned some things from working.
8. It's not like school.
9. You have to be there to get paid.
10. The boss isn't always fair.
11. Sometimes she is impatient.
12. As a lowly clerk, you don't get any respect.
13. The boss seemed annoyed when I brought back the shopping carts.
14. There were long lines at the registers.
15. She told me to help bag groceries.
16. There's a pecking order in most companies.
17. My boss is under pressure from the manager.
18. I'm trying to stay on top of the situation rather than just reacting.
19. I ask the boss how things have been going.
20. I try to anticipate what she'll ask me to do and offer to do it first.
21. Sometimes I feel frustrated about being low on the totem pole.
22. The manager doesn't even know who I am.
23. There's not much incentive to do good work.
24. You can always be replaced by another minimum wage worker.

<u>SET D.</u>
1. DEATH OF A SALESMAN is a book that influenced me because of the connections between the play and my own life.
2. Each time I had a different reaction.
3. I read the play once in high school, again in college, and then saw it on TV.
4. In high school, Biff was a good-looking football hero.
5. The play is about a salesman named Willy, his wife, and two sons, Biff and Happy.
6. Happy was just an ordinary kid, living in his brother's shadow.
7. When Biff learned that his father was not perfect, he began to drift around.
8. I realized I was only hurting myself.
9. I had an older brother who was a star.
10. I was always trying to get my parents' attention.
11. I even tried to get their attention by doing poorly in school.
12. At first, I identified with Happy.
13. Biff had a big ego because of all the attention he received.
14. Biff became a bum because of all the attention he received as a teenager.
15. When I read the play in college, I sympathized with Willy.
16. He never received any respect from his boss.
17. I have been working at a supermarket.
18. Clerks are a dime a dozen, just like salespeople.
19. I want a career where a paycheck is not the only satisfaction you receive.
20. The TV version made me admire the mother.
21. She held the family together.
22. She was completely loyal to Willy.
23. We all want someone to stick by us like she did.

SET E.
1. Earning credit for my choice of courses and activities will give me a chance to integrate course work and real experience.
2. Reading Methods is a required course.
3. I'll learn how to assess a student's reading level.
4. I'll learn about various methods for teaching reading skills.
5. I plan to work as a literacy volunteer.
6. I want to know why people don't learn to read.
7. I'll learn about methods for teaching adults.
8. I'll learn how illiteracy affects a person's life.
9. I'll realize what's at stake if the education system fails.
10. I want to take either an advanced composition course or an independent study in composition.
11. I would like to keep a journal of my experience as a literacy volunteer.
12. I would like to write about the connections I see between the methods course and my tutoring experience.
13. I would like to write some feature stories about illiteracy for the college newspaper.

COMPOSE YOUR ESSAY WITH CLEAR SIGNALS FOR THE READER

Your essay is judged on how well the essay communicates a whole message. If you keep the reader in mind, your essay is likely to communicate more effectively. The most important signals to use are topic sentences to state the main idea of each paragraph and transitions to link sentences within the paragraphs. One basic pattern you might use in composing your paragraphs is the five paragraph essay. Here is one example of such an essay written in response to Prompt 1, Exercise B. Study the way in which the topic sentences give the reader a preview of what will be discussed.

Paragraph I.   Lead and thesis statement.

Lead   Some students may have time for sports, clubs, or volunteer organizations. Unfortunately, my schedule of classes and part-time work does not give me much time to devote to other activities. However, my job has been quite a learning experience.

Thesis   <u>Although I am just a supermarket clerk, I have gained insight into the demands of a job, the behavior of supervisors, and my ability to influence a situation,</u>

Paragraph II   Topic sentence developed with sufficient detail.

Topic Sentence   <u>I realized that the demands of a job re not always like the demands of school.</u> Maybe that is something that other people know from the start, but it did not work that way for me. In fact, I can remember how the equation between work and pay dawned on me; if I missed an afternoon of work, I missed an equivalent amount of money in my paycheck. The connection between work and rewards is not quite so clear in school. A student can study hard for a test and do poorly. On the other hand, a student can sometimes bluff through a test and get a good grade.

Paragraph III.	Another topic sentence with supporting detail.
Topic Sentence	<u>I did not work for very long before I also realized that bosses can be difficult.</u> At first, my supervisor seemed like a nice enough person. However, I had a look at her other side one day when I returned to the store, pushing a long line of shopping carts which she had told me to gather from the parking lot. Lines had formed at all the registers, and she snapped at me to bag for one of the cashiers. It was as if it my fault that she had sent two of the cashiers out for supper just as it was getting busy in the store.
Paragraph IV.	Another topic sentence followed by detail.
Topic sentence	<u>After my initial anger at the boss's behavior, I decided to try to influence the situation rather than just reacting to it.</u> I realized this approach might work as I was bagging groceries. I saw the store manager peering down at my box from her office window. My boss had a boss who had a boss who had a boss. She was part of the pecking order just like me. Now I try to make small talk with her, ask how things have been going, and so forth. Also, I try to anticipate what she might ask me to do and then offer to do it first. This gives me the feeling that I can be an actor rather than just a puppet.
Paragraph V.	Conclusion with restatement of thesis.
Thesis Restated	Sometimes I still get frustrated at work. As a lowly clerk, I do not get much respect in a large, impersonal company. <u>However, my job has shown me that even the most ordinary parts of my life can give me an opportunity to learn something about myself and other people.</u>

Topic sentences do not always occur at the beginning of paragraphs. In fact, at times it seems stilted to put the topic sentence at the start of a paragraph. You may need a sentence or two that makes a bridge with the preceding paragraph. For example, the fourth paragraph in the sample essay above might have been written more chronologically, following the sequence of events more closely.

Example:	After my initial anger, I noticed the store manager peering down at my boss from the upstairs office window. I realized that my boss had a boss who had a boss; She was just a part of the pecking order like me. <u>I decided to try to influence the situation instead of just reacting to it.</u>
Thesis Statement	

Placing the topic sentence at the start of a paragraph gives the clearest signal to a reader, but it is not always essential to place the topic sentence at the beginning. It is important, however, to have a sentence that holds the rest of the paragraph together. It can come at the beginning, the middle, or the end of the paragraph. Here is a paragraph without a topic sentence:

Ms. Rodriquez always had a word of encouragement on each test she handed back. Furthermore, she taught me the difference between an intelligent mistake and a dumb one. An intelligent mistake occurs when a learner applies a rule or procedure to a special situation where it does not apply. For example, if a young child says, "I taked the book," she is applying the rule to use a "d" sound for a past action. Ms. Rodriguez also had a way of making math problems exciting mysteries. We watched her solve equations on the board like Sherlock Holmes in pursuit of a suspect. The work was never easy, but she always made us feel that it was possible to succeed if we put in enough time.

One way to phrase a topic sentence for the paragraph above would be:
Ms. Rodriguez was one of the best teachers I ever had.

Even if you think that the point of the paragraph is perfectly clear without a topic sentence, put one in. You are now writing this essay for a sophisticated magazine; you are taking a test to show that you can get an idea across clearly to a reader.

EXERCISE F.

1. Each paragraph below lacks a topic sentence. Create a topic sentence for each paragraph and decide where best to place it.

   a. I would be happy if I could make some difference in the lives of the students I will teach. It might just mean making them more curious about the world or more accepting of themselves. I realize that it is difficult to reach each student, but that does not mean that I will not try.
   b. Mr. Wright began every class by putting the homework on the board. Then he would announce what we were going to do that day. Usually, we went over the homework problems first. Students were asked to put their solutions on the board. After discussing them and making necessary corrections, Mr. Wright would turn to the new material. Using three or four pieces of colored chalk, he illustrated and commented on the examples in the book. Finally, if we finished all of the scheduled lesson, there was time at the end of class to start on the homework.
   c. Every teacher spends a minimum of 35 hours in school. In addition, teachers must often supervise activities such as the drama club or school newspaper. Conferences with parents, staff meetings, and required professional development activities also add to the total hours required. A teacher usually has three different course-related preparations, each of which may take an hour or more, depending on the teacher's experience. English teachers who have 25 to 30 students per class may assign a short piece of writing each week, and may spend 4 to 5 minutes reading each paper. This may add 13 hours of additional work per week.

2. Go back to the material that you brainstormed and organized in Exercise D. Pick at least one batch of material and turn it into an essay following the pattern of the five-paragraph essay described previously.

TRANSITIONS

Transitions are signals to your reader about how your ideas are connected. Certain words and phrases prepare the reader for what is to follow. Examples of important transitions to use in your essay are:

1. Words that indicate sequence of events or ideas: first, second (etc.), finally, last, ultimately, eventually, later, meanwhile, afterwards;

2. Words that indicate examples: for instance, for example, specifically, in particular;

3. Words that indicate addition of similar ideas: and, also, furthermore, moreover, similarly, equally important, another;

4. Words that indicate addition of contrasting ideas: however, but, on the other hand, on the contrary, still, yet, in contrast, nevertheless.

Transitions between sentences can also be achieved by repeating key words, using synonyms, or using pronouns.

1. Example of a repeated key word: *Literacy* is not just a matter of learning the ABC's, *Literacy* means having sufficient control of the language to function in one's society.

2. Example of use of a synonym: *Literacy* is not just a matter of learning the ABC's. One's ability to read and write must be equal to the demands of one's society.

3. Example use of a pronoun: *Literacy* is not just a matter of learning the ABC's. It means having sufficient control of the language to function in your society.

EXERCISE G.

1. Look at the paragraphs you wrote in Exercise F and underline all the transitions.

2. Go back to the essay you wrote in Exercise F. Underline any transitions you used. Find places where you might insert additional transitions.

PROOFREAD FOR WORD CHOICE, GRAMMAR, AND MECHANICS

Under ideal conditions, you would complete a first draft and then evaluate it for content and structure. However, a subtest, lasting approximately one hour, does not allow time for true revision. You may want to think of your brainstorming as a type of first draft and your focusing as a type of revision. As you focus and compose your essay, you will do a certain amount of revision, deciding to change the order of paragraphs, inserting or deleting details, trying out sentences in your head before you put them down on paper. Once you have completed the essay, you need to proofread to make sure you have used words correctly and avoid errors that will detract from your essay and subsequently from the score you receive for your essay.

WORD CHOICE

In choosing words to express your ideas, keep in mind that the directions on the examination writing subtest are likely to specify an audience that requires you to use a professional tone. You should avoid slang and cliches. On the other hand, don't go overboard and complicate your essay with fancy terms and inflated language. Aim for a clear and direct expression of your ideas.

Here are a few examples of the kinds of words and expressions to avoid:

1. One activity that I've really *gotten into* lately is sailing. (Substitute *became involved in, become interested in, become enthusiastic about*).

2. The person sitting behind me talked *a lot* during the class. (Try to be as specific as possible about what *a lot* means in the sentence where you are tempted to use it. Here, you might use *continuously* or *incessantly*, but at other times, you might want to substitute *a great deal* or *often*.)

3. My first class was *awful*. (General words such as *awful, perfect, beautiful*, etc. are acceptable if you are going to follow up with more specific description. However, it is almost always better to use specific language. In what respect was the experience or the person awful, perfect, or beautiful? In the example above, was the class dull, disorganized, too demanding?)

4. I was faced with a *number of alternatives*. (Strictly defined, an alternative is a choice between two things. If you mean more than two, use options *or* choices.)

5. Computers are a *new innovation* in the classroom. (Innovation means *new*; therefore, the phrase is redundant. The same would be true of expressions such as *personal friend* and *advance planning*.)

Our language is constantly changing. At any period in history, some words and expressions are considered suitable for formal writing while others are considered colloquial and appropriate only for informal settings. As you prepare for the writing subtest, you might want to use a dictionary or a glossary of usage in a handbook. These references will provide guidance in currently acceptable choices. You might also want to keep in mind that no references will be available during the test. Therefore, if you have any doubt about the appropriateness of a word or phrase, you might want to avoid using it, and choose words about which you feel more confident.

Excess words are as much a problem as inexact words. When people don't know what to write, they often try to pad the paragraphs with sentences that say the same thing in slightly different words or fill up the sentences with empty phrases. Superfluous words and sentences may bore, frustrate, or even confuse your reader. You will be spared these problems if you practice brainstorming for relevant and interesting details before you compose your essay. Here are some examples of padded writing:

Wordy: Education faces a crisis today. At the present time, a number of problems are troubling concerned citizens. Not a day goes by that you do not hear about one problem or another.

To the Point: Many problems in education call for our attention.

Wordy: Due to the fact that a problem arose concerning the time our committee should meet, we decided in the final analysis that it would be best to postpone our decision until the new chairperson took over.

To the Point: Unable to agree on a meeting time, our committee postponed the decision until the new chairperson took over.

EXERCISE H

1. Find places in your own writing where you could eliminate words without losing meaning.

2. Trim unnecessary words from the following sentences and rewrite.

   a. The aspects of teaching that I imagine I will most enjoy are the diversity of students and the freedom to organize my own classes.

   b. The problem that I foresee causing the most difficulty in the future is that a few years from now we are going to have even more non-native English speaking students than we do now and people don't understand the need for bilingual education.

   c. In conclusion, the final point that I want to make is to say that the productivity of our economic system will decline unless we do something to tackle the problem of illiteracy among the many people who can't read at all or who can barely read.

EXERCISE I

There are a number of commonly confused words. Use a dictionary or handbook to check the correct choice for each of the sentences that follow.

1. I _____ your invitation to the party. (accept, except, expect)
2. I _____ to do well on my math exam. (accept, except, expect)
3. Everyone is going _____ Susan. (accept, except, expect)
4. I went to my guidance teacher for some good _____. (advise, advice)
5. I always _____ my students to take French literature. (advise, advice)
6. The _____ of the hurricane was horrendous. (affect, effect)
7. Does this test _____ my grade? (affect, effect)
8. _____ never too late to try. (Its, It's)
9. The committee reported _____ decision. (its, it's)
10. Please place the books over _____. (there, they're, their)
11. _____ my brother's friends. (There, They're, Their)
12. The boys have lost _____ shoes. (there, they're, their)

13. Most of the students could not choose _____ the four answers. (between, among)
14. Mary is trying to decide _____ two majors: History and French. (between, among)
15. John arrived at the game, _____. (to, too, two)
16. Please place _____ books on this corner. (to, two, too)
17. David gave the ball _____ Mark. (to, two, too)
18. Peter ran the mile _____. (bad, badly)
19. I feel _____ when it rains. (bad, badly)
20. Teachers often have to _____ packaged materials to the special needs of their students. (adopt, adapt)
21. Our school would like to _____ a dress code for all students. (adopt, adapt)
22. This corner will be the _____ for the reading materials. (site, cite)
23. Students must learn how to _____ source materials in a research paper. (site, cite)
24. Individualized activities are needed to _____ group activities. (compliment, complement)
25. Teachers should _____ children often on the work that they successfully complete. (compliment, complement)

GRAMMAR AND MECHANICS

An occasional error in grammar or mechanics in an essay written without access to a dictionary will not result in failing the writing portion of the exam. However, frequent errors will detract from the effectiveness of your message and can cause failure. There are so many possible errors, that they cannot be covered in this brief guide. A discussion of the most serious errors will be followed by a set of sentences you can use to test your proofreading skills.

1. Sentence Boundaries: Running two or more independent clauses together without linking words or proper punctuation violates basic rules. A grammatically incomplete sentence is equally distracting.

    a. Run-on, fused sentence, or comma splice: Teaching is not an easy field, the rewards aren't always there. (A comma is not sufficient to separate two independent clauses. Substitute a period, a semi-colon, or a linking word, such as *because* for the comma.)

    b. Fragment: The best example being the difference between the way we see a character on TV and the way we visualize a character in a story. (The *ing* form of the verb creates a fragment. Substitute *is* for *being* to correct the sentence.)

2. Agreement of Sentence Elements: Verbs must agree with their subjects; pronouns with the nouns to which they refer. Similar elements must have parallel structure. Parts of the sentence must fit together grammatically.

    a. Lack of subject-verb agreement: The problems that young readers have seems to come partly from the environment. (*problems* calls for the verb form *seem* not *seems*. In sentences where several words come between subject and verb, it is easy to lose track of the elements.)

b. Lack of pronoun agreement: Everyone wants to achieve their potential. (*Everyone* is singular and calls for *his/her*, not *their*.)

c. Lack of parallel structure: I learned to operate the computer, write some simple programs, and the fundamentals of word processing. (*Operate* and *write* set up a pattern which calls for a similar word. Therefore, the last part of the sentence should be rephrased to include a verb; for example, *...and use the fundamentals of word processing.*)

d. Lack of grammatical fit: While taking an elective course in design my freshman year sparked my interest in art. (The introductory phrase, *While taking an elective course*, calls for a subject to come before the verb. This sentence could be revised in at least two ways:
While taking an elective course in design my freshman year, I became interested in art.
Taking an elective course in design my freshman year sparked my interest in art.

SELECTED CAPITALIZATION RULES

A few of the rules governing capitalization are reviewed below. Consult a dictionary or handbook for more complete coverage of this topic.

1. Capitalize proper nouns and adjectives.
   Example: Capitalize: *Judy Blume* and *Southington High School*.
   Do not capitalize *the author* or *my high school*.

2. Capitalize titles when they precede proper names, but not when they follow proper names or are used alone.
   Example: Professor Kent Curtis
   Kent Curtis, professor of history
   the history professor

3. Do not capitalize the names of academic years or terms.
   Example: spring semester
   my sophomore year

4. Capitalize the names of specific courses, but not fields of study unless they are languages.
   Example: Capitalize *English, Spanish,* and *Math 101*
   Do not capitalize *math, physics,* or *education*.

5. Capitalize the important words in titles of books and underline the titles.
   Example: <u>Catcher in the Rye</u>
   <u>Grapes of Wrath</u>

PUNCTUATION

Punctuation is another area that you should review with the help of a good handbook or dictionary. One simple rule to remember is: Do not use the dash as a substitute for the proper punctuation. Example of a punctuation error: Although I took up swimming—the doctors said it would be good exercise—but I found that I did not have the ability to make the team

(The problem with relying on dashes is that, as in the example, dependence can lead to sloppy sentence construction. The sentence above should be revised: I took up swimming because the doctors said it would be good exercise, but I found that I did not have the ability to make the team.)

EXERCISE J

1. Proofread the following essay to identify errors in grammar, mechanics, and word use. Underline or cross out all errors.

2. Rewrite the essay, using correct grammar, mechanics, and wording.

The extent of illiteracy in the Country is documented in Illiterate America—a book by Jonathan Kozol. When I read this book and realized the extent of illiteracy gave me a shock. Kozol claims that 25 million people can not red warning labels or a simple news story, another 35 million do not read well enough to survive in the Modern Age—Like being able to follow printed instructions. For someone who can't read and has to support himself or a family could be a real disadvantage.

The problem of illiteracy will be difficult to solve. There being many causes that go deep into our society. Schools have failed to halt the problem and may be contributing to it. My parents say that the problem with schools today are a lack of respect for authority. Years ago, everyone know what would happen if they disobeyed a teacher. Today, teachers must contend with students who are often bored, rarely prepared and frequently they defy the teacher. Some respect and discipline is needed to create a learning environment.

Another problem with the schools is poorly prepare teachers. Students graduating from college without being able to read or write well. During the 1960s was the decline of strict academic standards. Students failed to learn what they should of learned. The decline may be ending, new tests and requirements are in place. For example, the college of arts and sciences at Northeastern State University changed their requirements because entering students were so poorly prepared. Some of them unable to identify Sophocles or locate spain on a map.

Kozol's book interested me in the larger issues of literacy—it is more than learning the ABCs. Literacy is when you can read and write well enough to survive in a complex technology and making informed opinions about government policies. Teachers can help to create a literate America. After reading about the problems of illiteracy facing this country, I want to become one,

19

PUTTING IT ALL TOGETHER

PRACTICE TOPICS

You will not know in advance the topic on which you will be asked to write an essay for the examination. However, the topic is likely to involve your education, education in general, or your choice of a career.

The best way to prepare for the writing subtest is to practice the skills presented in this book and to write whole essays under conditions similar to those found in examinations. Below are several topics you may use for practice.

Practice Prompt 1

The Academic Standards Committee of your college is considering changes in the current grading system and they have asked you to write a statement about the impact of the letter grade system (ABCDF) on learning. You may want to consider how the letter grade system affects certain types of students, how it is viewed by students, teachers, or prospective employers, whether there is a practical alternative, or whether modifications should be made. Write a statement of your opinion of the letter grade system and the reasons for your opinion.

Practice Prompt 2

A screening committee is reviewing your application for a teaching position and has asked you to submit a statement of your strengths and weaknesses for the position. Imagine a specific teaching position for which you might apply and write a statement about how well you qualify for that particular job. You might want to consider how your educational background, work experiences, internships, or special interests make you a suitable candidate. You might also want to consider whether there is anything about the position, the type of students you might face, the location, or the responsibilities that might be a challenge to you. Describe the teaching position for which you are applying and explain why you would be a good candidate for the position.

Practice Prompt 3

The committee considering your application to enter a teacher training program wants to learn about your awareness of students' non-academic needs. They have pointed out that a teacher must often do more than teach subject matter. Consider the psychological, physical, social, and economic problems that affect a student's ability to learn. Describe your understanding of the ways in which the role of a teacher goes beyond teaching academic subjects.

Practice Prompt 4

Your college is hosting a conference for state high school teachers to address the problem of the inadequate preparation of the average student for college work. The conference is focusing on the average student because college teachers are concerned about the many students entering freshman courses who are unable to meet the demands of college. You might want to describe how serious the problem is, whose problem it is, and to what extent high schools should consider changing what they are doing. Use your experience, observations, and knowledge to write a statement which gives your perspective on the gap between the academic requirements in high school and those in college.

POST-TEST

Writing Subtest Directions

This part of the examination consists of one writing exercise. You should allow approximately 60 minutes to complete this assignment. You may NOT use a dictionary during the subtest. Make sure you have time to plan, write, review, and revise what you have written.

Before you begin to write, read the topic carefully and take some time to think about how you will organize what you plan to say. Your writing exercise will be evaluated on the basis of how effectively it communicates a whole message to the intended audience for the stated purpose. Your writing exercise will be judged on the success of its total impression by a panel of language arts experts. When evaluating your ability to communicate a whole message effectively, the scorers will also consider your ability to:

1. state and stay on the topic;
2. address all specified parts of the writing assignment;
3. present your ideas in an organized fashion;
4. include sufficient detail and elaboration to statements;
5. choose effective words;
6. employ correct grammar and usage; and
7. use correct mechanics (spelling, capitalization, paragraph form).

PROMPT

The screening committee considering your application for a teaching position is concerned about teacher stress and burn-out. They would like to learn about your awareness of this problem and your susceptibility to it. You might want to discuss how you have handled stressful situations in the past and any techniques that you use to cope with stress. Describe in writing how you would confront the problem of stress and burn-out in the teaching profession.

NOTES/OUTLINE

21

KEY (CORRECT ANSWERS)

In some cases where there is no one right answer, possible answers are given. If your answer is significantly different, discuss it with a teacher or tutor.

EXERCISE B

1. I must describe an activity and tell the committee why it is important to me.

2. I must explain to the superintendent why I want to teach and how an experience or subject helped me make this decision.

3. I have to select three courses or activities and justify why they would be worthwhile.

4. I have to write a letter to the director of admissions at the college of my choice and explain why I want to go there.

5. I have to describe to the committee a significant book and concentrate on what I got out of it.

EXERCISE C

Answers will vary.

EXERCISE D

Answers will vary.

EXERCISE E

1. Answers will vary.

2. A. An ideal wheel:

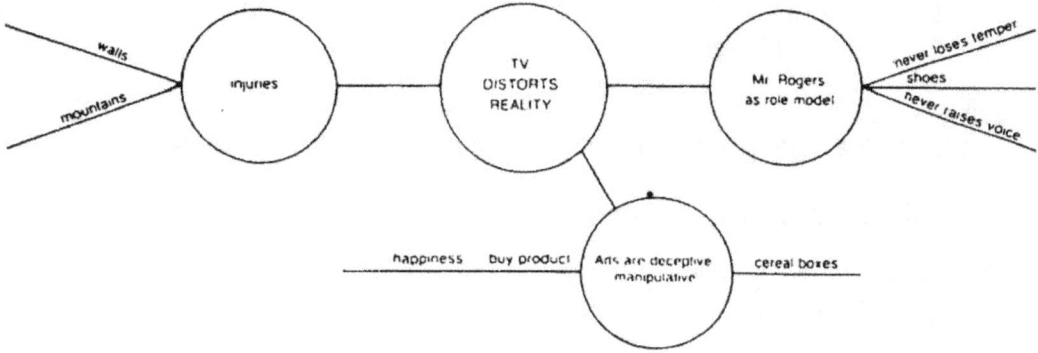

223

B. A flow chart:

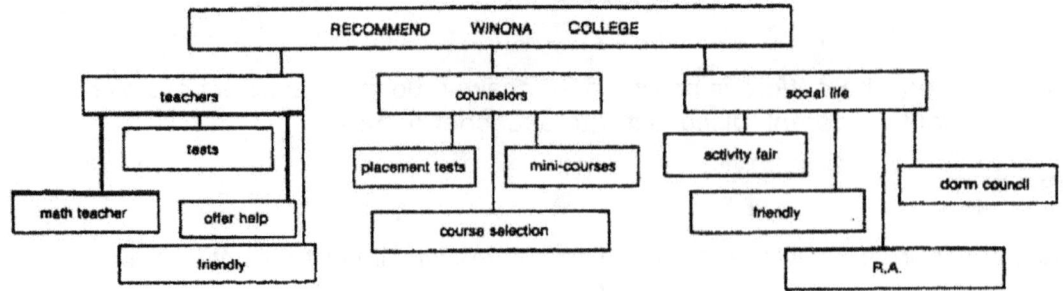

C. Using an outline:

Thesis: My job as a clerk has taught me about the reality of work and how to get along with supervisors.

I. I don't have time for special activities.
   A. School
   B. Need job
   C. Friends

II. Work is not like school because if you don't work, you don't get paid.

III. Boss is not always fair.
   A. No respect for clerks
   B. Gets impatient
   C. Got annoyed about lines

IV. I'm trying to get on top of the situation rather than just reacting.
   A. Boss is part of pecking order
   B. Make small talk
   C. Anticipate orders

V. I am still frustrated.
   A. No recognition
   B. No incentive
   C. Easily replaced

D. Using a list:
Death of a Salesman – connections between the play and my life

1. Different readings – different reactions

2. Describe characters
   Willy: salesman
   Linda: wife
   Biff: good looking, football hero breaks with Willy, drifts around
   Happy: ordinary, shadowed by Biff

23

      3. Identified with Happy
          My older brother
          Wanted parents' attention
          School troubles
          Realized I was hurting myself
          Attention hurt Biff

      4. Sympathy for Willy
          No respect from boss
          My job as a clerk, dime a dozen
          Want more than a paycheck

      5. TV version – admiration for Linda
          Held family together
          Loyal to Willy
          Want someone like her

  E. Another list:
     Choices: integrate courses and experiences

      1. Reading Methods Required – would choose it
          What I'll learn; assessment, skills

      2. Activity – literacy volunteer
          Why don't people learn
          How to teach skills
          Effect on a person's life
          Failure of system

      3. Course or individual study in writing
          Keep journal
          Make connections
          Write feature stories for newspaper

EXERCISE F

1. Answers will vary.

2. A. One benefit of teaching is personal satisfaction.
   B. Mr. McGrath ran a tightly structured class.
   C. Many teachers work harder than people realize.

EXERCISE G

1. Example: furthermore, for example, also, like, but
   A. but
   B. then, after, finally
   C. in addition, also, another

2. Answers will vary.

EXERCISE H

1. Answers will vary.

2. A. I will enjoy the diversity of students and the freedom to organize my own classes.

    B. The failure of people to understand the need to provide bilingual education to the increasing numbers of non-native English speaking students will be our biggest problem.

    C. Finally, failure to tackle the various forms of illiteracy will cause a decline in our economic productivity.

EXERCISE I

1. accept
2. expect
3. except
4. advice
5. advise
6. effect
7. affect
8. It's
9. its
10. there
11. they're
12. their
13. among
14. between
15. too
16. two
17. to
18. badly
19. bad
20. adapt
21. adopt
22. site
23. cite
24. complement
225. compliment

EXERCISE J

The extent of illiteracy in this country is documented in *Illiterate America*, a book by Jonathan Kozol. When I read this book and realized the extent of illiteracy, I was shocked. Kozol claims that 25 million people cannot read warning labels or a simple news story; another 35 million do not read well enough to survive in the Modern Age because they are unable to follow printed instructions. Someone who can't read and has to support himself or his or her family is at a real disadvantage.

The problem of illiteracy will be difficult to solve. Its causes go deep into our society. Schools have failed to halt the problem and may be contributing to it. My parents say that the problem with schools today is a lack of respect for authority. Years ago, students knew what would happen if they disobeyed a teacher. Today, teachers must contend with students who are often bored, rarely prepared, and frequently defiant of the teacher. Respect and discipline are needed to create a learning environment.

Another problem with the schools is poorly prepared teachers. Students graduate from college without being able to read or write well. During the 1960s, strict academic standards declined. Students failed to learn what they should have learned. The decline may be ending because new tests and requirements are in place. For example, the College of Arts and Sciences at Northeastern State University changed its requirements because entering students were so poorly prepared. Some of them were unable to identify Sophocles or locate Spain on a map.

26

Kozol's book interested me in the larger issues of literacy, Literacy means more than learning the ABCs. It means reading and writing well enough to survive in a complex society and making informed opinions about government policies. Teachers can help to create a literate America. After reading about the problems of illiteracy facing this country, I want to become a teacher.

www.ingramcontent.com/pod-product-compliance
Lightning Source LLC
Chambersburg PA
CBHW082034300426
44117CB00015B/2477